Inclusive Masculinity

Routledge Research in Gender and Society

Inclusive Masculinity

The Changing Nature of Masculinities

Eric Anderson

Routledge
Taylor & Francis Group

LONDON AND NEW YORK

First published 2009
by Routledge

This paperback edition published 2012
2 Park Square, Milton Park, Abingdon, Oxon OX14 4RN

Simultaneously published in the US
by Routledge
711 Third Avenue, New York, NY 10017

*Routledge is an imprint of the Taylor & Francis Group,
an informa business*

British Library Cataloguing in Publication Data
A catalogue record for this book is available from the British Library

Library of Congress Cataloging in Publication Data
Anderson, Eric, 1968–
    Inclusive masculinity : the changing nature of masculinities / by Eric
Anderson.
        p. cm. —(Routledge research in gender and society ; 22)
    Includes bibliographical references and index.
    1. Masculinity. 2. Gay athletes. 3. Homophobia. I. Title.
    BF692.5.A53 2009
    306.76′62—dc22
            2009009255

ISBN13: 978-0-415-80462-2 (hbk)
ISBN13: 978-0-415-89390-9 (pbk)
ISBN13: 978-0-203-87148-5 (ebk)

Typeset in Sabon by IBT Global.

*This book is dedicated to Michael Messner,
Michael Kimmel and Donald Sabo~*

*Men who were advocating and modelling inclusive
masculinities long before they were fashionable*

Contents

Acknowledgments

This book is dedicated to the creative, compassionate and committed emancipatory scholarship of three of the fathers of masculinities studies, Dr. Michael Messner, Dr. Michael Kimmel and Dr. Don Sabo. For almost three decades, these men have published academically accessible, cutting edge, meaningful gender scholarship. They have also been my personal friends, my academic heroes, and my greatest source of academic support. I was also fortunate to have the friendship and feedback from Dr. Lauren Joseph, Dr. Cheryl Cooky, Dr. Linda Faye Wachs, Dr. Sheri Dworkin, Dr. Don Barrett, Dr. George Cunningham, Professor Judy Treas and Professor Ellen Staurowsky.

I have also been fortunate to have two sharp graduate students during the research and writing of this book. Mark McCormack not only read multiple drafts, but he helped with the publications that fed into it as well. The same is true of Shaun Filiault. The quality of each of their scholarship is such that, perhaps they have taught me more than I have taught them. I am also grateful to the board members of the American Institute of Bisexuality, who generously funded much of this research. Their efforts, in memory of Dr. Fritz Klein, are as appreciated as their enthusiasm and support.

Finally, I thank my partner, Grant Tyler Peterson. Although he was lazy on this one, never once even proofreading a chapter, he did cook 100 meals. He begrudgingly, but nevertheless changed the playlist from modern rock, to my favorite writing music, Barry Manilow (I know it's a weakness). What Grant really did for me, however, is simply survive. The first draft of this book was written just a few months after he completed 13 months of chemotherapy. It took me twice as long to complete the final manuscript as it should have. This is because after Grant beat one of the deadliest cancers known, I gladly put the project aside so that we could cuddle, travel, and take long walks with our dog, Lewie, in the quiet English countryside. For as long as we are fortunate to have life together, Grant, I can only hope to accomplish half of what I otherwise would have.

Introduction

In 2005, I was invited to speak to several dozen radio sports personalities and shock jocks about my book, *In the Game: Gay Athletes and the Cult of Masculinity*. One morning I was talking to Deter, an on-air radio personality from a city far from the liberal comfort of Los Angeles or London, where I split my time. Deter looks like a typical sports fan. His attire is sloppy, and other than an emerging belly, he looks like he once ran track, or maybe hit a ball of some sorts. Deter tells me that he is intrigued with my research on the changing nature of heterosexual masculinities and the decreased gay-male phobia I find in competitive teamsport environments. Like every sportscaster on whose show I appear, he is clear to preface that he has no problems with gay men, or gay athletes by extension (cf. Nylund 2007). But of the dozens of sportscasters who interviewed me about my research during that autumn, Deter stands out because he tells me that he has several gay friends. He even tells me that he is a staunch supporter of gay rights. After a few minutes of off-air conversation however, Deter says, "My on-air personality is quite different." Deter informs me that he is known for his brash, brazen and (much to my surprise) homophobic on-air sentiment. "It's an act," he says. And, just a minute before we go on air, he asks if I'm willing to "roll with it."

Deter's transformation from gay rights supporter to raging on-air homophobe is reminiscent of many of the attitudes expressed by high school and university heterosexual teamsport athletes I interviewed between 1999 and 2004. When speaking privately, very few said that they were homophobic, yet all assumed that their teammates were. Not wanting to be out of step with other men, most athletes told me that they too used homophobic language. Although they did not explain it this way, they maintained that using homophobic discourse was a method of retaining their heteromasculine capital among their teammates. However, they insisted that their homophobic discourse was not meant to express personal homophobia. Instead, these men argued that it was designed to say, "I am not gay" and "I am not weak" to their friends and teammates. Thus, rather than homophobia being reproduced through personal prejudice, for both Deter and these other men, it served as a form of heterosexual and masculine social currency.

I am not excusing their discourse. Certainly it shapes frameworks of stigma around homosexuality. Also, while most of the openly gay athletes I interviewed said that their teammates' usage of terms like 'poof' and 'fag' did not bother them, many said that when they were closeted such language made it difficult for them to assess the level of homophobia among their teammates. Accordingly, I do not support using homophobic language in this or almost any other way. However, as part of the process of learning to see the social world through informant's perspectives, it *is* important to understand intent. In this case, homophobic discourse permitted these men to prove to each other that they were both masculine and (more important) that they were not gay. Interestingly, I found many openly gay men saying, "That's gay," too. It was for this reason that I subtitled the book, *and the cult of masculinity*. Men, it seemed, were more interested in keeping up masculine appearances, than standing up for what they believed.

As vexing as it was to hear members of a team individually pledge support for gays, but collectively suggest they were not ready for openly gay athletes, this was still considerable progress compared to the way sport scholars defined the relationship between homosexuality and sport during the 1980s and earlier part of the 1990s. Michael Messner (1992: 34) influentially described the degree of homophobia in the sports world as 'staggering.' For example, Messner's interviews with heterosexual men clearly indicates that during the 1980s and early 1990s there was no place for a 'fag' in sport. This was something I experienced, personally.

At 25 years of age, I broke the guiding principle of masculinity: I came out as gay. More so, I came out of the closet as an openly gay distance running coach at a conservative high school, in a conservative county. Here, I experienced just how much privilege heterosexuals have, not only in sport, but also in the dominant culture. Whereas before I was a privileged white, middle-class, athletic, young, ostensibly 'heterosexual' male, after coming out, things radically changed. My public identity transformed from 'the outstanding coach' to 'the faggot coach,' and the school letters that adorned my proud athletes' varsity jackets quickly lost their symbolic representation of a nationally revered distance running squad, instead gaining social stigma. Accordingly, my heterosexual athletes and I began to face the discrimination that accompanied the stigma of the time. Athletes ceased to join my team and those remaining found themselves immersed in daily battles with ignorance and violence.

My status as the first publicly recognized gay male coach in the United States went relatively unnoticed until a football player brutally assaulted one of my heterosexual athletes in 1995, believing him (through a guilt by association process) to be gay. Although the vicious attack was witnessed by other football players, none bothered to intervene. It seems they enjoyed watching a 'faggot' get his ass kicked. Without intervention, the 250-pound football player knocked my 150-pound runner to the ground, sat atop him, and pummeled his face. While gouging at his eyes, a woman emerged from her home and pleaded for the assailant to stop. "Stop it! Stop it!" she yelled. "You're going to kill him." The assailant responded, "It aint over until the faggot's dead." This is all that my athlete heard.

Knowing his life depended on it, my runner somehow squirmed from beneath the legs of his assailant. He rose to his feet, and although his vision was obscured with blood, he managed to sprint away and scale a fence, one the football player was too heavy to get over. My athlete was left with four broken facial bones, two permanent screws in his pallet, and a copy of a police report that described the incident as 'mutual combat.' This, according to the police, was *not* a hate crime. It was not an assault, or a crime in any way.

I was not a sociologist when I first wrote of these experiences in my autobiography *Trailblazing: The True Story of America's First Openly Gay High School Coach*. Nor had I read the works of Michael Messner, Brian Pronger, Michael Kimmel or Donald Sabo, but I realized that the beating was influenced by a number of events, institutions, as well as his football team's culture. I knew the football player was taught to hate. Although I could not articulate it this way at the time, I knew that the assailant played within a hyper-masculine arena, in which homophobic discourse marked certain types of people as sacred and others as profane (cf. Durkheim 1976). What was clear to me was that the assailant's aggression was influenced by indoctrination into an extreme form of masculinity predicated on homophobic hate. He was rewarded by his teammates, and encouraged into homophobia by his coach. Indeed, after the beating, the football player earned hero status among his teammates.

Today, I understand that this abusive football player, his teammates and coach, were not entirely to blame. Rather we, a sports obsessed, homophobic and hyper-masculine culture, created him. His Christian-conservative, American upbringing influenced him into a violent, masculine ethos with the promise of masculine glory and praise should he succeed. In football, he was taught that the most important principle was an othering of a largely invisible group of demonized men—'faggots.' Should we then be surprised that this 16-year-old boy would take the opportunity to show that he received the message well? When faced with an actual homosexual, or the sympathizer of a homosexual, not beating him would be to violate his sanctified beliefs. Had he *not* assaulted this 'homosexual,' he would have failed his teammates, and failed as a man.

As much as I still hate this player today (I am not good enough to forgive), I understand that his homophobic violence was a logical consequence of the position he found himself in. It was because of the valorization of heteromasculinity and its associated violence that I returned to graduate school in 1998. I desired to know the cultural mechanisms that influenced a young boy to hate, and I desired to better understand the relationship between gay athletes, sport and compulsory heterosexuality.

Under the supervision of Francesca Cancian, Michael Messner and Brian Pronger, and with the support of Michael Kimmel, Don Sabo and Judy Treas, I began to better understand the intersection of masculinity, sport and homophobia. As a sociologist of some years now, I better understand the operation of hegemony, and the near-seamless manner in which groups of people can maintain power by policing ideologies both through the threat of force, and the willing compliance of those oppressed. I now work with the complex role that sports play in society, particularly in producing a violent, homophobic masculinity. I have a better understanding of how the very structure of teamsports influence boys and men to develop a narrow sense of heteromasculinity, and I understand sport's influence in teaching boys to accept risk, to out-group others, and to use violence in order to raise their capital among other men. However, I now also realize that matters are beginning to change.

In 1999, I began collecting in-depth interviews of openly gay high school and university athletes. Much to my surprise, I found openly gay athletes playing, surviving, and sometimes thriving on their teams. Although most of these athletes swam in a sea of heterosexism (and often contributed to it themselves), all played in absence of overt homophobic violence and marginalization. None were called faggots directly (at least not with intent to wound), and none experienced the violence that my athletes and I endured. These almost exclusively white, openly gay men from various locations, sports and levels, challenged the hegemonic form of masculinity. In other words, on-air personalities like Deter are beginning to represent an archaic archetype of masculinity. In light of this, I wrote:

> If the softening of masculinity continues, the older conservative form of masculinity may be less alluring, and the masculinizing context of sport may have to adjust to the new version of masculinity or risk losing its effect on socializing boys and men in the culture as a whole. In other words, if everything changes around sport, sport will either have to change or it will lose its social significance and be viewed as a vestige of an archaic model of masculinity. (Anderson 2005a: p. 16)

In the years preceding my research on gay athletes, my research agenda included multiple ethnographies about the experiences of straight men in sports, too. In my studies of white, university rugby, cheerleaders and soccer players, as well as the members of a racially mixed university fraternity, I show that university-attending men are rapidly running from the hegemonic type of masculinity that scholars have been describing for the past 25 years.

Heterosexual men in these studies no longer physically assault their gay teammates, and heterosexual men increasingly refuse to symbolically wound gay men with homonegative discourse (cf. McCormack and Anderson forthcoming). Instead, perhaps influenced by the decreasing rates of cultural homophobia of the broader society, many of these men are politically charged to change the landscape of masculinity. Others simply adopt an inclusive approach to masculinity because it is what their teammates are doing.

I am not alone in suggesting that the dominant form of masculinity, in sport or any other cultural location, *can* change. The sociologist primarily responsible for promoting the study of hegemonic masculinities, Robert (now Raewyn) Connell (1987, 1995, 2005) also accounts for the contestation and replacement of *any* given form of dominant masculinity. Accordingly, as gender scholars, we all knew that the homophobic, sexist, and violent form of masculinity propagated in competitive teamsports *could* change, but since scholars started studying it seriously in the late 1980s, it had not. This book is significant because I show that things are now finally beginning to change.

DECREASING SOCIAL STIGMA

The premise of this volume is that the esteemed versions of masculinity among university-attending men are changing. However, before discussing inclusive masculinity theory, it is important to note that the changes I see occurring among young men are not germane to gender alone. Recent decades have brought a lessening of orthodox views and institutional control of all types of gender, sexual, and relationship types, in North American and Western European cultures. This is made evident in the growing percentage of people who engage in pre-marital intercourse (Laumann et. al. 1994; Johnson et al. 2001), the social and legal permission for divorce (Jackson and Scott 2004), what some would suggest is a lessening of the traditional double standard for heterosexual intercourse (Tanenbaum 1999; Wolf 1997), and most important to inclusive masculinity theory, the markedly expanded social and political landscape for gays and lesbians (Anderson 2005a, 2008b; Barnett and Thomson 1996; Loftus 2001).

The impact of these shifting cultural attitudes—the increasing loss of our puritan sentiment—is perhaps best illustrated by examining teenagers. For example, whereas teenagers once traded baseball cards, today they trade digital pornography clips obtained from websites. There are no age controls for many of these websites, and no need to register a credit card. The Internet provides anyone the ability to instantly access a display of sexual variety. Here bodies fuck (predominantly for straight and gay men's pleasures) in all combinations, styles, mixtures, manners and video quality. I am not necessarily critiquing this, instead, I think it provides what some feminists concerned with pornography have been calling for all along: not an abolition of pornography, but an explosion of the subjectivities of differing kinds of people in pornography (Ellis, O'Dair and Tallmer 1990).

Gone is the expectation of heterosexual missionary sex (Segal 1994). The Internet has sparked a sexual revolution. How this relates to decreasing stigma about homosexuality is a related matter.

Today's Porntube.com generation see, early and often, sexual images that arouse or entertain them: Whether accidentally or intentionally, my students tell me that they view video clips of gays, lesbians and others once stigmatized by the Victorian cult of heterosexual boredom. Often a heterosexual cannot find his preferred images of heterosexual intercourse without filtering through the images of the acts once so socially tabooed. Curiosity of the other, or perhaps a desire to simply see what others enjoy, tempts the heterosexually-minded young male into clicking on the link, watching what their fathers despised so much. The Internet, I propose, has therefore been instrumental in exposing the forbidden fruit of homosexual sex, comodifying and normalizing it in the process. This, combined with a strategic and political bombardment of positive cultural messages about homosexuality through youth media, MTV, reality television, and other popular venues, has sent a message that while homosexuality is okay, homophobia is not.

Kids are not the only ones working at reducing homophobia, of course. In the years since my athlete was beaten we have seen tremendous cultural and institutional gains for gays and lesbians. Vermont passed Civil Unions in 2000, giving gays and lesbians all the state rights of marriage. And in the summer of 2003, the U.S. Supreme Court ruled that the 13 states with remaining sodomy laws could no longer enforce them. Just five months after this landmark ruling, the Massachusetts State Supreme Court granted gays and lesbians the right to marry, opening the door to constitutional challenges for gay marriage across the nation. In 2008, California and Connecticut followed, and in 2009 so did Vermont and Iowa.

Important changes have also occurred in Britain. In 2001, the United Kingdom's law (Section 28), prohibiting the discussion of homosexuality in schools, was repealed. In 2006, Britain passed a domestic partnership act granting same-sex couples legal (but not cultural) equality with heterosexuals. And, in 2008, Britain published 'best practice' guidelines for schools, stating that homophobic bullying is not to be tolerated, and recommending that schools include gay history in their curriculum, and introduce youth to gay role models.

These events, and myriad other legal municipal, state, national and European Union rulings, have sparked public debates regarding the status of gays and lesbians in nearly every sector of American and British culture, including cherished American institutions like the Boy Scouts (which has come under increasing fire for their discriminatory practices), and most Judaeo-Christian churches (which frequently fracture over issues pertaining to homosexuality). Furthermore, gays and lesbians are increasingly gaining a normative, albeit mostly desexualized, representation on mainstream television, gaining popularity not only in a large number of shows with gays and lesbians, but also with shows *about* gays and lesbians. It seems that in the new millennium, Anglo-Americans are increasingly accepting of, perhaps even desensitized to, homosexuality.

All of this is crucial to the discussion of inclusive masculinity theory because my driving theoretical hypothesis is that homophobia directed at men has been central to the production of orthodox masculinity. Homophobia has been used as an ordering principle of valued or subjugated individuals in western cultures (Plummer 1999). Homophobia made hyper-masculinity compulsory for boys, and it made the expression of femininity among boys taboo. When one combines a culture of homophobia, femphobia, and compulsory heterosexuality, one has the makeup of what I call 'homohysteria.' Homophobic discourse has therefore been used as a weapon for boys and men to deride one another in establishing this hierarchy (Burn 2000). And because femininity was so deeply entwined with male homosexuality (Kimmel 1994), misogynistic discourse not only served to reproduce gender inequality among men, and between men and women, but it reproduced homophobia, too.

But what happens to the traditional, conservative, orthodox version of masculinity when our culture of homohysteria decreases? What implications might this have on men who were once forced into a narrow ascription of masculinity? I argue that the existence of inclusive masculinities means that there is an awareness that heterosexual men can act in ways once associated with homosexuality, with less threat to their public identity as heterosexual. I show that this has socio-positive effects for straight men, gay men, and women as well.

In the process of explaining my results, I highlight that Connell's (1987) notion of hegemonic masculinity is unable to capture the complexity of what occurs as cultural homohysteria diminishes. Accordingly, in this book I not only show that masculinities are changing among university-attending, heterosexual youth, but I propose a new social theory to explain this occurrence—inclusive masculinity theory.

INCLUSIVE MASCULINITY THEORY

In this book, I use multiple ethnographies (mostly of athletes) to show that there is significant change occurring to heterosexual masculinities among university-aged (mostly) white men, athletes and non-athletes, alike. Inclusive masculinity theory conceptualizes what happens concerning masculinities in the cultural zeitgeists of three periods within Anglo-American societies: Moments of elevated cultural homohysteria, diminishing cultural homohysteria, and diminished homohysteria. I use the term homohysteria to describe the fear of being homosexualized, as it incorporates three variables: 1) mass awareness that homosexuality exists as a static sexual orientation; 2) a cultural zeitgeist of disapproval of homosexuality, and the femininity that is associated with it; and 3) the need for men to publicly align their social identities with heterosexuality (compulsory heterosexuality) in order to avoid homosexual suspicion. In other words, a homophobic culture might look disparagingly at homosexuality, but without mass cultural suspicion that one might be gay it is not a culture of homohysteria.

Key to inclusive masculinity theory is that, in moments of higher cultural homophobia, homophobic discourse has traditionally been the most important policing agent of masculinity. Here, homonegative discourse is used to stratify men in deference to a hegemonic mode of dominance (Connell 1987, 1995). And, as multiple masculinity scholars have shown (cf. Plummer 1999), in periods of high homophobia boys and men are compelled to act aggressively and to maintain homophobic and sexist attitudes. In such periods, men are also encouraged to raise their masculine capital through sport and muscularity (cf. Pronger 1990) and they remain emotionally distant from one another. In this culture, boys and men are also expected to boast about their heterosexual accomplishments. It is in this cultural zeitgeist that Kimmel suggests homophobia *is* masculinity (1994), and it is in this zeitgeist that I suggest a culture is homohysterical.

In periods of high homohysteria, men's gendered terrains are severely limited, as is physical intimacy between men (cf. Ibson 2002). Accordingly, men's demonstrations of intimacy are generally relegated to the public sphere (such as playing sports), and soft tactility is prohibited. Thus, boys and men have traditionally been prohibited from holding hands, softly hugging, caressing, or kissing (Kaplan 2006). In such cultural moments, boys and men who *do* display physical or emotional intimacy are socially homosexualized and consequently stripped of their perceived masculinity.

However, inclusive masculinity theory argues that in cultures of diminishing homohysteria, two dominant (but not dominating) forms of masculinity will exist: One conservative and one inclusive. Because the conservative masculinity is not culturally hegemonic, I call this form 'orthodox masculinity.' Here, men remain homohysterical, and therefore tactically and emotionally distant from one another. Conversely, heterosexual men ascribing to an 'inclusive masculinity' demonstrate emotional and physically homosocial proximity. They include their gay teammates, and are shown to value heterofemininity. Important in this cultural moment, however, is that neither form of masculinity retains cultural hegemony. In this stage, men who value orthodox masculinity might use homophobic discourse with specific intent to demonize homosexuals, while inclusive acting men may use homophobic discourse but without intent to degrade homosexuals.

Finally, inclusive masculinity theory argues that in an Anglo-American culture of diminished homohysteria, homophobic discourse is almost entirely lost, or the meanings associated with it no longer maintain homosexualizing utility. In such a setting, the esteemed attributes of men will no longer rely on control and domination, thus intentional homophobic stigmatization will cease. Inclusive masculinity theory therefore highlights that there will be social inclusion of the form of masculinities that were once traditionally marginalized by hegemonic masculinity. Accordingly, inclusive masculinity theory maintains that, in such a zeitgeist, multiple masculinities will proliferate with less hierarchy or hegemony. There will also be an expansion of acceptable heteromasculine behaviors. In other words, when archetypes of inclusive masculinities proliferate, they do not seem to also 'dominate.' This is not simply a matter of a protest version of masculinity competing for cultural hegemony. Inclusive masculinity theory serves as a social-constructionist theory that simultaneously incorporates (during high periods of homophobia) and challenges (during diminishing and diminished periods of cultural homophobia) Connell's (1987) theorizing.

The theme of this book is therefore as much about the equal inclusion of gay men as it is about the inclusion of straight men's femininity. However, there are other socio-positive variables that come from decreased homohysteria. I show that inclusive masculinities also lead to decreased sexism, and I suggest that this may help in the erosion of patriarchy. Inclusive masculinity theory also maintains that the gendered behaviors of boys and men will be less differentiated from girls and women in periods of diminished homohysteria. In other words, inclusive masculinity theory maintains that in periods of diminished homohysteria there will be a reversal of what gender scholars sometimes describe as the separation of gendered spheres (Cancian 1987). In such a culture, the differences between masculinity and femininity, men and women, gay and straight, will be harder to distinguish, and masculinity will no longer serve as the primary method of stratifying men. Claiming that inclusive masculinities exists, explicating the claim through rich, qualitative data from a variety of men in a variety of geographical locations, and framing it with a sophisticated new gender theory, is the project of this book.

ETHNOGRAPHIC METHODS

To illustrate the changing relationship between men, masculinity and homohysteria, I utilize multiple ethnographies and qualitative investigations in both America and Britain, alongside other researchers' findings. I examine sports that Messner (2002) describes as being *at the center* of masculine production (such as football and basketball), as well as those in the semi-periphery (such as soccer, tennis, and track). I also examine men in sports traditionally marginalized by mainstream, competitive sports (cheerleading, bowling, and figure skating), to see if masculinity operates differently throughout this stratification. Also, because Michael Messner (2004) theorizes that the more competitive a team is, the less freedom there is for variable conceptions of athletic masculinity, I interview athletes from both low and high quality teams, hoping to better understand the operation of masculinity throughout the institutional progression of sport. Data represented in this research is drawn from the following ethnographies.

Gay Athletes (see Appendix 1)

I first utilize interviews with 68 gay athletes (from all over the United States), taken between 1999 and 2004. Forty-eight of these men are out of the closet on their ostensibly heterosexual high school and university teams, and the other 20 remain closeted. These men are interviewed about their experiences in sport, how they are treated by their teammates, and for general information about the degree of homophobia and heteromasculinity present on their teams. Athletes came from a variety of states and school sizes. Many of them came from regions that are traditionally considered highly homophobic. However, only nine of the 68 men are of color.

Heterosexual Male Cheerleaders (see Appendix 2)

I next chose to examine heterosexual male athletes. However, because I desired to see what happens when male athletes are structurally compelled to rely on both women and (often) gay male teammates, I studied competitive university cheerleaders. The sample I chose, however, is unique. I only selected heterosexual men who had once played high school football. These athletes, unable to make their university football teams, were literally wooed into cheerleading by female cheerleaders.

Athletes from this sample come primarily from four teams, from four separate geographical regions of the United States (South, Midwest, West and North-East). All of the athletes are university-attending, and they are almost exclusively white. I conducted participant observations with these teams before doing semi-structured, in-depth interviews. These men are interviewed about a variety of topics related to masculinity and sexuality, but the primary questions centered on how they feel about homosexuality, how they construct heterosexuality, and how they feel about women and gay men as teammates.

The phenomenal results—the outright acceptance of gay men among half of the cheerleading teams studied in 2001–2002, and the men's acceptance of women as capable athletes—is sometimes met with a sort of "of course you found that, aren't they all gay anyhow" response. In other words, the heterosexual informants are homosexualized simply for playing a feminized sport. Nonetheless, the results were groundbreaking because they show that things are being done radically different than in previous investigations of masculinity, in the same sport (Davis 1990). I find that sport, today, is at least as much affected by the broader culture as it has influence over that broader culture. My findings show that improving institutional and organizational cultures is highly influential in shaping men to radically alter their gendered perspectives. In short, men came in as homophobes, but very quickly lost their homophobia because of their team's organizational culture.

A Mainstream Fraternity (see Appendix 3)

After publishing my cheerleading data, I began investigating university men in more masculinized settings. I was looking for a contestation of the traditional, homophobic and sexist version of masculinity that has been shown to dominate in youth culture. Thus, I next conducted a two-year long ethnography, alongside 32 interviews, of a mainstream American fraternity in Southern California, between 2002 and 2004. Here, 40 percent of the men were of color.

Although not members of an organized sporting team, these men nonetheless maintain high masculine capital through their association with their fraternity. This fraternity research adds to my body of work on inclusive masculinities, not only because fraternities are described as highly homophobic and sexist institutions (Boswell and Spade 1996; Martin and Hummer 1989; Sanday 1990) but because nobody has ever previously described fraternities as being aligned with an inclusive project of masculinity. Not only do I find the men of this fraternity promoting a more inclusive form of masculinity, but after one of their more agentic members came out of the closet, they elected him to lead their fraternity. Thus, data from this investigation elucidates the power of the individual in contesting and shaping organizational culture.

A Rugby Team (see Appendix 4)

Because I had found various forms of inclusive masculinity among ex-high school American football players, and among non-athletes of a mainstream American fraternity, I next decided to examine the relationship between sport and masculinities among 24 men of a highly masculinized teamsport. Accordingly, I investigate the construction of masculinity within a nationally recognized British university rugby team. Unlike the cheerleaders or fraternity men, these athletes have no openly gay teammates to influence their gendered perspective. And, unlike the cheerleaders, they represent men who reside atop the masculine stratification. Yet, these men are found to have come to the same gendered perspectives as the informants in the other studies. Most interesting, the men in this study are not influenced by institutional directives (as the men in cheerleading are) or influential openly gay individuals (as men in the fraternity study are). Instead, these men highlight that even those at the center of masculine production can be influenced by what is occurring in the broader culture.

A Soccer Team (see Appendix 5)

The British study of university rugby players is supported by research on a top-notch British university soccer team. Here, I show that not only do the mostly white players of this team wish to distance themselves from homophobia, but they proudly partake in all sorts of homoerotic kissing activities, even posting the photos on the Internet site Facebook.

Other Influential Data

I am also influenced by, but do not formally present, data from four other ethnographic studies. I do not present the data here because it is still in the process of being written. One of these is conducted on the men of a small, Catholic university in the American Midwest. These men almost exclusively hail from small, religious towns. Yet, these men exhibit as inclusive a form of masculinity as the other American men I study. I add to this another ethnographic study of soccer players at a major East Coast U.S. city. Here I find that while these men are not quite as 'soft' in their masculinity as men within my (major British city's) university, they nonetheless exhibit the characteristics of inclusive masculinity. These men maintain their support for homosexuality, and display a variety of homosocial bonding and homosocial tactility.

I am also influenced by data currently under review. This research, conducted on British high school male students (both athletes and non-athletes) finds that homophobic discourse is not accepted. Students do not even say, "that's so gay." These heterosexual male students are also physically demonstrative with one another. They sit on each other's laps, dance together, and kiss each other out of heterosexual affection.

I also draw considerable influence from the unpublished work that I conducted on male nurses for my PhD dissertation (Anderson 2004). Here I found heterosexual men varied in their rationale for nursing, with older men justifying their transgression into the field through having first served in a hyper-macho institution, like the military. I also found these men to be defensive about their heterosexuality. For example, I timed that on average they managed to signal to a new patient that they were heterosexual in less than a minute. Conversely, heterosexual male nursing *students* felt no need to justify their career choice, and avoided signaling heterosexuality.

Finally, although not formally coded, other data that I use to create my conceptualization of the growing influence of inclusive masculinities comes from the personal relationship that I maintain with my students. My university is widely recognized as a sporting centre of excellence. Men and women in my program come with a sporting background, and most desire to have a career in it. Here at the university, I anonymously survey them (before they know me) and I find decreasing degrees of homophobia with each subsequent year's cohort. This year for the first time, no incoming freshman suggested that gay men should be excluded from playing on straight teams; and no men thought that gay coaches should be barred from locker rooms. Furthermore, all of the second year students report having kissed another guy (on the lips).

More important than the surveys, however, is the personal relationship I maintain with my students. I do not believe in social distance between lecturer and student. I maintain that the best teachers are mentors, and the best mentors are friends. I therefore join my students for lunch, run with them after class, and socialize with them in my office. I even go clubbing and drinking with them. I desire to project this open attitude from the first day, providing them with my mobile phone number. Finally, every Tuesday night is 'Pint with Eric' night in our university's pub. Here, students come and socialize with me about all types of things.

It is in these relationships, the countless informal interviews, that I develop my deepest understandings of what it means to be a young man today. It is here that I often develop my best social theories to explain their lives. Of course, one might also argue that I am only drawing inclusive students to interview, suggesting that I am only tracking changes amongst an already inclusive group. However, I often have the occasion to meet these men's friends who are not thought to display inclusive masculinities. Furthermore, they share with me how they think their friends from other groups view things, too. And, because they have learned something about the sociological imagination through my lectures, they make excellent key informants.

SITUATING MYSELF WITH THE INFORMANTS

Because this research involves sexuality, I reflected upon the influence of disclosing my sexual identity to my informants. Politically, I align with the feminist mantra that the personal is political, and I maintain that remaining closeted constitutes a deeply socio-negative political act (Rofes 2000). It is possible that my coming out positively influences the data, but it does not bias it. This is because it has been shown that disclosure of homosexuality helps to minimize power disparities between researcher and informant. Kong, Mahoney and Plummer (2002) suggest that when researchers come out as gay, informants reciprocate by divulging more of their lives.

Thus, because much of my research deals with stigmatized behaviors (including same-sex sexual behaviors among heterosexual men) I decided it best to be not only open about my homosexuality, but open to discussions of my own sexual desires, behaviors and beliefs as well. And, just as Kong, Mahoney and Plummer suggest, I find that the more I disclose about my sexual activities, the further disclosure it elicits among my informants. It also significantly reduces social distance. This helps facilitate invitations into my informants' worlds.

I am frequently invited to their parties, where I drink and often get drunk with them. I am invited to their homes, and introduced to members of their non-athletic social networks. I become friends with many of these informants, many of which have lasted for years. My willingness to be so open, and my desire to be comfortable in my informants' social worlds, enabled me to collect much of the 'sensitive' data I show.

I recognize that it is possible that my openness influences informants to overstate their socio-positive beliefs about gay men and inclusive masculinities, too. However, this fits with my political aim of conducting emancipatory research. My research *is* political, and I make no pretense to enter the field as a strictly neutral observer. It is for these reasons that I maintain that a heterosexual researcher, or even a homosexual researcher who is unwilling to engage in lengthy and personal discussions about one's own sexual behaviors, will not elicit the same response or perhaps even come to the same conclusions as with my methods.

PUBLIC SOCIOLOGIES AND ACCESSIBILITY

I try to examine men's social arrangements with a critical eye, in order to help emancipate people from oppressive structures of gender and sexuality (Silk and Andrews forthcoming). Questioning metanarratives, myths, stereotypes, and hegemonic processes of social matters is the job of a sociologist. In this case, questioning assumed knowledge and dominant norms and values enables me to better comprehend the relationship between sport and society. To do this, I use social-feminist thinking, viewing power and stratification as embedded within institutions, in order to ask critical questions about the relationship between sport, gender and sexuality.

However, my standpoint is one of a public sociologist. I believe in emancipatory research that is accessible for public consumption. Thus, it is not my intention to write an academically inaccessible work. Instead, I desire to explicate my data using sophisticated sociological theories, but accessible language. Additionally, to help illuminate my systematically collected data, I sometimes attempt to then personalize, and sometimes even editorialize, my findings. I do so because these examples resonate with readers less familiar with sociological principles.

CONTEXTUALIZING RESULTS

Most of the data I draw from represents undergradute men. Furthermore, these studies are mostly conducted on white men. Accordingly, there is simply not enough data to make generalizations beyond that of white, university-attending men. Also, although I did not ask for socio-economic data from my informants, it is assumed that this research reflects middle-class men because this demographic is overrepresented in university attendance. I recognize that this contributes to a culture of normalizing middle-class whiteness. However, my sample is not intentionally designed to exclude people of color or people from lower socio-economic status.

For example, I searched (for years) to find openly gay athletes of color to interview, but I could locate very few. Furthermore, although the sport of cheerleading had some men of color, few are drawn to and/or can afford the sport. Eighty percent of these informants are white. I am also limited to a dominance of white men in my British studies. The population of Britain is 90 percent white, and this demographic is reflected in both the ethnographies I report.

Furthermore, it is not possible to extend my analysis of race or class by drawing on the works of other researchers. This is primarily because there is little, if any, current literature to draw on. And comparing the results of older research of men of color would make the fundamental error of comparing old results with new. Hopefully, other researchers will apply the theoretical framework I propose here to empirical research of young men of color and varying socio-economic status.

But while this research is limited by its focus on white, middle-class men, it is strengthened by the multitude of geographical locations in which data is collected. Participant observations and interviews come from men in the American South, North, East and West, as well as four locations in the Southwest of England. This research also offers considerable validity through the high number of men interviewed. If one adds the 68 interviews of gay athletes, to the 68 interviews of heterosexual cheerleaders, along with the 32 mostly heterosexual informants of a California fraternity, the 24 heterosexual informants of a British university's rugby team, the 22 interviews of the heterosexual soccer players at that same university, there are a total of 214 interviews that formally feed the results discussed in this research.

There are another 22 interviews of heterosexual British High School students, 20 interviews of heterosexual soccer players from a small Catholic university in the American Midwest, and another 20 interviews among the heterosexual soccer players of a major Eastern U.S. university that informally shape my analysis, but are not formally included here. Accordingly, there is ample evidence to suggest that while the changes I see occurring among university-attending men might not be occurring equally in all places, there seems to be a broader trend of a shift toward masculinities favoring inclusivity among university-attending men.

This sample is also strategically positioned to permit me to assess what is occurring amongst men who perhaps have (or will have) significant cultural capital to influence social understandings in the broader culture, thus influencing the construction of masculinity for the next generation. The informants in my research are individuals who are more likely to coach sports, and teach physical education. Perhaps some will even become professional athletes. Equally significant, because they have a university education, those who leave sport are more likely to become leaders of businesses and governments, where they might potentially maintain more agency in influencing organizational or institutional culture. So, while my sample is not representative of all university-aged men, it does account for a demographic that is likely to have significant influence in shaping the culture of masculinity in the future. Furthermore, although university-attending men may represent more inclusive versions of masculinity than poorer, or lesser educated young men, this should not be assumed without empirical investigation.

While these studies are over-representative of athletes (86 non-athletes, compared to 196 athletes) it is plausible to suggest that results of university-attending athletes are generalizable to non-athletes, as well. This is because teamsport athletes traditionally exhibit more conservative masculinities than non-athletes. If I show change occurring among teamsport athletes, one can reasonably determine that non-athletes will demonstrate the same. Indeed, research on the non-athletes seems to support this. The considerable evidence of the emergence of inclusive masculinities, even among university athletes (which have traditionally been described as conservative in their approach to gender), means that we should be cautious about relying on older data which shows university-attending men to value orthodox notions of masculinity. The results I present in this book should make us more measured in our claims about the degree of homophobia, homohysteria, and heteromasculinity that exists in *any* given youth culture.

Collectively, these various investigations provide a wide-ranging sample upon which to draw general conclusions about the relationship between university-attending men, sport and masculinity. However, I am not trying to claim that all men are performing inclusive masculinity. I do not, for example, claim that middle-aged men are more inclusive than they used to be. I do not even maintain that *all* university attending men, everywhere, are inclusive in their approach to masculinity. However, the results from these various ethnographies suggest that a broader trend is occurring among university-attending men, and that we need to examine how men may or may not be changing their approach to masculinity in other settings. Accordingly, my thesis, that decreasing homohysteria is leading to more inclusive versions of masculinity among university–attending men, manifests itself differently in various cultures. So when readers read of a particular result presented here, and maintain that this particular result is not occurring in their culture, I would encourage that instead of discounting the general premise, readers investigate what *is* happening in their own locale.

Finally, the behavioral results described within each ethnographic study presented are likely to be somewhat unique to each location. For example, I did not find men performing same-sex kisses in California as I did in the study of men at a British university. Men are not emotionally bonding in the Midwest as they are in California. However, this does not mean that men in the Midwest are not doing something to challenge hegemonic notions of masculinity. It simply means that they are doing things differently. This is one reason I describe these changes as inclusive 'masculinities,' as opposed to inclusive 'masculinity,' even if I refer to the theory as 'inclusive masculinity theory.'

OUTLINE OF THE CHAPTERS

In Chapter 1, I describe how women and gay men grew to become the 'other' upon which heterosexual men are constructed and valued in American societies. I examine the traditional construction of heterosexual masculinity, and discuss how hegemonic processes of dominance and oppression are used to explain the stratification of men. I examine the relationship between homosexuality and masculinity, and the threat that homosexuality poses to the maintenance of patriarchy. I clarify different forms of masculinity, and highlight how they operate in the masculinized culture of teamsports and other masculinized arenas. In doing so, I lay the framework necessary to understand the developing relationship between men and masculinity throughout the rest of the book.

In Chapter 2, I take a different perspective on patriarchy and homophobia in sport. Instead of theorizing a grand narrative about gender, I examine the particulars of how *sport* has resisted the advancements of women and gay men. I explicate sport as a perfectly integrated, self-reinforcing system with few internal contradictions or conflicts, by explaining the cultural and structural variables that combine to make it so resilient to change. Consistent with hegemony theory, however, my thesis is that as resilient as patriarchy has been, no form of masculinity can be entirely self-reproducing. The reproductive process is laden with social tension and ultimately it can fail. Although the analysis I provide in this chapter focuses on sport, the model I propose is easily extrapolated to other institutions.

In Chapter 3, I highlight how orthodox masculinities not only oppress others, but how those who exhibit the traits of orthodox masculinity suffer for their masculine adherence. I first discuss the outcomes for the 'others,' namely violence. I then move to a discussion of the ways orthodox masculinity polices the social terrains that heterosexual men can occupy, and the types of relationships they are denied with other men. I suggest that the collective nature of the manner in which athletes matriculate through sport (as discussed in Chapter 2), and the way in which the cultural and structural environment of sport is used to place an athlete into an agenticless state, articulates how sport has not only managed to reproduce itself over the years, but how it has managed to resist the impact of more liberalizing broader cultural trends. However, I suggest that if it can be shown that there exists a competing paradigm within or between groups, it can help athletes see an alternative pathway to constructing their masculinity. If broader social trends become so divergent from what occurs in sport, it may also highlight the barbarism of competitive sporting culture. I suggest inclusive masculinity theory is that model.

In Chapter 4, I apply the well-recognized and highly influential social psychological literature of Zimbardo, Milgram (1974) and Asch (1951) to sport, describing how men are trained to be complicit to authority, and how sport teaches men to accept and inflict masculine policing.

In Chapter 5, I lay the foundation for inclusive masculinity theory. I first describe orthodox masculinity as a 20th century archetype predicated in the marginalization of other types of men, alongside patriarchal oppression. I describe the policing mechanism of men's borders as being homophobia and misogyny, theorizing homophobia as being particularly central to the production and stratification of masculinities as an ordered system of valued or subjugated individuals in Western cultures. This has led to a culture of homohysteria.

In Chapter 6, I suggest that if our culture were to value homosexuality and femininity differently, we might also expect a shift in the way gender is carried out and valued. Accordingly, I specify what inclusive masculinity theory is. I describe what happens to heterosexual men's masculinity in three cultural phases: one of high homohysteria, one of diminishing homohysteria, and one of diminished homohysteria. I argue that, in the later stages, multiple masculinities will proliferate without hegemony or hierarchy. This is the foundation of inclusive masculinity theory.

In Chapter 7, I suggest that if inclusive masculinities exist within competitive teamsports and/or the broader culture, we should also expect to see the lived experiences of gay men, and the attitudes of heterosexual men toward them, improve. I first outline the findings of my 1999–2004 in-depth interviews of openly gay high school and collegiate athletes, showing a significant variance between what researchers theorized would happen to openly gay athletes in sport and what their lived experience is. More so, this research highlights the use of individual agency in contesting and reshaping organizational attitudes toward homosexuality.

I next present data concerning the relationship between heterosexual male athletes, and their gay male teammates in the collegiate sport of cheerleading. Here, I discuss the utility of contact theory in breaking down traditional homophobic sentiment. Straight men in this sport unlearn their gendered perspectives before relearning a more inclusive approach. While the influence of openly gay men on their teams is significant in this process, I also highlight the influence of progressive organizational norms in changing long held homophobic sentiment.

I next present data collected among the men of a mainstream U.S. fraternity. This data not only finds these fraternity men recruit gay members, but that they elected an openly gay man to be their chapter president. I show that this fraternity is influenced by an institutional mandate to promote inclusivity, and highlight that this policy makes it easier for members to come out to his fraternity brothers. This serves to further promote inclusivity within the organizational setting.

Finally, I share the results of an ethnography on an English university's rugby team. Although there are no openly gay players on this team, and although both their institution and coaches remain highly homophobic, these men nonetheless exhibit inclusive attitudes toward homosexuality. I suggest that (unlike men in these other studies) they learned their inclusive attitudes not from gay men or female teammates, but instead from the broader culture. Accordingly, the various ethnographies I draw upon in this chapter highlight the varying influences of organizational, institutional, and the broader culture, alongside individual agency in contesting orthodox inscriptions of masculinity and shaping a more inclusive zeitgeist.

In Chapter 8, I show that the reduction of homohysteria (and the embracing of one's gay teammates and friends) has a greater impact on gender relations than just how gay men are treated. This is because homophobia and anti-femininity are intricately related. The reduction of cultural homophobia might therefore have an effect, in some measure, on eroding patriarchy. Also, in a culture of decreased homohysteria, homophobia no longer polices men into narrow masculine boundaries. Once heterosexual men are freed from the burden of having to reprove their heterosexuality, and once they no longer care if others think they are gay, they maintain more liberty to explore and embrace once tabooed social spaces, behaviors, and ideas. As men increasingly occupy traditionally feminized terrain, the gendered and stigmatized nature of those gendered spaces is destined to change. Accordingly, I next examine how men whom I describe as aspiring to the principles of inclusive masculinity associate with femininity in ways that men in both masculinized and feminized terrains previously have not. I begin by looking at the institutional attitudes of two university cheerleading associations, and how their variance influences men to adopt either an orthodox or inclusive perspective. However, even here I suggest that the men labeled as orthodox are not 'as orthodox' as men of previous investigations. I next return to fraternity members, showing how their organization has created an atmosphere of respect for women, unlike other research on fraternities. Finally, I discuss how, despite the misogynistic views of their coaches, the rugby men nonetheless take a more inclusive perspective with women.

In Chapter 9, I show that the incongruous relationship between heterosexual men's own desire for emotional intimacy and the hegemonic norms by which they are supposed to express themselves has traditionally prevented many heterosexual men from developing physically intimate relationships with other men. I show how heterosexual men are eroding at the one-time rule of homosexuality. Forty percent of the men in my cheerleading ethnography have had some form of sexual behavior with another man, yet none consider themselves to be gay, nor (importantly) are they homosexualized when they make this knowledge public. I then show how same-sex kissing no longer maintains stigma among the players of a UK-based soccer team. Essentially I suggest that the one-drop rule of homosexuality has been betrayed by a kiss.

In the concluding chapter, I suggest that inclusive masculinities rival or outnumber orthodox masculinities as an esteemed category of masculine archetypes. In addition to having a plethora of socio-positive benefits for gay men, this means that there is also a decreasing polarization of gendered behaviors. I suggest that many of the long-held codes, behaviors and other symbols of what separates masculine men from feminized men are blurring, making behaviors and attitudes increasingly problematic to describe as masculine, feminine, gay or straight. The culture has shifted so that behaviors coded as feminine no longer represent the stigma they once did. In the process, they have been stripped of their homosexualizing significance. Accordingly, I argue that the efforts of the first, second and now third wave of feminism, combined with the gay liberationist and gay assimilationist efforts of the past four decades, are slowly eroding at the gender binary. This is particularly true for gender *within* masculinity.

I argue that the existence of inclusive masculinities highlights that there is awareness that heterosexual men can act in ways once associated with homosexuality with less threat to one's public identity as heterosexual. This then is a positive influence for men to associate with women, femininity and gay men. The influence of this change is multiple and varied. Accordingly, this concluding chapter examines the influence of these various forces on constructing inclusive masculinities through culture, institutional, organizational and individual agency.

Part I
Orthodox Masculinity

1 Orthodox Masculinity and Hegemonic Oppression

Various attributes are associated with sporting participation for boys and men in Western cultures. One of these concerns indoctrination into manhood. Raphael (1988), for example, argues that without historic rites of passage modern men are confused about what it means to be a man, proposing that competitive sports help fill this void. Others view sport as a mechanism for socializing boys into a host of socio-positive psychological characteristics necessary in an industrial culture. Others, like Sage (1990), suggest that sports permit governments to transmit dominant social and political values the way religion once did. Still others suggest that competitive teamsports are an effective solution to many social issues related to the social integration of racialized people (Girginov, Papadimitrious, & Lopez De D'Amico 2006). And, of course, if you ask my first year university students why sports are 'good' they will repeat the lore of sports' mythical attributes: sports promote teamwork, cooperation, fitness, and self-esteem. They might suggest that sports help minorities find employment out of ghettos; that they help promote school attendance; and that sport helps certain athletes earn scholarships to pay for the rising costs of university attendance. There are absurd beliefs, too. Some believe that sports help men (who they perceive as naturally violent) vent their anger in an acceptable manner (cf. McCaughey 2007). While others maintain that sports 'teach' boys to win and fail in public view, perhaps letting them learn from their triumphs and tragedies in the process. Somehow failure and it's public ostracizing even 'builds character' in kids too young to understand the rules of a game.

My analysis of sport however is quite critical. This is not to say that sports do not have some socio-positive value, but I reject most of the supposed socio-positive aspects of sport, instead believing them to be far more psychologically and socially damaging than beneficial. Brackenridge (1995) supports this belief, writing that sport:

> . . . has held a special place in the affections of western industrial societies for its supposed virtues and its potential as a tool of economic and social development. The special status of sport has also protected

it from critical scrutiny and meant that social inequalities and other problems, such as sexual harassment and abuse, have all-too-often been ignored or tacitly condoned. (p.16)

The socio-negative aspects of sport I highlight in this chapter are not solely because of the competitive nature, or the gender-segregated structure, on which sport is built. It also reflects the masculine ether in which most competitive sports swim. I would love to debunk each of the aforementioned myths—but that's mostly the project of another book. For now, a more measured claim is to suggest that sports (for males) are a somewhat unique cultural location where boys and men gather to bond over physical joy, pain and labor. In sport, men relate in emotional and physical ways, not acceptable in other cultural spaces. In this chapter, I examine the historical/political project of sports concerning this bonding process, and the importance of segregating women and gay men away from heterosexual men in order to preserve heteromasculine privilege. I show how women and gay men grew to become the 'other' upon which heterosexual men are constructed and valued, and the manner in which heteromasculine men are given immense institutional and cultural privilege because of their introduction into sport.

I examine the relationship between homosexuality and masculinity, and the threat that homosexuality poses to the maintenance of patriarchy. I also examine the construction of heterosexual masculinities, and how hegemonic processes of dominance and oppression are used to stratify men. I clarify different forms of masculinity, and highlight how they operate in the masculinized culture of teamsports (and other masculinized arenas). In doing so, I lay the framework necessary to understand the developing relationship between men and masculinity throughout the rest of the book.

SPORT, SEXUALITY, AND THE SECOND INDUSTRIAL REVOLUTION

Although the invention of the machinery and transportation necessary for industrialization began early in the 1700s in Anglo-American cultures, the antecedents of most of today's sporting culture can be traced to the years of the second industrial revolution—the mid 1800s through early 1900s. During this period, sturdy farmers exchanged their time-honored professions for salaried work. Families replaced their farm's rent for that of a city apartment, instead. The allure of industry, and the better life it promised, influenced such a migration that the percentage of people living in cities rose from just 25 percent in 1800 to around 75 percent in 1900 (Cancian 1987).

However, just as cities attracted people, the increasing difficulty of rural life also compelled them to leave their agrarian ways. This is because the same industrial technologies that brought capitalism also meant that fewer farmers were required to produce the necessary crops to feed a growing population. With production capacity rising and crop prices falling, families were not only drawn to the cities by the allure of a stable wage and the possibility of class mobility, they were repelled by an increasingly difficult agrarian labor market as well as the inability to own land.

For all the manifestations of physical horror that was factory life, there were many advantages, too. Families were no longer dependent on the fortune of good weather for their sustenance, and industry provided predictable (if long) working hours. Having a reliable wage meant that a family could count on how much money they would have at the end of the week, and some could use this financial stability to secure loans and purchase property. Also, the regularity of work meant that between blows of the factory whistle, there was time for men to play. The concept of leisure, once reserved for the wealthy, spread to the working class during this period (Rigauer 1981). It is the socio-cultural impact of this great migration that is central to the production of men's sport in Western cultures.

Sport gave boys something to do after school. It helped socialize them into the values necessary to be successful in this new economy, to instill the qualities of discipline and obedience, and to honor the hard work that was necessary in the dangerous occupations of industrial labor and mining (Rigauer 1981). Accordingly, workers needed to sacrifice both their time and their health, for the sake of making the wage they needed to support their dependent families. In sport, young boys were socialized into this value of sacrifice (in this case for team), so that they would later sacrifice health and well-being for family. But most important to the bourgeoisie ruling class, workers needed to be obedient to authority. Sports taught boys this docility. Carter (2006) nicely summarizes these points, saying that sports teach, "a clear hierarchical structure, autocratic tendencies, traditional notions of masculinity and the need for discipline" (p. 5). Accordingly, organized competitive sports were funded by those who maintained power of the reproduction of material goods. And, just as they are today, organized youth sports were financially backed by business, in the form of 'sponsors.' This, alongside the inclusion of physical education as part of a compulsory state-run education, was an economical way of assuring a docile and productive labor force.

This shift to industry had other gendered effects, too. Although there was a gendered division of labor in agrarian work, there was less gendering of jobs and tasks compared to industrial life. Here, both men and women toiled in demanding labor. Accordingly, in some aspects, heterosexual relationships were more egalitarian before industrialization. Factory work, however, shifted revenue's generation from inside the home to outside. Mom's physical labor no longer directly benefited the family as it once did, and much of women's labor therefore became unpaid and unseen. Conversely, men's working spaces were cold, dangerous and hard places. Men moved rocks, welded iron, swung picks and operated steam giants. These environments necessitated that men be tough and unemotional.

Cancian (1987) describes these changes as a separation of gendered spheres, saying that expectations of what it meant to be a man or woman bifurcated as a result of industrialization. Men grew more instrumental not only in their labor and purpose, but in their personalities, too. As a result of industrialization, men learned the way they showed their love was through their labor. Being a breadwinner, regardless of the working conditions upon which one toiled, was a labor of love. Because women were mostly (but not entirely) relegated to a domestic sphere, they were reliant upon their husband's ability to generate income. Thus, mostly robbed of economic agency, women learned to show their contribution through emotional expressiveness and domestic efficiency. Accordingly, the antecedents of men's stoicism and women's expressionism were born during this period.

In one sense, the separation of spheres created a new foundation for masculine power and privilege, especially to the extent that men increasingly came to control the family wage (Hartmann 1976). Men were also given more time away from home and family, as labor both inside and outside the home grew increasingly divided (Hochschild 1989). For example, when discussing the division of masculinity and femininity in doctoring and nursing, Williams (1993) writes that "Prior to this modern division, both men and women performed diagnostic, curative techniques as well as caregiving functions (although on very different clienteles). Separating these functions involved barring women from schools of medicine, and excluding men from nursing programs" (p. 3).

Even today, the work performed seems to be the predominant factor in determining whether a job is coded as masculine or feminine. They are also classed. Lower-class men's occupations require strength and physical danger, while upper-class men's occupations require leadership. Oppositely, women almost exclusively work in fields requiring nurturing, caregiving, or those concerned with cleaning up men's messes. Occupational gender segregation is so profound that Reskin and Hartmann (1986) showed that in order to balance out the gender segregation in the workforce (and make an equal number of men and women in all occupations) more than half of all men or women would have to change their job categories.

Conservative theorists, such as Parsons and Bales (1955) and Simpson and Simpson (1969), have argued that this is a natural outcome of the differences in socialization patterns, while others (Eisenstein 1979; Hartmann 1976) instead looked to patriarchy as the cause. For whatever reasons, however, labor grew divided as a result of the second industrial revolution—and this included child rearing.

During this period, fathers left for work early, often returning home once their sons had gone to bed. Because teaching children was considered 'women's work,' boys spent much of their days in presence of women where they were thought to be deprived of the masculine vapors supposedly necessary to masculinize them. Rotundo (1993: 31) writes, "Motherhood was advancing, fatherhood was in retreat . . . women were teaching boys how to be men." Messner (1992: 14) adds, "With no frontier to conquer . . . and with urban boys being raised and taught by women, it was feared that men were also becoming 'soft,' that society itself was becoming feminized." A by-product of industrialization, it was assumed, was that it was capable of creating a culture of soft, weak and feminine boys. Boys were structurally, and increasingly emotionally, segregated from their distant and absent fathers. This set the stage for what Filene (1975) called, *a crisis in masculinity.*

Simultaneous to this, however, was the first wave of women's political independence (Hargreaves 1986). The city provided a density of women upon which activism was made more accessible. Smith-Rosenberg (1985) suggests that men felt threatened by the political and social advancements of women at the time. Men perceived that they were losing their patriarchal power. The antidote to the rise of women's agency largely came through sport.

However, a much under-theorized influence on the development and promotion of sport comes through the changing understanding of sexuality during the second industrial revolution. Particularly concerning the growing understanding of homosexuality.

Agrarian life was lonely for gay men. One can imagine that finding homosexual sex and love in pastoral regions was difficult. Conversely, cities collected such quantities of people that gay social networks and even a gay identity could form. This coincided with a growing body of scholarly work from Westphal, Ulrichs and Krafft-Ebing, early pioneers of the gay liberationist movement. These scholars sought to classify homosexual acts as belonging to a *type* of person; a third sex, an invert, or homosexual (Spencer 1995). From this, they could campaign for legal and social equality. Previously, there were less entrenched heterosexual or homosexual social identities. In other words a man performed an *act* of sodomy, without necessarily being constructed as a sodomite. Under this new theorizing, however, homosexuality was no longer a collection of particular acts, but instead, as Foucault (1984: 43) so famously wrote:

> We must not forget that the psychological, psychiatric, medical category of homosexuality was constituted from the moment it was characterized–Westphal's famous article of 1870 on "contrary sexual sensations" can stand as its date of birth–less by a type of sexual relations than by a certain quality of sexual sensibility, a certain way of inverting the masculine and the feminine in oneself. Homosexuality appeared as one of the forms of sexuality when it was transposed from the practice of sodomy on to a kind of interior androgyny, a hermaphorodism of the soul. The sodomite had been a temporary aberration; the homosexual was now a species.

And while I think Foucault overstates matters, it is evident that the visibility of the homosexual grew during this period. The 1895 conviction of Oscar Wilde for 'gross indecency' animated this newly created deviant identity. So extensive was the media coverage and public discussion around the trial of Britain's celebrated author and playwright, that it breathed public awareness into homosexuality, and consequently engendered elevated social homophobia. In Wilde, homosexuality found a spokesperson.

All of this is to suggest that the cultural awareness that some men existed as a different type of sexual person, a homosexual, came into existence during this period. Thus, one might describe the trials of Oscar Wilde as giving birth to homohysteria. For example, the day news of Wilde's conviction became public, gay men fled England in droves.

But whereas Wilde put a face on homosexuality, Sigmund Freud explained its etiology. In his *Three Essays on the Theory of Sexuality* (1905), Freud theorized that sexuality was not innate. Instead he suggested that childhood experiences influenced men to become heterosexual or homosexual, something he called inversion. Homosexuality, Freud said, was a process of gendered wrongdoing, particularly through the absence of a father figure and an over-domineering mother. In one of his footnotes he wrote, " . . . the presence of both parents plays an important part. The absence of a strong father in childhood not infrequently favors the occurrence of inversion" (p. 146). Freud even gave child-rearing tips to help parents lead their children to heterosexual adjustment.

Freud's theories are certainly more complex than I present, and my aim is not to paint Freud as homophobic. Freud actually tried to humanize homosexuals by explaining their 'condition.' Yet in the process of explaining how homosexuals came to be, Freud cemented the notion and value of a nuclear family into popular culture. Also, what is important about Freud is not what he said, thought or wrote, but what others attribute to him. So while Freud was certainly more complex in his thinking, what the populace heard was that an absent father and an over-domineering mother could make kids homosexual. This created a moral panic among Victorian-thinking British and American cultures. It seemed that industrialization (because it pulled fathers away from their families for large periods of time) had structurally created a social system designed to make kids 'inverts.'

Accordingly, in this zeitgeist, what it meant to be a man began to be predicated in not being like one of those sodomite/invert/homosexuals; homohysteria. Being masculine entailed being the opposite of the softness attributed to homosexual men. Kimmel (1994) shows us that heterosexuality therefore grew further predicated in aversion to anything coded as feminine. Accordingly, what it meant to be a man in the 20th century was to be unlike a woman. What it meant to be heterosexual was not to be homosexual. In this gender-panicked culture, sport was thrust upon boys. It was implemented as part of a political project to reverse these feminizing trends. Sports, and those who coached them, were charged with shaping boys into heterosexual, masculine men. Accordingly, a rapid rise and expansion of organized sport was utilized as a homosocial institution principally aimed to counter men's fears of feminism and homosexuality.

Another key element in this project was elevating the male body as superior to that of women. Men accomplished this through displays of strength and violence, so that sports embedded elements of competition and hierarchy among men. Connell (1995: 54) suggests, "men's greater sporting prowess has become . . . symbolic proof of superiority and right to rule." But sport could only work in this capacity if women were formally excluded from participation. If women were bashing into each other and thumping their chests like men, men wouldn't be able to lay sole claim to this privilege (Bryson 1987). Without women's presence in sport, men's greater sporting prowess became *uncontested* proof of their superiority and right to masculine domination. Thus, sport not only reproduced the gendered nature of the social world, but sporting competitions became principle sites where masculine behaviors were learned and reinforced (Hargreaves 1995).

Unfortunately, when we think of sport today, few consider its origins and intent. Few recall that Pierre de Coubertin's reinvention of the ancient Olympic Games was *because* he saw French men becoming soft. Few people, outside of a select group of sport sociologists, think of sport as a social mechanism to demonstrate support for masculine hegemony today. Most are misled into believing that all is equal in sport because women have multiple sporting opportunities. Furthermore, we scarcely think about what types of sports we culturally esteem—those that highlight the differences between the male and female body, such as American football and rugby (Burton-Nelson 1994). We value sports were bodies clash, jump and sprint, and not those where finesse, extreme endurance or balance determine success. In other words, we value sports that favor whatever biological advantage men as a whole maintain.

Christianity also concerned itself with the project of masculinizing and heterosexualizing men during this period. Muscular Christianity concerned itself with instilling sexual morality, chastity, heterosexuality, religiosity and nationalism in men through competitive and violent sports (Mathisen 1990). This was a project that extended to Native Americans as well; here sport was used to introduce natives to Anglican ways of thinking about the individual, opposed to the collective their cultures valued. This muscular movement aimed to force a rebirth of Western notions of manliness, to shield boys and men from immoral influences by hardening them with stoic coaches and violent games. Ironically, some of those pushing hardest for masculine morality began the Young Men's Christian Association (YMCA), which almost immediately served as gay pickup joint (something reflected in the Village Peoples' song, 'YMCA').

Modern sport was therefore born out of the turn of the 20th century notion that it could help prevent male youth from possessing characteristics associated with femininity. It was designed to compel boys to reject all but a narrow definition of masculinity: One that created good industrial workers, soldiers, Christians and consumers. The construction of sport as a masculine and homophobic enterprise was both deliberate and political, and over a hundred years later, little has changed.

Sport, it would seem, has served well the principle for which it was designed. It has created a social space in which boys are still taught to value and perform a violent, stoic and risky form of masculinity: one based in antifemininity, patriarchy, misogyny and homophobia. Sport, in the latter parts of the 20th and throughout the 21st centuries was and remains used to teach boys a form of masculinity that Sedgwick (1990) calls 'orthodox'.

ORTHODOX MASCULINITY AS HEGEMONIC

Sociologists recognize that there are various forms of masculinities found among differing cultures, and that there is no singular way of being masculine within any given culture. We recognize that, in response to social forces, the definitions of what it means to be masculine shift within the same culture—and that not all masculinities are treated equally in any culture. In her influential book *Masculinities* (1995), Connell gives an excellent discussion of the various and often competing forms of masculinities in Western cultures, especially in regard to understanding the operation of hegemony as it relates to masculinity.

Hegemony, a concept created by Antonio Gramsci (1971), refers to a particular form of dominance in which a ruling class legitimates its position and secures the acceptance—if not outright support—of the classes or archetypes below. While a feature of Gramsci's hegemony theory is that there is often the threat of force structuring a belief, the key element is that force cannot be the causative factor that elicits complicity. This is what separates hegemony from overt rule.

In order to compel people to empathize with the ruling class or identity, those who do not fit within the dominant ideal must believe that their subordinated place is both *right* and *natural*.

Of relevance to this research, the concept of hegemony has only recently been applied to a more nuanced understanding of how men and their masculinity and sexuality are stratified in society (Connell 1987, 1995). Much of the study of masculinities examines how men construct hierarchies that yield decreasing benefits the further removed one is from the flagship version, hegemonic masculinity. But this whole process, is also (confusingly) known as hegemonic masculinity, and this is where scholars most often go wrong with Connell's theory.

It is important to clarify that hegemonic masculinity is not an archetype, "It is, rather, the masculinity that occupies the hegemonic position in a given pattern of gender relations, a position always contestable" (Connell 1995: 76). And while Connell does describe the contemporary form of hegemonic masculinity as including the tenets of homophobia and anti-femininity, she does not assign a categorical label to this group. This makes it easy to conflate the process of hegemonic masculinity with an archetype of masculinity, and this explains why there is such usage confusion among scholars. Accordingly, Donaldson (1993) highlights that the concept of hegemonic masculinity is unclear, carries multiple contradictions, and fails to demonstrate the independence of the gender system.

In order to avoid confusing hegemonic masculinity as a social process from hegemonic masculinity as an archetype, I do not use 'hegemonic masculinity' as a categorical label in this book; instead, I use the archetype of 'orthodox masculinity.' I do this for two reasons. First, I clarify that hegemonic masculinity is a social process of subordination and stratification. Melding an archetype with the process weakens the theoretical significance of Gramsci's hegemony theory, and decreases the contribution that Connell makes to masculinities studies in explaining how the stratification of masculinities operates. And in order to avoid this problem with my theory, I use 'inclusive masculinity' to indicate the theory and 'inclusive masculinities' to discuss the archetypes.

I also avoid using hegemonic masculinity or inclusive masculinity as an archetype because the thesis of this book is that there exist multiple masculinities among men, whether they be multiple orthodox masculinities or multiple inclusive masculinities. Thus, in this book, the difference between an archetype and a social process of dominance is understood by delineating the traditionally hegemonic category of masculinity as orthodox masculinity. The final and perhaps most important reason I avoid using hegemonic masculinity as an archetype is that it conflates too many ascribed variables (such as race) with achieved ones (how one acts).

Connell was not the first to describe a certain group of men as having a dominating identity. Goffman (1963: 128) described many of the tenets of the archetype, saying that in America there is only one complete, unblushing male:

> A young, married, white, urban, Northern heterosexual, Protestant, father, of college education, fully employed, of good complexion, weight and height, and a recent record in sports. Every American male tends to look out upon the world from this perspective. . . . Any male who fails to qualify in any one of these ways is like to view himself . . . as unworthy, incomplete, and inferior.

Orthodox masculinity has historically remained at the top of the masculinities hierarchy, while men belonging to gay, nonathletic, or feminine-acting men have occupied the lower rungs (Messner 1992, 2002). Conversely, inclusive forms of masculinities reject the homophobia, sexism, stoicism and compulsory heterosexuality implicit in orthodox masculinities. I therefore describe orthodox and inclusive masculinities as two (sometimes competing) categories of archetypes, but I do not wish to essentialize these as coherent and easily definable categories of masculine performance. There is no *one* way of constructing masculinity, there always exists competition for dominance among men of any group, culture or institution. Thus, when it comes to men's gendered expression in masculinized settings, different organizations might adhere to different sets of gendered values and masculine norms, even within the same institution or across members of the same team or organization.

I recognize the slipperiness of trying to define the behaviors and attitudes that make up any ascription of gendered behavior, particularly when analyzed as a binary. However, I settle upon the limitations of categorizing men as belonging to the polarized categories of orthodox or inclusive archetypes because these concepts prove useful to me in understanding a macro analysis of men as they culturally engage with gendered identities. Inclusive masculinities, just like orthodox masculinities, are a configuration of gender practices. Accordingly, I accept the limitations of identity categorization, sometimes pulling together various and intersecting forms of inclusive masculinities and various forms of orthodox masculinities into a singular archetype. This simplifies the complexities of describing men's gendered attitudes and behaviors and permits me to make meaningful discussion of an otherwise nebulous social matrix.

I principally rely upon a social constructionist framework for understanding how gendered and sexual identities are achieved. I use inclusive masculinity theory in order to frame my data. I do this for several reasons. Principally, it is because what I see occurring in my investigations (of white university-aged men) is not accounted for with hegemonic masculinity theory. Times have changed, and this requires new ways of thinking about gender. There are other reasons, however, for utilizing new social theory regarding masculinities. Many scholars have suggested that an over-reliance on hegemonic masculinity theory may lead to selective accounts or diminished lines of research inquiry (Sparkes 1992). Studies using hegemonic masculinity have also been critiqued as unduly examining the negative aspects of sporting culture, and perhaps trivializing some of the positive aspects of sport (Mckay, Messner, and Sabo 2000), although I do not support this critique. Gramsci's hegemony theory (built to expand on Marx's materialism) may also overstate a top-down power system, squashing the agency out of the analysis of the individual. For this purpose, many scholars have relied on Foucault to analyze sport and gender (cf. Pringle and Markula 2005). This is because Foucault views power as emanating from both institutions and individuals, so that all retain various types and elements of power (1977, 1984). However, in my work on inclusive masculinity theory, I borrow from both social constructionists and poststructuralists.

I understand that some reject the use of blending these epistemologies (Pringle 2005; Pringle and Markula 2005), but I view this to be academic fundamentalism. I find that poststructuralist notions of identity and power nicely compliment social constructionist accounts of gender and sexual identity formation. As a social scientist, my job is to help make sense of the social world, utilizing whatever tools fit. Thus, in this book, I willingly utilize Foucault's (1977, 1984) theoretical accounts of the multiplicity of power, and Butler's (1990) conception of the power of discourse, to augment hegemony theory. I do this because I see Foucault and Gramsci as being symbiotic in the arena of progressive gender politics (Cole 1993). Each paradigm is borne of anti-essentialism and each has been used to advance our understandings of sex and gender.

However, when I discuss poststructural concepts, I avoid the language in which most poststructuralists frame their ideas. This is because much of poststructuralist thought comes in extremely inaccessibility writing. Butler (1990), for example, is so inaccessible that she commits a violent, shameful act of academic exclusion. Furthermore, poststructural inaccessibility often leads scholars to differently interpret what the author means, like preachers arguing over varying interpretations of biblical passages.

Finally, it should be said that I limit deconstructive discussions of breaking down identity types. This is not because I do not agree with this school of thought, but rather I find it lacks political agency. A central tenet of poststructuralist theory is the fluidity and multiplicity of identities, and a resistance of categorizing them. But how does one conduct an emancipatory political project, if one cannot define the group one's research is intended to emancipate? How can one complain about being 'gay bashed' if the term 'gay' is so deconstructed it is rendered useless?

Highlighting an example of this, when men who retain exclusive sexual desires for men tell me, "I don't want to be labeled," I appreciate their philosophical position, but question the practicality of it. After all, it's not how they personally identify that is all important; instead, it is how others, those with particularly cultural dominance, see and label one who maintains desire for sex with men. Without gay men advocating for their own identity, they leave *heterosexuals* to define the characteristics of their archetype. This is a dangerous proposition. The history of how heterosexuals construct homosexuals is not favorable (cf. LeVay 1996; Spitzer 2003). A man desiring to avoid being labeled does not have to identify as gay, in order to be treated as such. And while the argument for deconstructing sexual identities may someday have its time and place in emancipatory research, it needs to begin with heterosexuals refusing to categorize themselves, first. Furthermore, only when heterosexuality is no longer presumed, can sexual minorities safely disregard sexual categorization. Identity politics, based in empirical research, is how we have gained rights for sexual minorities, not post-structuralist philosophies.

I also borrow from both Gramsci and Foucault because both discuss the varied and problematic manner in which people maintain power, asserting that dominant groups limit access to outsider power as a way of maintaining their privileged position (Holub 1992). While a Marxian-Gramscian perspective maintains that power is unevenly distributed according to hierarchical positioning, Foucault (1988) problematizes this, suggesting that power is more diffuse, that each individual shares in power. On this matter, I challenge each paradigm. I do not take the view that just because there is a hierarchy, power is fixed in running one way. Nor do I suggest that all people share in power equally. I therefore suggest that instead of having two paradigmatic camps, we blend these epistemologies to nuance social constructionism while keeping its political viability. This is something I hope to accomplish with inclusive masculinity theory. Accordingly, I will interchange between Gramscian and Foucaultian operations of power throughout this book. As Adams (2008: 13) says, "I resolve to intertwine them on the same page, in a theoretical melting pot, bridging the gap between the philosophical and the empirical and facilitating a more thorough articulation of the powers that congeal in this social location." Hopefully, I can then breathe life into my work, by writing it a manner that is accessible to a wide body of scholars and readers.

ORTHODOX MASCULINITY AND SEXISM

For aforementioned reasons, it is difficult to come up with a precise archetype of what orthodox masculinity (or orthodox masculinities) is/are. Nonetheless, there are central tenets that all scholars (of all epistemological orientations) use in their work to describe orthodox/hegemonic masculinities. Most highlight that the first rule is that of sexism (Kimmell 1996). Here, the primary element toward being a man has been not to *be*, *act*, or *behave* in ways attributed to women. Robert Brannon (1976) summarizes this nicely, saying that the first rule toward being a man is "no sissy stuff." However, the reason for this underlying discontent of femininity is because effeminacy among men is correlated with homosexuality.

This rigid contention carries with it a measurable cost, damage that begins as early as primary school. For example, psychologist William Pollack (1998) maintains that fear of homosexual stigmatization prevents young boys from engaging with anything that is designated feminine. Sociologist Michael Messner (1992) suggests that men, too, avoid compassion, weakness, fear, or the appearance of vulnerability because these are traits also associated with women. Both Pollack and Messner agree that if one violates these rules, he risks being labeled a sissy or a fag. And when this happens, one must either deflect attention by calling someone else a fag, or stand and fight for one's heteromasculinity (Kimmel 1994). This is a social condition I discuss as homohysteria.

Although she is not much utilized today, Nancy Chodorow's psychoanalytic theorizing is important to understand for the growth of masculinity studies. Revising the Freudian model I earlier spoke of, Chodorow links the construction of gender identity to the process of mothering. In her 1978 book, *The Reproduction of Mothering*, she maintains that since mothers and daughters share the same sex, mothers teach their daughters to be feminine and heterosexual through a top-down socialization process. Here, girls are relatively passive in the construction of their sexual identities. She argues that the socialization of girls into heterofemininity is near-seamlessly accomplished because young girls merely have to identify with their mothers—their heterosexuality and femininity simply follow.

In contrast to the smooth construction of women's sexed and gendered identities, however, Chodorow describes the development of masculinity among boys as much more difficult. This is primarily because masculinity in boys is constructed through object relations. For Chodorow, masculinity is abstract because it is constructed in opposition to the gender identity of a boy's mother. Chodorow therefore borrows from Freud in explaining the male characterization of woman as "the other." She argues that because men learn to define themselves as *not woman* and *not mother*, masculinity is inevitably a negative identity. Chodorow maintains that in order for boys to construct a masculine and heterosexual identity, they must break the attachment to their mother, and align themselves with their father. Thus, while the homogeneity of sex with a mother/daughter relationship practically ensures femininity and heterosexuality of adult women, the heterogeneity of sex between mother and son makes the production of heterosexuality and masculinity fraught with potential "wrongdoings."

Furthermore, Chodorow's explanation of masculinity and heterosexuality also implicates sexual identity with gender identity. Essentially, her theory entangles male homosexuality with feminine expression, and male heterosexuality with masculinity. For Chodorow, a male who maintains a feminine identity must also be homosexual. These polarized constructions of male/female and homosexual/heterosexual over simplify a rich diversity of human behaviors, rather than understanding them as a more complex and fluid continuum.

I critique Chodorow for viewing gender identity as cemented within one's formative years (my gender identity certainly has changed over the years) and I also critique her simplified binaries of sexual and gendered identities (there is more than just gay and straight). But while I view Chodorow, Freud, and his followers psychoanalytic theories as being too reductionist, this does not mean her theory should be entirely discarded. First, Chodorow does understand these processes to be somewhat malleable (gender is not fixed at birth), and this is something that social constructionists of gender later picked up on and further developed (West and Zimmerman 1987). Furthermore, her ideas have cultural resonance. Just as with Freud, her ideas have filtered down from the academy and resonate with many people.

Another reason for highlighting Chodorow is because it drives my larger theoretical point that, when it comes to the study of masculinities, whether one subscribes to a psychoanalytical, social constructionist or poststructuralist paradigm, gender scholars basically agree. Although they differ in focus, there is no argument against the paradigm that masculinity has traditionally been constructed in opposition to femininity. Whether one calls this abstract masculinity, relational masculinity, orthodox masculinity, hegemonic masculinity, or heteromasculinity, there is a very durable finding across a spectrum of scholars that the traditionally esteemed version(s) of masculinity look disparagingly at femininity. Accordingly, the sexism embedded in masculinity, is a major variable in the reproduction of men's patriarchal rule over women. Sexism is one component of patriarchy.

ORTHODOX MASCULINITY AND PATRIARCHY

In the 1970s, several general theories addressing patriarchy were advanced, including Rubin's (1975) work on the exchange of women in marriage. Others followed this line of thought regarding domination of one group by another via economic, social, and cultural hierarchies. But the origins of men's dominance are multifaceted. Masculine domination is likely produced by an interlocking system of cognitive oppositions and social patterns in families, schools, and the state, all of which are grounded in the opposition of the dominant male and submissive female (Bourdieu 2001). It is the interlocking system of cognitive categories and objective social differences that produce the (false) perception that there are deep-seated differences between the sexes (Burton-Nelson 1994).

Rich (1980) also did much to advance our notion of the operation of patriarchy, and how regulation of homosexuality is also an important factor. She contends that in a society in which men control most aspects of women's institutional lives, women are essentially bound to a binary system of oppression. She suggests that this oppression is facilitated due to the fact that women face nearly the same cultural pressure to be heterosexual as men, and that women are part of the equipment which men use to prove their heterosexuality. Examining this in the domestic sphere, Rich suggests that compulsory heterosexuality, and the devaluing of women, promotes a political institution of symbolic and real domestic violence. The naturalization of heterosexuality helps excuse men's violence against women because, "that's just the way it [biologically] is" (p. 154). Rich therefore stresses that compulsory heterosexuality is largely used to control and subordinate women in order to maintain men's privilege.

Connell (1987) was perhaps the next most influential thinker in explaining how patriarchy is maintained in modern society. She suggests that the purpose of having one hegemonic archetype of masculinity is not just about stratifying men along a continuum of diminishing returns. She suggests that the current hegemonic form of masculinity (the archetype that I call orthodox masculinity) contains sexist and misogynistic tenets in order to help men maintain their patriarchal privilege over all women. Non-hegemonic (orthodox) men may pay (or lose out) for not maintaining the characteristics associated with the elite form of masculinity, they may even be harassed, bullied, or exploited because of it. Nonetheless, with everyone looking 'up' to the dominant version of masculinity, simply *being* male permits all men to benefit from the marginalization of all women, something Connell calls the patriarchal dividend. In other words, all men invest into their symbolic (hegemonic) form of dominating masculinity, so that they might hold this version as symbolic proof of their rite to rule. This is why Connell does not develop a process of hegemonic femininity. Instead, she suggests that because men are collectively positioned over women in society, the elite form of femininity is best described as *emphasized femininity*.

Later, Bourdieu (2001) described the need to highlight how a social movement committed to "symbolic subversion" can erode upon men's privilege. Bourdieu suggested that the gay male (who is so marginalized in Connell's theorizing that he is hardly within the terrain of masculinity) possesses the unique circumstances necessary toward undermining masculine orthodoxy. Bourdieu maintained that the gay male has the ability to invisibly gain access to male privilege, so that he can then become visible (as gay) with full citizenship. In other words, Bourdieu saw the gay male as being able to penetrate masculinized terrains while closeted, to raise their worth among men, and then to come out as gay, exposing the fallacy upon which the system is built. Thus, he thought the gay male was uniquely positioned to align with feminists in a terrain or progressive coalition politics to attack male dominance materialistically, symbolically, and domestically.

While this may have real saliency in sport, the point seems to ignore the actual history of gay liberation politics. The connection between masculinity and sexism has been trumpeted since the 1970s, yet the alliance between gay and feminist groups has been tenuous, at best. The potential for gay liberationist ideas of undermining patriarchy, I argue, have also passed. This is because, by the mid to late 1970s, much of the radical impulse in gay liberation had been eclipsed by a more pragmatic approach to the obtainment of civil rights that focused on individual rights and lifestyle alternatives—an assimilationist approach. Gay marriage (which I favor) serves as a perfect example.

Furthermore, Peter Nardi (1999) adds that the idealized gay family also changed from one of kinship to the heterosexual model in the previous few decades. Gay men even began to lose the camp expressionism and liberating political overtones that characterized gay males of the late 1960s and early 1970s. Instead it seems gay men today are mostly concerned with adopting every other attribute of heterosexual masculinity (Connell 1992). In fact, to some degree, I suggest that while university-attending straight men are seemingly running away from hyper-masculinity, many gay men are running toward it.

This however is not to suggest that gay men do not still pose a threat to heteromasculine dominance. I suggest that one arena in which gay men maintain considerable agency is in sport. Accordingly, I agree with

Connell (1987, 1995) in that hegemonic masculinity helps reify and reproduce patriarchy. I also agree with Burton-Nelson (1995), that sport symbolizes and legitimates this dominance. I agree with Chodorow (1978), that the reproductory process and mothering structurally generates inequality. I agree with Rich (1980) in that compulsory heterosexuality prevents patriarchy from being contested. And I agree with Bourdieu (2001), in viewing male dominance from a historical materialist (radical feminist) perspective. Ultimately, however, I think New (2001: 735) says it best, suggesting that in order to better understand patriarchy we must drop the fantasy that,

> there is a group of timeless heterosexual men sitting around somewhere outside social relations, devising a world that would keep their slippers handy, their dinners nicely served, and their sexual desires met for all eternity. Men's interests in patriarchy are inseparable in the social relations in and through which they are expressed, and cannot therefore be invoked to explain those relations.

In other words, patriarchy is just much more complex than can be addressed with any one single theory. Oppression comes in many forms, and has many different etiologies.

None of this is to suggest that we should not intellectually investigate the pathways that we may take to undo patriarchy. Thus, what I am concerned with in this book is the role that sport plays in promoting patriarchy. What I am driving at is that homophobia (particularly against gay men) and sexism are intricately linked (Pharr 1997).

Accordingly, I do not use Chodorow, Rich, Connell, Bourdieu or Butler unquestioningly or unaccompanied. In fact, I do not take a theoretical explanation from just any one gender theorist, to explain heteromasculine dominance. Instead, I simply suggest that almost all men and women who theorize about masculinity, homophobia and sexism understand their inter-relatedness. As blasphemous as it may sound to sociologists concerned with gender, when it comes to theorizing about men's dominance over women, and heterosexual dominance over bisexuals and homosexuals, there really is not that much variance between theories or theorists. We may argue about how passive children are to gender (sex role theory), or the role of the family in the process (psychoanalytic theory), we may demonstrate that gender is nothing but a performance (dramaturgical theory), or what form of feminism is best to undo it all, but we all understand that heterosexual men have collectively controlled women and, despite the advancements of the first, second and now third waves of feminism, they continue to do so. Finally, in more recent years we have begun to understand the processes by which orthodox masculinities also help reproduce heterosexual privilege. Of course, orthodox masculinity also help reproduce heterosexism, too.

ORTHODOX MASCULINITY AND HETEROSEXUAL HEGEMONY

Because men's femininity is conflated with men's homosexuality (Kimmel 1994), orthodox masculinity not only helps retain patriarchy, but also the dominance of heterosexuality. Heterosexual hegemony (also called heterosexism) enables heterosexuals to retain power and privilege over non-heterosexuals. Accordingly, as part of the operation of hegemony, only the minority (in this case homosexuals) are examined for fault. Thus, while homosexuality is academically and culturally scrutinized, heterosexuality escapes critical questioning from popular culture and sometimes even critical academics (cf. Richardson 1996). There have, for example, been a large number of investigations into whether gay men can through some form of psychological or biological "therapy," become heterosexual (cf. LeVay 1996) but only one study to determine if straight men can become gay (Meijer 1993). Similarly, there have been a large number of studies to locate a biological predisposition toward homosexuality, but fewer investigations into the biological determinants of heterosexuality. In this aspect hegemonic processes conceal important structures of inequality. Hegemony shifts all analysis to the subordinated group, concealing the cost that those with power might also pay for their privilege.

I find the works Adrienne Rich important to understanding heteronormativity. Her influential article, *Compulsory Heterosexuality and Lesbian Existence* (1980) popularized the term compulsory heterosexuality, which critiqued the cultural assumption that both males and females are either biologically or psychologically predisposed to heterosexuality. Whereas Chodorow described a near-seamless socialization among females who passively receive the gendered and sexed identity of their mothers, Rich responded by questioning why and how, if theories like Chodorow's are tenable, women would redirect their emotional attachment from that of either mom or other women on to men. She charges Chodorow's theorizing as being void of a political astuteness to the historical manner in which men have controlled women's lives.

Rich argues that the assumption that biology excludes a naturalized explanation of homosexuality limits human existence and experiences. Rich maintains that the operation of compulsory heterosexuality as a product of nature reifies and naturalizes heterosexuality, while homosexuality is considered the product of either psychological dysfunction or deviant personal choice. From this understanding, homosexuality is stigmatized because it is thought to go against the supposed natural inclinations of the individual. Rich argues that the naturalization of heterosexuality manifests itself in cultural and institutional inequality for non-heterosexuals, denying their sexual and gendered identities as a valued reality and a source of knowledge. She presses for the recognition that there is nothing innate or free in the compulsory understanding of heterosexuality—it is a political institution. Clearly, there remain important elements of her argument today.

One does not have to use Rich to understand heterosexism and homophobia this way. There are a number of other ways of examining how society is structured so that heterosexuality is good and homosexuality is bad. One might use Durkheim's "Sacred and Profane" (1976); Douglas's "Purity and Danger" (2002); Butler's "Heterosexual Matrix" (1990); Rubin's "Charmed Circle" (1984); or, perhaps the most appropriate for this book, Kimmel's notion of "Masculinity as Homophobia" (1994). All explain the cultural matrix of a bifurcated sexual regulatory system in which (at best) homosexuality is equated with denigrated behavior. They highlight the power of hegemony in that they show that all cultural focus, all critical inquiry, falls on to those that do not exist within the heterosexual, monogamous, married norm. However, in culturally over analyzing homosexuality we fail to see the serious problems associated with heterosexuality, too. Heterosexual governance has its burdens. This is the subject of the next chapter.

2 Costs Associated with Orthodox Masculinity

While sexism and homophobia are central tenets in constructing orthodox masculinities, there are a number of activities that men can partake in, and a number of attributes that men can ascribe to in order to achieve this archetype. In this chapter, I examine how men jockey for position to raise their masculine worth, and how masculine capital is used to purchase privilege among peers. However, there are many costs associated with the fulfillment of orthodox masculinity, too. Men who adhere to orthodox principles of masculinity produce a great deal of symbolic and real violence, not only against women and other men, but against themselves, too. In a culture that values orthodox masculinity, men are limited in the arenas in which they can work or play, the entertainment they can partake in, the emotions they can express, and the sports they can enjoy. Essentially, in an orthodox valuing society, everybody suffers. This chapter explicates these ideas.

MASCULINE CAPITAL

Collectively, not associating with homosexuality or femininity, being a muscular leader, and reserving all unacceptable emotions, will certainly raise the masculine worth of an individual. He may even achieve orthodox masculinity. But these tenets alone do not permit one to achieve the form of masculinity that Connell suggests (1995, 2002) maintains hegemonic dominance. This is because defining the hegemonic form of masculinity (as difficult as it is to do) not only necessitates that one act in accord with the behaviors of masculinity, but one must also have the requisite ascribed variables.

These variables, like race, class, height and good looks fall in line with dominant power positions in current culture, and are largely out of the locus of an individual's control. Essentially, if I presented the case of two NFL quarterbacks, both act macho and both are homophobic and misogynistic, yet they are different races (one being white and the other black), it would be difficult (perhaps not impossible) to suggest that the black man maintains cultural hegemony. This is because whiteness still exists as the dominant race. It is because of these complexities that Connell avoids listing the traits needed to fill the 'hegemonic' archetype of whatever form of masculinity is currently in power.

To help clarify matters, whereas one must maintain all of the culturally ascribed and achieved variables to be truly dominant (hegemonic) in society, in order to achieve my notion of orthodox masculinity one need only to act masculine: to be homophobic, misogynistic, willing to take risks, muscular etc. Race, class, religion and age are not part of the equation in achieving my notion of orthodox masculinity. Another way to look at this is to say that one can achieve orthodox masculinity without being capable of achieving hegemonic masculinity, but one cannot be hegemonically masculine without also having orthodox masculinity. For all intents and purposes orthodox masculinity is more (although not entirely) about how you act, while hegemonic masculinity is more (though still not entirely) about what you are born with. It is how one acts that I am concerned with in my research. And it is in the attitudes and behaviors that heterosexual men retain, regardless of their race or class that's important for the expression of inclusive masculinities. Thus, to describe the social currency that one uses to achieve orthodox status, I propose the notion of *masculine capital*. Similar to Becker's (1964) notion of human capital or Bourdieu's (1984) symbolic capital, I use masculine capital to describe the 'masculine level' of a man, as achieved through attitudes and behaviors.

Traditionally, there have been good reasons to raise one's masculine capital. Boys with the most masculine capital use that capital to acquire goods, services and privileges. Essentially, masculine capital is the fuel of masculinity, regardless of one's color or sexuality. And, once a man's masculinity fuel tank is near full, I suggest he has (albeit temporarily) 'achieved' orthodox masculinity (or a version of orthodox masculinities). Conversely, acts of femininity deplete one's masculine levels. Of course, nothing drains a man's fuel away like homosexuality. Masculinity therefore becomes a currency, in which privilege and esteem are traded.

Maintaining a high degree of masculine capital helps men refute suspicion of homosexuality, and one of the most reliable ways of building one's masculine capital comes through teamsport involvement (Pronger 1990). This effect is largely a product of the association between athleticism and masculinity. Because masculine capital is achieved through athleticism, and because athleticism is thought to be incompatible with homosexuality, it follows that athletes cannot be homosexual. This assures them a higher degree of masculinity. Put simply, the notion of a gay athlete is something of an oxymoron (Pronger 1990).

Another way to examine this is to say that the better an athlete is, and the more masculine the sport he plays, the less homosexual suspicion there is about him. Consequently, American football players and British rugby players are provided near immunity from homosexual suspicion, while cheerleaders and ice-dancers are inundated with it (Adams 1993).

Surprisingly, boys at the top of the masculine hierarchy are actually provided more leeway to temporarily transgress rigid gender boundaries that few other boys are willing to challenge. This is because lower status boys are met with enhanced social or physical reprisal for violating these norms, while high-status boys are not. This is why I say that men can use their masculine capital to purchase privilege. It explains why teamsport athletes can partake in amazingly homoerotic rituals and still maintain their publicly perceived heterosexual identities. Conversely, athletes from lower masculine-ranked sports cannot perform these same behaviors without being publicly homosexualized.

The ability for highly ranked orthodox men to transgress feminized boundaries is something that occurs at multiple levels of boys and men's social worlds. For example, one time a well-muscled athlete walked into my class of 400 in a dress, where he was cheered for his transgression. However, the next week when an unathletic, feminine boy also came to class in a dress, he was treated like a pariah. Quite literally, a void of unoccupied seats spread around him. Similarly, elite boys on elementary school playgrounds have been shown to possess more freedom in transgressing norms by (temporarily) playing so-called girl games (McGuffey and Rich 1999). And Schroeder (2002) shows that high-ranking members of military academies are able to commit 'mock' homosexual acts against first-year cadets without being homosexualized by these behaviors.

While this masculine hierarchy is mainly built around athleticism, repeated association with femininity, or things considered to be consistent with gay males, are important determinants in the downgrading of one's masculine capital—whether the association is real or perceived. One does not even have to associate with femininity; one only needs to be accused of it. Sociologist David Plummer (1999) points out that an accusation of homosexuality is the primary manner in which to verbally marginalize another male. He maintains that homophobic terms come into currency in elementary school, even though the words may not yet have sexual connotation. Still, he posits that these terms are far from indiscriminate, they tap a complex array of meanings that are precisely mapped in peer culture.

Young boys who slip out, or are pushed out, of heavily-policed masculine zones may be able to recoup some of their masculinity and be reabsorbed back into the masculine arena by deflecting the suspicion of homosexuality onto another boy. A higher status boy, for example, who transgresses gender boundaries, might call a lower status boy a "fag" in attempt to displace suspicion. By negatively talking about and excluding members who are presumed gay, boys delineate their public heterosexuality, while collectively endorsing orthodox masculinity. In such a manner, the marginalized attempt to gain power and control by marginalizing a subordinate other, almost as if it were a game of "fag, you're it", with the 'it' being homosexuality. More so, in certain highly masculinized social locations, demonstrating one's heterosexuality is not sufficient to maintain an unambiguous heterosexual masculinity. In these locations, such as within American football culture, it is has also been theorized to be necessary to show opposition and intolerance toward homosexuality (Curry 1991).

The labeling of boys and men as gay stratifies men in a king-of-the-hill style competition for the upper rungs of a masculine hierarchy. Much like the game, where the most dominant male occupies the top of the hill and physically pushes weaker boys down it, the contestation for masculine stratification is played out on flat sporting fields and courts in the institutions of both sport and public education where sport, through physical education or teamsport participation, is made compulsory. Those on sporting teams have their associations glorified publicly, and those excelling are sanctified.

Connell (1995) highlights that there exists a belief that true masculinity almost always proceeds from men's bodies. As a result, jocks often embody what orthodox masculinity entails. In his 1999 movie, *Tough Guise,* Jackson Katz calls this a 'jockocracy.' Here boys that score the most touchdowns, goals, or baskets symbolically occupy the top of the hierarchy. Here, they reify their status by marginalizing other males with homophobic and misogynistic discourse. Thus, masculinity and athleticism are interlinked, providing for a cornerstone of contemporary gender ideology in which patriarchal and heterosexual privilege is maintained. In fact, the term jock is so engendered within the male body that "jock" is also used as slang for penis.

Those who are softer, weaker, or more feminine, are decidedly not jocks. These men are often regarded as homosexual (whether they are or not) and they are either normally relegated to the bottom of the masculinity stratification, or cast down from masculine terrain altogether. Boys who reside atop the masculine hierarchy (that is, those with the most masculine capital) are required to maintain their social location through the continuous monitoring of masculine behaviors in order to ensure complicity with masculine expectations at nearly all times. Michael Kimmel (1996 p. 74) describes these processes by saying, "Masculinity must be proved, and no sooner is it proved that it is again questioned and must be proved again— constant, relentless, unachievable, and ultimately the quest for proof becomes so meaningless than it takes on the characteristics, as Weber said, of a sport."

The system of using athleticism to stratify men along an axis of power has been described as hegemonic because it is maintained not only through the real and symbolic forces of those who occupy the upper tiers, but through the willing participation of those who are subordinated. This is what makes it hegemonic. A high school jockocracy provides a clear understanding of the process of masculinity as hegemonic oppression because ancillary players (those occupying subordinated positions of masculinity) keep this volatile framework in place by lauding social merits on to the kings of the hill, literally cheering them on. Women, adult men, and other marginalized boys pay tribute to elite men by supporting them in the very arena in which they struggle to maximize their influence—athletic competitions. The epitome of this is when women cheer for male athletes, relegating themselves to symbolic subservience. The public celebration of masculine domination makes orthodox masculinity a popular identity to adopt, and therefore has traditionally ensured compliance by other males seeking such admiration.

The praise of these 'kings,' by individuals and institutions, naturalize and legitimate the power of those who control the jockocracy. However, as an operation of hegemonic oppression, the system is not necessarily understood in this context. Rather, hegemonic processes conceal problems with sport via myths of school, community or national pride. Subordinated members of the in-group do not view their cheering as praise for the elite and powerful men who dominate and subordinate them. Rather, they view their participation as cheering for 'their' team. And when 'one's' team wins, men draw masculine significance from it. Associating with dominance not only permits one to feel superior to those who associated with the losers, but biological research shows that men's testosterone levels actually increase when the team they root for wins, and it dips when they lose (Bernhardt et. al. 1998).

This social process is similar to how all men gain symbolic power over all women when *some* men beat all women at an athletic event, or when men prevent women from competing against them in the first place (Burton Nelson 1994). By associating with dominating men, even men who cannot beat women gain power over women because their gender won. This, in essence, is one link between homophobia and patriarchy: Homophobia keeps all men in line, so that all men can benefit from the privileges of patriarchy. However, this game is not a 'winner takes all' bet. There are considerable costs associated with orthodox masculinity for dominating men, too.

COSTS ASSOCIATED WITH ORTHODOX MASCULINITY

There are *many* costs associated with those not possessing orthodox masculinity. Several researchers examine masculine hierarchies, and how those who are marginalized by this stratification suffer emotionally (Pollack 1998), socially (Plummer 1999) and sometimes physically (Messner 1992, 2002). This is particularly true for gay males, who are almost altogether marginalized by athletic culture. Still, few heterosexuals escape social victimization under this system, too—and none escape the physical. This is made salient when watching the violence men inflict upon each other in most teamsports, violence that is naturalized as "just part of the game" (cf. Papas, McHenry and Catlett 2004).

Bourdieu (2001) also suggests that males suffer under a patriarchal culture. This is because they have to respond to collective expectations of being male. Thus, males become mastered by their own dominance. New

(2001: 729) adds that, "Men may have conflicting interest in relation to the gender order. While men are frequently agents of the oppression of women, and in many senses benefit from it, their interests in the gender order is not pre-given, but constructed by and within it." She adds, "Since in many ways men's human needs and capacities are not met within the gender orders of modern societies, they also have a latent 'emancipatory interest' in their transformation."

Yet, Bourdieu implies that even if men wished to reject their lot, they would be inhibited from doing so. This is because of their deeply socialized gender patterns. Accordingly, inclusive masculinity theory has implications for patriarchy, too. Inclusive masculinity theory maintains that at least university-attending, white men are beginning to lose their orthodox gender patterns. I later show that this has positive implications for men's oppression of women. MacInnes (1998) has also hypothesized such. He suggests that as the gender-polarized zeitgeist of the industrial revolution erodes, so does the very notion of gender. Implicit in this argument is that gender is only made salient when it is bifurcated.

We, of course, are not yet living in a gender-neutral society. Men still rule, and orthodox masculinity still exits. Men wedded to this framework are more apt to suffer, and more apt to cause social unrest than men who are not. Accordingly, I have previously described the construction of orthodox masculinity as a public health crisis (2005a), pointing that masculinity both causes health problems and influences men to avoid seeking help for medical issues—all in order to gain and retain their esteemed orthodox masculinity. This is not solely the fault of the individual. Some make the decision to choose inclusive masculinity, but they are permitted this choice largely because of the willingness of their local culture. Others remain socially compelled to exhibit orthodox masculinity.

For example, Pollack's (1998) research on boyhood finds that boys, just like girls, are capable of the same emotional expression, and that they are just as emotionally vulnerable as girls. However, boys experience early and harsh pressure to disconnect from their families in pursuit of individualism, masculinity, and other attributes that boys are not cognitively and developmentally prepared for. He astutely calls the collective nature of social expectations 'the boy code' and highlights how social gender roles are oppressive to both men and women. This culture places boys into a gender straightjacket that forces them to mask their feelings, deny their need for help, disconnect from their families, and ultimately it leaves boys with a host of psychological disorders that follow them into adulthood.

Another way to examine this is to say that masculinity brings undue consequences, for men; consequences that researchers all-too-often fail to consider when analyzing patriarchy. In his 1974 book, *The Liberated Man*, and again later in his 1993 book, *The Myth of Male Power*, Warren Farrell makes such an argument. Farrell points out that men are drafted, women are not; men die on average seven years younger than women; men kill themselves in much higher numbers than women; men are twice as likely to be victimized by crime, and three times more likely to be murdered. Farrell makes other interesting comparisons about how men are limited in certain other social freedoms, too.

There are problems with Farrell's analysis. He often lacks contextualization to his arguments, and he often chooses one example to extrapolate more broadly. Furthermore, Farrell doesn't highlight that men are much more likely to commit crimes that have nothing to do with men's social roles as warriors or breadwinners. In other words, while men are more likely to be victimized by crime, the majority of violent crime is committed by men (Bowker 1998). Farrell also avoids an institutional account of the way power operates. However, his basic point is worthy—sexism carries a price tag. And under patriarchal rule, men are encouraged to adopt conservative forms of masculinity, which maintain serious costs to their emotional and physical health; masculine narratives that cause all types of social ills, too. Or, as Edwards (2006: 44) says, "From pub brawls to building bombs, and from forced prison buggery to battered wives, the problem seems to be men: men swearing, men punching, men kicking, men smashing, men bashing, men destroying other things, men, women, themselves, even the world."

Essentially, whether one analyzes the gender order the way Farrell does, calling it 'bisexism,' or the way New (2001) does, expressing that oppression is multi-dimensional, the point remains that this is not a system in which men are all-privileged and women are all-disadvantaged. This is a point that I believe sociologists have not paid adequate attention to: the costs of orthodox masculinity to those possessing it. And, much of the cost that men pay for their adherence to orthodox masculinity comes from the same institution that builds their masculine capital, the violent ether of men's teamsports.

ORTHODOX MASCULINITY AND THE PROMOTION OF VIOLENCE IN SPORT

The violent nature of sport promotes the social exclusion of many types of people. First, the physical violence in many sports prohibits those without enough muscle mass from effectively participating. More significantly, the violence associated with playing through pain, taking risks, and giving it all, means that a large number of athletes are excluded from participation due to injury. Finally, the inter and intra-personal violence associated with fighting and intimidation influences some parents to withhold their children from these types of sports, preventing many individuals from voluntarily playing them; which some children view as denying their citizenry into boyhood.

While much of the violence (against self and others) of sport is attributed to the culture of sport, much can be attributed to the structure of sport, too. This is particularly made clear in the purpose of collisions and intentional fouls in contact sports. But other learned violence comes from the fact that we have structured sports so that there is one individual winner (or one winning team). Thus, success is achieved only at another's loss. In this manner Lester Thurow (1985) describes sports as a zero-sum game. Sport is a social situation in which one person's success must come at the expense of another's. Accordingly, coaches and athletes frequently express ill feelings toward their competitors as they have been socialized into an in-group/out-group perspective that is predicated upon establishing the other team as the enemy. Rather than viewing competitors as agents in cooperation to bring about one's best, others are viewed as obstacles in the path of obtaining cultural and economic power. 'In order for me to win, you must lose.' Violence, intentional or not, therefore becomes an acceptable tool in achieving this victory.

There are, however, other ways to structure sport. Sports can, for example, be re-structured to determine that both teams must reach parity within an allotted period of time while still playing ones best, or both lose. Or, if teams were given a task that must be accomplished together, in an allotted period of time, then athletes from both teams would win or lose together—minimizing this in-group, out-group process. Unfortunately, the existing structure is so powerful in its influence, basked in decades of 'tradition,' that many maintain that without winning, there is no purpose to sport. This ethos moves sport far from the field of leisure and recreation, and closer to the act of war.

Much of the violence is also traceable to the ethos that a coach brings to the team. The problem, of course, is that what counts as evidence of 'good coaching' is the result, not the process. There is only one attribute that counts in determining whether a coach is of quality, and that remains the win-loss record. So although we say that we promote sport because it teaches our kids and young adults valued experiences, equipping them to deal with various socio-emotional situations, when it comes to the hiring and firing of coaches, what counts is not the quality of people the coach produces, what counts is the victories. Athletes are not interviewed or asked to rate their coaches. And if they are, these ratings are not used in a formal system for hiring and firing coaches between institutions. Employers do not look at the performance of a coach's athletes on university attendance, or measures of their self-esteem, or other indicators of the 'character' coaches were supposed to have inculcated in their players in the coaching process. Instead, all evaluation comes from 'success.' Winning remains not only the benchmark for judging the 'quality' of a coach, but the only category of importance. Accordingly, someone like Bobby Knight can be continually fired and then rehired at another institution because he wins.

Worse, when coaches win, they are permitted more freedom to exploit their athletes' fears of social rejection, of being de-selected for playing time, or not making the team the following season, which in turn helps the coach win further matches. 'Sacrifice' (defined here as violence against the self) becomes part of the game, as athletes (particularly those with low self-esteem or poor social support networks) are willing to risk their health because they are overly eager to be accepted by their coach and peers. Thus, coaches frequently push athletes too far and often knowingly have them play with injuries. In fact, research shows that over 80 percent of the men and women in top-level intercollegiate sports (in the United States) sustain at least one serious injury while playing their sport, and nearly 70 percent are disabled for two or more weeks (Edwards 2006).

But violence occurs not only against the self in sport. Teamsport athletes are also influenced to commit violence against others. This is played out on sporting pitches and fields across nations. Here, athletes are taught that it is better to foul an opponent than permit him to score a goal. In American baseball, for example, pitchers are sometimes encouraged to throw a brush-back pitch: One that comes dangerously close to the batter in order to back him away from the plate. Other times, pitchers are actually encouraged to hit the batter, sacrificing a base, rather than letting the hitter score a run. In this manner, the structure of the sport (the need for one's team to win) creates the culture of the sport (acceptable violence). It essentially institutionalizes, sanctions, and normalizes violence. This is something that is quite visible in the employment of goons in American hockey (large players with the specific job of beating up players from other teams). This violence is accepted because we are socialized into it as "just part of the game." Accordingly, Messner (2002) suggests that the aggression in sport is naturalized, ubiquitous, and all-inclusive. If we were serious about eliminating such violence, players would be kicked off their teams and arrested for it.

Of concern here, is that the socializing of men into a violent ethos of sporting masculinity may have serious implications for the symbolic and physical violence that men commit against not only themselves and other men, but against women as well. Although I problematize the argument that boys and men accept these risks when they play, because playing is near socially forced upon males, it is an entirely different manner when athletes transfer the violence they learn in sport outside of sport. Teamsports are *at least* partially responsible for the promotion of anti-feminine, sexist and misogynistic attitudes among male athletes (Muir and Seitz 2004). Accordingly, male teamsport athletes have been shown to objectify women—often viewing them as sexual objects to be conquered (Schacht 1996). Kreager (2007) shows that the socialization of men into teamsports might also influence symbolic, domestic and public violence against women. Explicating this, Crosset Benedict and MacDonald (1995) show that while student-athletes make up only 3.7 percent of the men at Division I universities, they are responsible for 19 percent of sexual assault reports to campus Judicial Affairs offices. Crosset (2000) has also shown that football, basketball and hockey players are responsible for 67 percent of the sexual assaults reported by student-athletes, although they only comprise 30 percent of the student-athlete populace. Despite these findings, hegemonic views continue to attribute sport as a socio-positive institution in Anglo-American culture. This conceals a great number of social problems that sport, or at least the way we do sport, generates.

LIMITING MEN'S SOCIAL SPACES AND BEHAVIORS

In addition to the violence created by and attributed to sport, the sexist and misogynistic ethos associated with the presence of orthodox masculinity means that the performance of femininity by men, or transgression of masculinized boundaries is deemed highly contentious. Feminized terrains are therefore heavily monitored and policed, and men are penalized for transgressing into them (Adler and Adler 1998). Men who play within feminized terrains, like cheerleading, gymnastics, and ice-skating, or men who enjoy a plethora of other feminized activities (such as sewing, attending the opera, or even seeing a 'chick flick') are generally subordinated by their participation. This makes them targets of homophobic and misogynistic discourse (Eveslage and Delaney 1998). In fact, the collective policing of these masculine borders can be so severe that I have previously described competitive teamsports athletes as members of 'a cult of masculinity' (Anderson 2005a). These are men who tithe their agency and vow complacency to rigid team norms. As members of this cult, these men express near uniformity in thought and action—reverent to the ideology of orthodox masculinity.

Most of the research regarding men who transgress gender boundaries concerns itself with work and occupations (Davis-Martin 1984; Jacobs 1993) and chiefly, the important issues of tokenism and the benefits men derive from male privilege within the occupational setting. Considerably less however is known about the costs and consequences for men who transgress gender boundaries. Williams (1989, 1995) studies men that enter the field of nursing, and Davis (1990) studies men who become cheerleaders, and each has been influential in helping us understand what happens to men when they do occupy feminized terrains, particularly, how they rectify this transgression with orthodox masculinity.

From these and other studies, we find that before entering feminized terrain, many heterosexual men have already established their masculine worth by engaging in highly masculinized arenas. For example, in my research on nursing, some heterosexual male nurses serve as medics in the military, or work construction before becoming a nurse (Anderson 2004). Similarly, in my cheerleading research, most heterosexual cheerleaders come from backgrounds as high school football players (Anderson 2005b, 2008c). Men who transgress into feminized terrain also maintain that they do their specific job (or part of their job) better than women, particularly when it comes to issues requiring physical strength. Alternatively, they contest the cultural ascription of their job-role as feminine in the first place.

In these efforts, most of these men attempt to associate with masculinity and disassociate with femininity. They self-segregate into masculine enclaves within the larger feminized space and perceive that excluding women and gay men from their peer circles raises their masculine capital. Heterosexual men in these studies are highly aware that their transgressions have rendered their heterosexuality suspect. In this aspect, men who work and play in feminized terrains find themselves in tension with their social space. Whereas the operation of cultural heterosexism normally means that one is assumed heterosexual unless otherwise told (Ingraham 2001), men in highly feminized arenas find themselves in an opposite paradigm—one in which they are suspected of homosexuality. Men in football are masculinized and heterosexualized, while men in cheerleading are feminized and homosexualized. Therefore, many heterosexual men feel the need to counter the assumption that they are gay in a way that they would not if they worked or played in a highly masculinized institution. This is a sign of homohysteria, and it results in homophobic and anti-feminine discourse.

What is not shown in these studies, however, is variance. These studies are nearly void of heterosexual men embracing femininity. Williams (1995) says that she found so few male nurses who she would describe as "gender renegades," and the narratives of her interviews were so defensive, that it led her to call for the creation of another form of masculinity that was based less in misogyny and more inclusive of femininity for heterosexual men. It is from this suggestion that I came up with the archetype name of 'inclusive masculinities.' I found what she did not—gender renegades. When I studied male nurses and male cheerleaders a decade after these investigations (Anderson 2004), I found that young heterosexual male nurses took a different approach to masculinity than older heterosexual male nurses.

WHAT ABOUT AGENCY?

What I have not discussed in this chapter however, is what happens to men's agency in sport? What happens to their moral conscience in order to permit such violence and panoptic self-regulation? How does sport manage to teach, influence, or instruct boys and men to commit crimes against others? How do coaches get athletes to follow their often sadistic or masochistic instructions, without athletes and parents standing up to cry foul?

In the next two chapters I explain how boys learn obedience to masculine norms, masculine role-models, and the masculinized nature of "authority" in general. I begin with a discussion of the structural mechanisms of sport that permit it to reproduce near-seamlessly generation after generation. Then, in Chapter 4, I discuss influential social science research concerning obedience and conformity, in order to help explain how the ethos of sport has also remained unchanged.

3 Reproducing Orthodoxy

In the first chapter, it was discussed how orthodox masculinity is principally constructed in opposition to femininity and homosexuality. I explained that around the turn of the 20th Century, the second industrial revolution influenced this new form of masculinity. In the second chapter, I discussed the role of sport in building masculine capital, and the considerable consequences that orthodox masculinity brought to gay men, women, and the very men who possess it. However, one might question just how orthodox masculinity has retained such cultural dominance throughout the previous century. How has orthodox masculinity resisted the first, second, and now third wave of feminism, the gay liberationist' ideals of the 1970s and 1980s, and the gay assimilationist efforts of the 1980s, 1990s, and 2000s? How, despite all of this progressive activism, cultural awareness, and even increasing legislative equality, has the symbolic and real power of the 'good-old boy' retained such power?

This chapter takes a different perspective on this issue. Instead of theorizing a grand narrative about gender, I examine the particulars of how one highly agentic institution, sport, has resisted the advancements of women and gay men. I explicate a near-perfectly integrated, self-reinforcing system, with "no internal contradictions or conflicts" (Bourdieu 2001) that permits the reproduction of orthodox masculinity in Anglo-American cultures. I explain the cultural and structural variables that combine to make sport so resilient to change. I then suggest that because nearly all boys are socialized into this patriarchial institution, they then carry the formal and informal ways of thinking about sex and gender with them into adulthood, and consequently other important institutions. This is sports unintentional link to patriarchy.

Although the analysis I provide in this chapter focuses on sport specifically, the model I propose can be extrapolated to other masculinized institutions as well. This is because the model highlights the mechanisms of both culture and structure in producing a gendered (and in this case, gender-segregated) institution. Sport is not the only important gender regime, most all influential institutions are embedded and institutionalized as masculine (Acker 1990). Accordingly, when reading about how I use my model to explain the reproduction of sport as a masculinized terrain, I encourage the reader to extrapolate it to fraternities, the military, the church, politics, and other masculinized institutions and organizations. I believe the similarities are striking. However, I conclude this chapter on a more positive note. My thesis is that as resilient as orthodox masculinity has been in Anglo-American cultures, no form of masculinity can be entirely self-reproducing. The reproductive process is laden with social tension and ultimately it *can* fail. This, as I suggest in part two of this book, is occurring among men with high social influence.

REPRODUCING ORTHODOX MASCULINITY IN THE INSTITUTION OF SPORT

Those who are thus far put off by my critique of sport might like to know that, in one sense, empirical evidence supports that there are at least some documented socio-positive advantages to socialize boys into sport. Researchers find that the most salient benefits of athletic participation are found in elevated self-esteem, better school attendance, educational aspirations, higher rates of university attendance and perhaps even post-schooling employment (Eccles and Barber 1999; Carlson et. al. 2005; Jeziorski 1994; Marsh 1992, 1993; Sabo, Melnick and Vanfossen 1989).

However, I maintain that these investigations are potentially misleading because they fail to examine whether the benefits associated with sporting participation are the result of something intrinsic to teamsports, or whether they reflect the political dominance that a socially elite group of males exhibit over marginalized others in a sports-obsessed culture. Are the higher rates of self-esteem attributed to athletes a result of their scoring goals? Or, does this reflect a statistical affect of the lowering of non-athletes' self-esteem in response to being subordinated by athletes whom are culturally and institutionally glorified in American and British school cultures?

Furthermore, when studies do investigate the socio-negative attributes of teamsport participation, they often examine variables that lend themselves to quantifiable analysis, like disciplinary referrals (Miller et. al. 2005). Thus, they fail to examine the more important socio-negative variables (those that do not lend themselves to quantification), like the volitional and unintentional damage inflicted upon those who do not fit this masculine model.

However, what is important toward understanding the role sport plays in our society is not whether sports deliver upon the socio-positive outcomes we are promised; rather, what is important is that both Americans and the British *believe* that they do. This is reflected in the high teamsport participation rates. Compared to the 6 percent of American parents that discourage athletic participation, 75 percent encourage it (Miracle and Rees 1994). This is largely due to the fact that the United States remains one of the few Western countries to intertwine public education with athletic programs (Gerdy 2002); some American high schools even report participation rates as high as 72 percent (Carlson et. al. 2005). Things are even tighter in Britain, where national curriculum guidelines *force* boys to play rugby. And as long as people believe, they unconsciously pick data that supports their belief and dismiss data which does not. Because we tend to attach an emotion of pleasure to data which supports our belief we will even feel connected to the author (personally) for telling us what we want to hear, and dislike those who do not.

As a result of the parental, cultural, and institutional pressures for boys to play sport, it often becomes *all-important* to the lives of boys and young men. They are socialized, rewarded and esteemed for playing it. Thus, boys are compelled to play sport from the time they are quite young. This frequently makes their fathers' happy, it makes them one of the boys, and it permits them to fit the dominant masculine mold, so they can feel that, as a boy, they are doing things right. But the damage I speak of comes not through simple participation in sport; it reflects the structural variables and cultural ethos embedded in sport. And much of the core of this problem results from the structure of gender-segregating sports.

With the exception of a few progressive sporting leagues, boys and girls play in gender-segregated sports. Here, boys and girls, men and women, occupy separate spaces. Although some youth leagues are gender integrated in the formative years, sport quickly establishes two camps in middle childhood, one for boys and the other for girls.

Few other institutions naturalize the segregation of men and women so near perfectly as do teamsports (Messner 2002). While occupational sex-segregation is declining in other institutions (Johnson 1998; Reskin and Roos 1990), formal structure and traditional reasoning has left teamsports a largely unexamined arena of gender-segregation. And, while this segregation has *many* male-driven purposes, it is important to note that feminist separation also occurs in sport.

One can certainly understand feminist desire to play sports away from men, particularly because women are protected from the violence of male athleticism in gender-segregated teams. But the ethos surrounding separate sporting programs is much deeper. The separation of the sexes in sport maintains a hegemonic stranglehold on our abilities to think differently, to imagine a better model for sport. For example, of all the topics that I encounter resistance from my undergraduates, segregating sport is the most contentious. This is because sport is naturalized through notions of 'opposite' phenotypes (Davis 1990) and (some) myths about boys' elevated levels of innate aggression and athletic advantage over girls (Butterfield and Loovis 1994). This is not to say that there are not some mean differences between boys and girls, men and women. But it is to say that focusing on that distracts us from examining difference between boys, and between men. Thus, my students (male and female) have no qualms about permitting a 100-pound male to play rugby against 250-pound men. But when I ask if a 300-pound woman should be permitted to try out for the men's rugby team, they protest that women have their own team and that they "might get hurt" playing with the boys. They maintain that it would be unfair to women to integrate, because men would have an advantage. Sadly, women agree. Thus, collectively, sex-segregation in sport, as Messner describes (2002: 12), is "grounded in a mutually agreed-upon notion of boys' and girls' 'separate worlds.'"

But it is more than just sexist-separation that keeps sport a masculinized arena. Homophobia is traditionally valued in men's teamsports, too. Therefore gay men are influenced to either avoid the institution altogether, or to keep their identities silenced. Indeed, even today, gay men are almost entirely absent at all levels of the sport-media complex. Over the previous decade I have known only two openly gay male sport reporters and only a handful of openly gay male high school or university coaches in America. I have known none in Britain. There are, to my knowledge, no openly gay men operating at the professional level on or off the pitch, with the exception of one rugby referee.

Perhaps this is not surprising. Sport was principally designed to turn boys away from homosexuality. Accordingly, men, who control sport, have a vested interest in reproducing the system, and they have managed to resist the creation of even a gay subculture within the school-based, university-based, and professional levels of sport. Gay men who wish to play, normally self-segregate into gay leagues, reminiscent of the way black men were once segregated into the 'Negro leagues.'

Why sport has managed to remain an institution that is run by and for straight men is simple: Sport resists change because it exists as an arena that is accepting of both sexism and homophobia. *How* sport has managed to do this, how sport has managed to normalize and even condone homophobia and misogyny is, however, more complicated. This comes through the idolization of a heterosexist and homophobic culture that is reproduced by a selection system that brings men who adhere to these principles to both the leadership and stakeholder positions in sport (coaches, managers, and owners).

SPORT AS A NEAR-TOTAL INSTITUTION

Athletes who emulate the institutional creed of orthodox masculinity are usually selected over players who break from its tenets, influencing them to adopt the gendered norms associated with orthodox masculinity. Ewald and Jiobu (1985) show that some athletes so overly adhere to the norms of sporting culture that they disrupt family relationships, work responsibilities, and even their physical health—all guided by a masculine creed of *giving it all* for the sake of sport and team. I have previously shown that gay athletes largely remain closeted for these same reasons, fearing that coming out will thwart their athletic matriculation (Anderson 2002, 2005a).

Hughes and Coakley (1991) describe this form of social deviance as *overconformity* to the sport ethic stating, "The likelihood of being chosen or sponsored for continued participation is increased if athletes over conform to the norms of sport" (p. 311). Of course, athletes do not see overconformity as problematic, rather " . . . they see it as confirming and reconfirming their identity as athletes . . ." (p. 311). Building upon Hughes and Coakley's overconformity theory, I examine the structural mechanisms that help reproduce sport as a site of orthodox masculinity by highlighting the near-total institutional aspects of teamsports.

Goffman (1961) describes a total institution as an enclosed social system in which the primary purpose is to control all aspects of someone's life. Foucault's (1977) description of the military serves a useful example. Here, Foucault maintained that through intense regimentation and implementation of a standard ideal of behavior, the military is capable of transforming peasants into soldiers. Men become more docile to the system because their growing identity as a soldier is essentially one of subordination from agency. Foucault suggested that the longer a soldier remains in the military the less agency he has to contest it.

Though I do not maintain that competitive, institutionalized teamsports *are* a total institution (athletes do have the legal freedom to quit sport), I argue that sport approximates a 'near-total' institution. This is because, much like the military, sport uses myths of glory, patriotism, and masculine idolatry, along with corporeal discipline and structures of rank, division, uniform, rules and punishment to suppress individual agency and construct a fortified ethos of orthodox masculinity (Britton and Williams 1995; Woodward 2000).

When individual athletes' thoughts are aligned with their teammates,' they are given social prestige and are publicly lauded. Athletes who toe the line are honored by their institutions and celebrated by fans and their community (Bissinger 1990). Hughes and Coakley (1991: 311) say, "Athletes find the action and their experiences in sport so exhilarating and thrilling that they want to continue participating as long as possible." Coakley (1998: 155) adds, " . . . they love their sports and will do most anything to stay involved." Thus, it is understandable that from the perspective of an athlete, particularly a good athlete, sport is a socially positive vessel. And while I think the reasons athletes will do almost anything to remain in teamsports are more complicated than just the thrill one receives from playing them, the point remains that athletes who withstand the selection process do so because of both their outstanding athletic ability *and* their willingness to conform to orthodox masculinity.

In conforming to the norms and excelling in sport, athletes limit whom they befriend. They shut out other cultural influences that might open their consciousness to new ways of thinking, and they are therefore less exposed to those who do not fit orthodox masculine requisites (Robidoux 2001). Men who spend their formative years in competitive teamsports are much less likely to meet gay men, feminized men, and other types of men who do not fit the jock mold. Similarly, men who spend their formative years in competitive teamsports are sheltered from growing to understand women's athleticism and leadership capabilities. They are sometimes even challenged to get to know women as friends; instead, women remain on the sidelines, sexually objectified and socially demonized for their femininity.

Conversely, athletes who do not adhere to the tenets of orthodox masculinity are sanctioned by verbal insults and are less likely to be given valued playing positions within sport. Coming out of the closet, 'acting feminine,' or being told that one is not a team player is a mark of shame that is likely to drive non-conformists away from the sporting terrain (Hekma 1998). This is why I appreciate students who fake an illness to be removed from physical education. They use agency to escape an oppressive environment.

Men who see things differently are less likely to crave the peer recognition and social promotion that sport provides athletes. These men are therefore less likely to put team expectations before their individual concerns and physical health. Conversely, those who thrive in the masculine arena sacrifice their individual agency and contribute to the reproduction of a rigid, masculine sporting culture. Of particular concern to this book, this virtually necessitates that those who aspire to the next level of sport must publicly disengage with any notion of sexual or gender ideology that is inconsistent with orthodox masculinity.

From an early age, athletes befriend each other, on and off the field. Their social lives are routinely dictated by a rigid schedule of athletic practices, competitions and other team functions. Teamsport athletes report that the further they matriculate through the ranks, the less freedom exists to inhabit any social space outside this network, and the more their identity narrows in order to be competitive with other men (Nixon 1994; Robidoux 2001).

I suggest that this might make gender construction in teamsports different from the type of agency-laden gender construction that West and Zimmerman (1987) or Thorne (1993) suggest occurs more broadly. This is because, from youth to adulthood, males socialized into competitive teamsports follow a subtle but increasingly institutionalized gender ideology: an incipient notion of gender that slowly erodes individual agency and restructures athletes as highly masculinized conformists in thought and action. The subordination required for retaining one's sporting status, or being selected for advancement, withers at their agency to contest orthodox masculinity. This is then justified by the prevalent belief that homogeneity is required in sports to produce desirable results (Sabo and Panepinto 1990), even though there is only a small and dubious relationship between a group's social cohesion and athletic success (Granovetter 1983; Mullen and Cooper 1994). This is sporting hegemony. And it is a structure which is then reproduced by selecting next generation's leaders from those that most overconformed.

REPRODUCING ORTHODOX MASCULINITY IN THE STAKEHOLDER'S POSITIONS OF SPORT

At the start of each year I ask my student-athletes to tell the class something about themselves. Without prompting them, the men and women alike, begin with "I play netball," or "I am a footballer." When I provide them a questionnaire asking them to fill in the statement preceding the two words, 'I am,' I receive the same. These students have been successful enough at sport to develop their master identity as that of an athlete. They do not list their race, sexuality, or even their religious orientation first. Instead they have come to recognize themselves, first and foremost, as athletes. They do this because they have been successful at sport and have therefore chosen to pursue it as their college degree.

Having a master identity of 'athlete' makes it all the more difficult for athletes to break from the gendered ideology embedded in the athletic institutions that they earned their identities from (Messner 1987). However, centering one's identity on athleticism carries risks. This is because sport is a volatile field where careers end on poor plays. Athletes can, at a moment's notice, be cut from a team. In fact, as an athlete, the only thing that one can be assured of is that one's career *will* end. And relative to other occupations, it will do so very early. Thus, whether an athlete suddenly loses his association with his athletic identity, or his body ages out of competitive form, all athletes must disengage with competitive sport. And when this happens, they are generally no longer valued in the sport setting (Messner 1987).

Men who drop out, are forced out, or otherwise do not make the next level of sport often find themselves detached from the masculine prestige they once enjoyed—something sport psychologists call the disengagement effect (Greendorfer 1992). Athletes who rode atop the masculine hierarchy feel the greatest loss upon disengaging from that elite status. So, for those with no further opportunity to play competitive sports, coaching becomes one of the few alternative venues for returning to the game. This coaching recruitment model means that sport almost always draws coaches, managers and other leaders from those who overconformed to the previous cohort's ideals, something perceived to give them expertise as coaches (Anderson 2009).

These individuals have had almost entirely positive sporting experiences and therefore hold unqualified acceptance of, and an unquestioned commitment to, its value systems (Hughes and Coakley 1991). As a result, the authoritarian method of coaching is viewed as a necessary part of sport, 'to get the best out of athletes' (Kelly and Waddington 2006). As coaches, these ex-athletes rely upon heteromasculine narratives to promote their individual experience and to inspire a new generation of boys into a similar ethos of orthodox masculinity.

Playing a specific sport before coaching certainly authenticates a coach. The more successful one's abilities as an athlete, the more he or she is assumed to be competent as a coach (Lyle 2002). In other words, athletes tend to think that a world champion athlete would make a better coach than a second-string athlete. This is because it is assumed that the journey one takes to become the 'worlds' greatest' necessitates having as much intellectual mastery over the sport as physical. For example, one of my informants suggests truly liking his coach, until learning that his coach did not actually play football. "I mean I really liked the guy, he had studied the sport and knew what he was doing; but once we [the team] found out he had not played, he got no respect . . . It's like if you haven't bled for the sport, you can't know it."

This, 'I did it so you can too' narrative serves several functions. First, it prevents those not weaned on a particular sport from coaching it, and it also influences the system to forgo a more rigorous manner for judging the abilities of a coach. This system limits the awareness, observations, or formally learned ways of thinking others might bring to the field. Furthermore, if a coach learns to coach via how he or she was coached, does this not make the system ripe for reproducing errors? Finally, this system limits the agency of athletes, because coaches can negate their players with, "I played professional and you have not."

Making the transmission of poor coaching practices easier, coaching positions (public or private), at almost all levels, require no university degree in coaching pedagogy, sport psychology, or physical education. Certainly one needs a bachelor's degree in physical education in order to teach physical education courses, but one does not need a bachelor's in physical education in order to coach. While many organizations and institutions may require coaching certification courses, they are generally not substantive of good coaching practices. Most of these workshops are concerned with litigation—teaching coaches how to avoid getting their institutions sued. Programs that talk about coaching at a more practical level tend to be focused on the basic motor skills and tactics of the sport. I cannot speak for all of these, but my experience, in talking to my students who earn coaching certificates in a variety of sports in England, suggests that they are vastly insufficient. They do not address sport as a complex field where identities, as well as bodies, are in peril. They do not address tactics and strategies for developing human beings; instead the focus remains on how to train and compete for victory.

COACHING POWER

Coaching, as a profession, stands out as odd in that a bachelor's degree (in the specific field) is not required. One cannot counsel patients without an MA or PhD, one cannot practice medicine without an M.D, and one cannot cut hair without a state-certified license. Without a similar institutionalized system of training, measurement and accreditation, there is little opportunity to evaluate or reform coaching practices outside of team victories. Thus, if a coach is a good technical coach, and wins matches, there is little reason for him to alter his coaching style, even if he's abusive. Accordingly, sports are *full* of men who predicated their identities as athletes, and were therefore drawn to coaching as a mechanism to remain within masculine margins. Here, they are provided with a phenomenal amount of power.

Collectively, coaches maintain an inordinate degree of power. French and Raven (1959), refer to five types of power, of which coaches normally possess all five. These powers are described as: 1) *Legitimate*, defined as power given by one's elected or appointed status; 2) *Coercive*, defined as power because of one's ability to take something away; 3) *Reward*, defined as power derived from the ability to give something desired; 4) *Expert*, defined as power accorded to individuals who have undergone formal training; 5) *Referent*, defined as power given because of the respect an individual might have. And while it is not absolutely necessary to understand exactly what and how each of these powers operates, it is important to understand that few other occupations/professions offer individuals the ability to associate with all five types of power (Jones, Armour and Potrac 2004). In fact, I can think of none.

Clearly coaches use reward power by offering players social promotions, more playing time, or public praise, and they use coercive power in punishing athletes with the opposite. Coaches establish their legitimacy in the eyes of their athletes primarily through having 'come up' through the system, often as a successful player first, and then by producing quality athletes. This legitimacy, coupled with the title 'coach,' is then thought (often erroneously) to make one an expert, as coaches are assumed to possess the technical knowledge beneficial to advancing athletes. In other words, a person does not need to be an expert in order to maintain expert power, they only need be perceived as an expert. As I have discussed, coaches most often lack the qualifications, knowledge and skills to be a safe and effective coach. Finally, coaches sometimes gain the respect of their athletes through referent power because athletes desire to accomplish the same feats, times, or levels of play, or because they look to the coach as a mentor or parental figure. This is the, "Look what sport did for me" attitude. Unfortunately, with young athletes looking up to the coach, the coach maintains a great deal of power in socializing individuals into a particular belief system. Thus, as gatekeepers, coaches maintain a great deal of sway in determining the social outcomes of sport. The combination of these five powers quite nearly gives a coach *absolute* power. When one adds these powers to the institutional autonomy coaches are given, it is a recipe for danger.

This absolute power leads to a plethora of coach related problems, including sexual, emotional, and physical abuse. In their study of abused professional athletes, Kelly and Waddington (2006) found that "no matter how abusive or violent the manager's [coach's] behavior may be, his authority was not to be questioned and those who did question it were punished, in this case by being withdrawn from the games" (p.153). Jones et al. (2004) suggest that a coach's power surpasses any other profession which ultimately encourages conformism (Hughes and Coakley 1991), obedience (Tomlinson and Yorganci 1997) and dependence (Cense and Brackenridge 2001). In his study of adult athletes physically abused by their coaches, Phil Doorgachurn (CoachAbuse.com) finds that the adult male athletes he studied suggested that their coaches believed that they were more qualified in diagnosing and curing injuries than registered professionals, such as physiotherapists and doctors. He gives an example of how one coach undermined medical professionals, by stating that they were wrong, and that the athlete needed to return to training despite severe medical warnings not to. Athletes are compelled to follow these directions, even against the advice of professionals, because if they do not, they lose favor in their coach's eyes and may lose valued playing positions and time.

Summarizing this, within competitive teamsports—and from a very early age—athletes are normally removed from the presence of women. They are only selected to the next level of play if they adhere to the tenets of orthodox masculinity, where they are influenced by the top-down modeling of the near-total institution. Finally, the institution itself excludes input from those not within its dominant framework. Thus, this system is more than just culturally hegemonic, it is also structural. Not just structural in the sense of a social, historical and institutionalized pattern, but literally structured by codified rules of segregation, reminiscent of the same rules that once formally segregated blacks from whites. It is a resilient system which reproduces a more conservative form of gender expression among men, helping make sport a powerful gender-regime despite the gains of second wave feminism that characterizes the broader culture.

INSTITUTIONALIZING PATRIARCHY

For every athlete who has been highly merited by sport, there are many more that did not make the cut, often those who had horrifying experiences in sport. Those who were marginalized or publicly humiliated in sport are rarely represented in coaching positions. Their stories are seldom told in popular culture. Books are not published, sponsorships are not given, and movies are not made about those who *did not* achieve success in sport. Even when stories of gay (or otherwise marginalized athletes) are told, they normally depict a heroic underdog, my own story included (Anderson 2000).

In this manner, only highly selective stories are being told about sport. These are stories that glamorize the struggle and romance of the sporting hero genre (Stangle 2001). These stories, fictional or real, make for great entertainment, but they falsely bestow upon sport qualities that only exist for a few. Conversely, when marginalized athletes drop out, are pushed out, or otherwise leave the sporting arena, their perceptions of how sport ought to operate go with them. Those who were marginalized by sport and those who were too intimidated to play them in the first place do not go on to coach. Their ideas about how sport ought to function go unheard. Accordingly, sport is essentially closed to voices of dissent.

Unfortunately, masculinity and men's dominance of athletes is bolstered, not just in sport, but it is also reproduced in other institutions as well. This is accomplished by coding masculinized values (which are learned in sport) as being important to work place "spirit" and productivity. Essentially, talking the masculine talk and walking the masculine walk builds trust and respect among other men, inside and outside of sport.

Teamwork, discipline, hard work and sacrifice are characteristics that are thought synonymous with business, too. Thus, the self and forced segregation of females from males in sport means that men and women are schooled in different institutions, and one sex is left severely lacking in valued training and social networking. Clearly, women have a hard time competing with the type of masculine and social capital that sport yields, not because they lack male genitalia, but because they are formally segregated from boys and men in sport. In this manner, what is learned in sport is reproduced outside of sport: People who learn homophobia, sexism and conservative forms of masculinity in sport learn cognitive patterns and leadership styles that then spill over into other institutions. Those who do not learn the cultural codes and behavioral conducts of sport (women, openly gay men and others), do not impress upon the masculine gatekeepers their worthiness of occupational performance. Water cooler questions are organized around, "What sport did you play" and not "What differing voice can you bring to this institution?" This helps explain patriarchal dominance and the over-representation of heterosexual men in positions of power, aside from willing homophobia and misogyny.

Supporting this, Howe's (2001) research into the professionalization of rugby highlights how institutional norms are highly influential in recreating identities among players on *and off* the pitch. Similarly, Parker (2001: 61) suggests that everyday routines construct masculine identities through official and unofficial norms, including a "professional attitude." These studies illustrate the power of social capital in constructing a certain type of valued individual for the leadership market. They signify the social connections and norms of relational cooperation that are embedded in trustworthiness of cooperation for mutual benefit of orthodox achieving men (Putnam 1995).

What I am suggesting here is that some senior managers *may* strategize to keep women and openly gay men out of positions of power themselves, but rather it is much more likely that the institutionalization of sexism and homophobia operates at a much more invidious manner. I suggest that even well-minded, gay friendly feminist men can unwillingly reproduce the culture of masculine privilege in sport and other institutions: Sexism occurs not just because heterosexual men decide that they do not wish women to join their club. We must instead look to the micro, meso, and macro layers of the social institutionalization of men's privilege in sport if we are going to understand how men's privilege is reproduced elsewhere.

In other words, while *some* might strategize to keep women and gay men out, it is more likely that the gatekeepers choose individuals that have social and masculine capital—factors that they assume will make *a heterosexual and sporting man* 'the best man' for the job. Gatekeepers (often ex-sportsmen) are likely to consider that their former sporting histories have well prepared them for their current occupation. Accordingly, New (2001: 736) suggests that, "The best 'man' could be anyone who might not threaten the ways of being and doing with which they are comfortable." Women and openly gay men might actually come to the workforce with a different perspective.

I hope to have shown that the system of reproducing the masculinized nature of sport, and its ancillary occupations and organizations, is much more than just culturally hegemonic, it is also structural. As I have previously said, not just structural in the sense of a social, historical and institutionalized pattern, but literally structured by codified rules of segregation, reminiscent of the same rules that once formally segregated blacks from whites. It is a resilient system which, despite the gains of second wave feminism that characterizes the broader culture, reproduces a more conservative form of gender expression among men. This helps the entire institution of sport reproduce itself as an extremely powerful gender-regime. And, because almost all boys are socialized into this institution in their formative years, they learn cognitive patterns and gendered behaviors that they carry with them into their adult years and other institutions.

But it is important to remember that the system by which men reproduce their dominance in sport (or any other social institution) is not seamless. Women have, and continue to make grounds at undoing formal sexism and the institutionalization of men's privilege. In sport, women have made considerable progress in gaining the right to play, albeit in their own segregated sporting spaces.

I argue that the next step in unraveling how boys learn sexism and thus help reproduce patriarchy needs to come through gender-integration in sport. Results from my cheerleading research (presented in Chapter 8) suggest that gender-desegregating sport would be useful in promoting inclusivity, which includes eroding at patriarchy (Anderson 2008c). Of course, I am aware that among traditionalists of sport, the potential implications of my suggestion may not be received with favor. But hegemonic perspectives that value gender-segregation in sport—whether they be masculinist or feminist in origin—should not stop us from academically examining a counter proposition. As Frye (1999: 361) writes, "If you are doing something that is so strictly forbidden by the patriarchs, you must be doing something right." Hopefully, my research will help men and women better understand the institutionalization of masculine privilege within sport and its ancillary settings, so that we may better wither at it—making sport something closer to the meritocracy for which it is esteemed.

4 Masculine Conformity

In the first chapter, I discussed how sport was developed to produce orthodox masculinity by turning boys away from femininity and homosexuality.
In subsequent chapters I explained the structural mechanism which permits
sport to near-seamlessly reproduce itself, and how the continued socialization of boys into an orthodox form of masculinity bleeds into their adult
lives, and other social institutions as well. Thus, at a macro-level, I have
discussed how sport promotes sexism, homophobia, and patriarchy. In this
chapter I investivate matters at a micro level.

Much of what masculinity is predicated in is wholly *unnatural*. Unnatural,
is a strange word for a sociologist to use. But I say it because much of what
orthodox masculinity requires men to do is to defy their natural instincts.
Men do not naturally limit the spaces they occupy, or the way they relate to
other men. Men do not naturally desire the plethora of mental, physical and
social consequences that also come with adhering to the orthodox requisites
of masculinity. For example, a batter does not naturally desire to lean into
a pitch, sacrificing his body's health for the sake of taking a base. Similarly,
men do not naturally charge into war. That, too, is learned. Whether this obedience is accomplished through submission to parents, teachers or coaches,
males learn early that questioning or contesting authority has serious consequences. Thus, boys and men normally learn to follow those in power.

Power is the fundamental concept in social science research (Russell
1938). In this section, I examine the use of power in terms of teaching men
to obey authority, limit their agency, and submit to the will of the dominant. I use three famous social psychology experiments to do this, beginning with Philip Zimbardo's 1971 prison experiment to illuminate the
power of conformist thinking. I use Zimbardo to show the ease in which
boys and men are made docile to authority, and how we readily adapt to
culturally determined roles. After explaining his experiment, and its much-
discussed implications, I apply to the field of sport. Next, I look to the social
interactions among men, showing how easily men are coerced into obey-
ing masculine authority. I do this through discussing the influential social
psychological literature of Milgram (1974) and Asch (1951), also relating
the findings to sport. Thus, I describe how men are trained to be complicit

to authority, and how sport teaches men to accept and inflict the damage and limitations of orthodox masculinities. Those readers already familiar with the groundbreaking research of Zimbardo, Milgram and Asch, may elect to skip to the end of each section in this chapter, to see how I link these influential studies to sport.

ZIMBARDO AND ROLE ADOPTION

In 1971, Philip Zimbardo paid 24 men to participate in his prison experiment. Depending on the flip of the coin, the university students were randomly assigned to take the role of either prisoners or prison guards. A Stanford University basement was turned into a makeshift prison to facilitate the experiment. The 'prisoners' were first collected by police car, stripped naked, 'decontaminated,' and placed in gowns with no undergarments. On his website, (www.prisonexp.org) Zimbardo says that this was designed to 'effeminize' the men, suggesting that they began "to walk and to sit differently, and to hold themselves differently—more like a woman than like a man." The men's heads were shaved, and shackles placed around their feet. In attempt to begin to wither at the men's sense of self (their agency), their names were replaced with identification numbers, dehumanizing them in the process.

The guards were given no instructions, other than to keep order in the prison. They too were given uniforms, along with whistles and Billy clubs. At 2:30 A.M, the first morning, the prisoners were awoken for "count," where the guards forced them to repeatedly recite their I.D. numbers. The scene was accentuated by jocose behaviors, as neither the prisoners nor the guards took their new role too serious. But the guards' control soon escalated, as the men began to *live* their roles.

The experiment, originally designed to last two weeks, was canceled after just six days. This was because the guards began to wield abusive power over their 'prisoners.' Push-ups at first, and then degrading, homophobic, and power-laden, guard-to-prisoner discourse. Disturbed sleep and humiliating behavior influenced a rebellion among the prisoners, who blocked the door and removed their prisoner hats. The guards then sprayed the prisoners with a fire-extinguisher, stripped the prisoners' nude and increased verbal humiliation. Then, borrowing a tactic used to stymie workers from forming unions, the guards gave privileges to some prisoners, and not to others. Prisoners who continued to rebel were starved. The guards soon reversed the 'privilege' which further set the groups of prisoners against each other.

When one prisoner broke down, crying and shaking, he was chided by the guards for not being "man enough." He was asked how he would make it in San Quentin (a notoriously rough American prison). When this prisoner said that he wanted to quit the experiment, he was told by the other prisoners to suck it up and not to quit. And, when visiting parents complained about the condition of their sons, the guards chided them. One guard even said to a father, "Why? Isn't your boy tough enough?" The father responded, "Of course he is. He is a real tough kid. A leader." The next day, Zimbardo (who was acting as the prison warden) heard there was to be an escape planned. He began to obsess about how to stop it.

But none of this—the abuse, the pleading parents, or the psychological harm—was enough for Zimbardo to cancel the experiment. What finally caused Zimbardo to cancel is as illuminating about masculinity, as his study is about role conformity. On Zimbardo's website he writes:

> I was sitting there all alone, waiting anxiously for the intruders to break in, when who should happen along but a colleague and former Yale graduate student roommate, Gordon Bower. Gordon had heard we were doing an experiment, and he came to see what was going on. I briefly described what we were up to, and Gordon asked me a very simple question: "Say, what's the independent variable in this study?" To my surprise, I got really angry at him. Here I had a prison break on my hands. The security of my men and the stability of my prison was at stake, and now, I had to deal with this bleeding-heart, liberal, academic, effete dingdong who was concerned about the independent variable! It wasn't until much later that I realized how far into my prison role I was at that point—that I was thinking like a prison superintendent rather than a research psychologist.

Even after Zimbardo (who clearly appears to have masculinity and homophobia issues of his own) began to realize that he, too, adopted a role (that of prison warden), he did not use his ultimate authority to cancel the experiment. It seems Zimbardo rather enjoyed the power. Later, several other young men then broke down, crying uncontrollably. One requested medical assistance, and others lawyers.

The students internalized their roles so well that when talking to one psychologically disturbed young man, Zimbardo said:

> Listen, you are not #819. You are [his name], and my name is Dr. Zimbardo. I am a psychologist, not a prison superintendent, and this is not a real prison. This is just an experiment, and those are students, not prisoners, just like you.

The point, of course, is that the prisoners adopted their roles so well, they ceased to remember that they were involved in a college experiment. Although, according to their contract, they were free to leave at will (only losing their pay) they seemingly lost their agency to leave. They formulated a form of self-imprisonment. Perhaps most illuminating, on the fifth day, when a new prisoner was brought into the scenario, he rebelled against their treatment. But this was no longer a favored tactic of the older prisoners. Accordingly, they viewed him as an unwanted trouble maker!

Zimbardo eventually did end the study. "I ended the study prematurely for two reasons," he says. "First, we had learned through videotapes that the guards were escalating their abuse of prisoners . . . Their boredom had driven them to ever more pornographic and degrading abuse of the prisoners." He continues, "Second . . . [another academic] strongly objected when she saw our prisoners being marched on a toilet run, bags over their heads, legs chained together, hands on each other's shoulders. Filled with outrage, she said, 'It's terrible what you are doing to these boys!'" Out of 50 or more outsiders who had seen our prison, she was the only one who ever questioned its morality. Zimbardo adds, "Once she countered the power of the situation, however, it became clear that the study should be ended. And so, after only six days, our planned two-week prison simulation was called off."

Zimbardo's study is well recognized in social psychology literature. The men (prisoners and guards) learned to conform to authority and to act according to their pre-conceived perceptions of the role they were placed into. Even Zimbardo was swept into overly associating with the role of warden. Thus, as horrific as this study is, there is also much illuminating data to emerge from it, much of which relates to sport.

The first lesson comes form role conformity, and the lesson is that if you put a uniform on people, they will enact the role that is signified by that costume. Second, degrading men, and challenging their masculinity for a short period of time (in this case with homophobia and misogyny), will erode at their will to stand up for themselves. This is where some of the usefulness of hazing is found in sports. It permits older team players to wither at the agency of new recruits, influencing them to replicate team norms. Highlighting how hazing can erode at an individuals sense of self, two months after the experiment, one prisoner said:

> I began to feel that I was losing my identity, that the person that I called "Clay," the person who put me in this place, the person who volunteered to go into this prison—because it was a prison to me, it still is a prison to me. I don't regard it as an experiment or a simulation because it was a prison run by psychologists instead of run by the state. I began to feel that that identity, the person that I was that had decided to go to prison was distant from me—was remote until finally I wasn't that, I was 416. I was really my number.

Third, those who were given power (the guards) so revealed in their ability to wield it, that many of the men volunteered to do extra shifts (guarding) without pay. The ability to dominate and control others was their reward. This has implications for coaches who assign students as 'captains,' anointing them with power over their peers.

There are other striking parallels for sport and masculinity. Boys are culturally compelled to play organized sport. In Britain they are even forced into it through 'educational' state curriculum. And similar to the prisoners being dehumanized through stripping and spraying, sport instead initiates boys through recruitment rituals, which often include nudity. Just as prisoners are assigned uniforms and numbers, athletes are too. Whereas prisoners are told to follow numerous institutional rules (often designed to diminish their will to resist), athletes are told that part of 'teamwork' is adhering to a set of often illogical rules, like punishing a whole team because one athlete was not able to keep up on a run.

And, just as prisoners are punished for violating the warden's rules, when athletes break the coach's rules, they are corporally punished with push-ups, running, early morning practices or other physical acts that are designed to cause physical pain and social ostracization. Just as homophobic and effeminizing words were used to further compel prison mates to comply with the psychologically demeaning behaviors they were subjected to, teammates are normally subject to the same homophobic and misogynistic words.

When an athlete shows fear, cries or hesitates, his masculinity is questioned and the coach or others tell him to "suck it up." If the athlete is lucky enough to find support among his parents, a coach simply dismisses accusations of violation with epithets that punishment or ostracization is 'good' for kids, that it 'builds character.' If a prisoner/athlete stands to contest the system, he is called a non-conformist, a rebel, and reminded him that there is no 'I in team.' If he continues to 'act-up,' a coach sets his fellow teammates against him by rewarding the prisoners who do comply with the rules and punish the athletes who don't. He sets teammates against each other and makes them compete for privileges. This prevents them from focusing their anger at the coach. For the warden, who becomes so consumed with winning, someone might eventually remind him that 'it's just a game,' but it won't do much good. By this time the warden has one, singular focus, winning. Accordingly, he will cast off the objections by calling the objector, a " . . . bleeding-heart, liberal, academic, effete dingdong . . ."

Is it absurd to say that teamsports are a prison? Yes, it is. But the intertwining of athletic and prison terminology in the previous paragraph highlights that is it not at all absurd to suggest that sports and prisons use many of the same mechanisms of social control to erode agency from individuals. The prison analogy is simply that of a total-institution, while sports are a near-total institution. Just as the prisoners and guards played a role (which they soon internalized), so do athletes. Even if we have no personal experience with these roles, they are mapped in our culture for us. All we have to do is don a team uniform or whistle and we begin to act accordingly. I've seen this occur numerous times with young, assistant coaches. In fact, I did it myself.

After graduating high school, I decided to return to my school and coach. Suddenly, I was in charge of the very friends and teammates that

I had trained with the previous year. Although I had no coaching experience, I adopted the role of 'coach' as I knew it. I began ordering my athletes around in an authoritarian voice. Of course my athletes (former friends) did not appreciate the style. But *I* was the coach, and just like Zimbardo was the prison warden, I had to keep control.

By the third year, most of my former teammates had graduated. Accordingly, the new runners only knew me as "coach." Consequently, my power and authority grew. One day I found myself in a shouting match with one of my athletes. I was modeling the way my coach had dealt with problems—anger, shouting and insulting. After a teacher broke it up, I thought, *there has got to be a better way.* The next semester I enrolled in an educational psychology course at my university. I began to undo the authority model and adopted a humanist approach to coaching, so my coaching relationships moved to one of friendship and mentorship, not control and power. I sought to increase my referent power, partially by decreasing my coercive power. I began decreasing social distance, and casting off traditional coaching models of authority. I became more democratic in my coaching, and even encouraged my athletes to intellectually challenge the workouts or race strategies I assigned. Occasionally, I would even prescribe preposterous workouts, just to see if they were thinking critically. I would then reward the individual who used his agency to contest me. The point is most coaches don't do this. Instead, they adopt the Bobby Knight, chair throwing, screaming, "respect my authority" type coaching. Most coaches *like* authority. This is why it is commonly known that once you are a head coach, you can never go back to being an assistant. Most coaches like power.

Today, I teach my student-athletes that using authority is one of the most problematic ways to get athletes/students to do what you want them to do. I encourage them to increase their referent power with their athletes, so that they can influence them to not only think on their own, but to contribute to the learning environment. Essentially, I stress that use of authority is abuse. There is almost always a better way.

MILGRAM AND OBEDIENCE TO AUTHORITY

There are other social psychology experiments that help us understand how athletes learn complicity, complacency and docility to a coach's authority and team norms. In the wake of World War II, Yale social psychologist Stanley Milgram set out to determine if Adolf Eichmann and other Nazi war criminals were simply following orders, making them accomplices to a crime rather than the assailants themselves. His study was designed to see if a person off the street would obey an authority figure to the point of violating their moral conscience. Accordingly, pretending to have subjects participate in a learning experiment, Milgram situates an actor to pretend he was being electrically shocked. The subject asked the confederate (actor) a question, and when it was wrong, the subject was to administer an electric shock. The actor would scream, and the subject would be instructed to continue with the experiment. With each wrong answer, the subject was to systematically escalate the level of electric shock. Milgram summarized the experiment in his 1974 article, "The Perils of Obedience," writing:

> The legal and philosophic aspects of obedience are of enormous importance, but they say very little about how most people behave in concrete situations. I set up a simple experiment at Yale University to test how much pain an ordinary citizen would inflict on another person simply because he was ordered to by an experimental scientist. Stark authority was pitted against the subjects' strongest moral imperatives against hurting others, and, with the subjects' ears ringing with the screams of the victims, authority won more often than not. The extreme willingness of adults to go to almost any lengths on the command of an authority constitutes the chief finding of the study and the fact most urgently demanding explanation.

As the intensity of 'administered' shocks increased, the actor would pound on the wall, begging for the experiment to stop. Milgram even had the confederate complain about a heart condition. Most of the subjects asked Milgram if they could stop the experiment. But Milgram upped the authority with each plea. First he simply said, "Please continue." The next request to stop was met with, "The experiment requires that you continue." Followed by, "It's absolutely necessary that you continue." Finally, the subject was told, "You have no other choice. You must go on." If the subject again asked to stop the experiment, it was halted. Otherwise, it wasn't halted until the subject had administered an unbelievable 450 volts (enough to kill you) three times in a row!

In the original experiment, none of the participants stopped before administering 300 volts, and 65 percent went on to the final stage of 450 volts, three times each. Many of the subjects continued to administer the shocks even though the confederate had ceased to scream (as if he had died). Since the original experiment, it has been replicated and altered in numerous ways. In one study the wall between the confederate and the subject was removed, so that the shocker could see the (acted) pain the other person was experiencing. Nonetheless, the consistent finding remains that 61–65 percent of people will administer the lethal dose of 450 volts (Blass 2000). And, of those who did cease, none demanded that the experiment stop for others. None bothered to check on the health of the person they thought they were shocking.

Milgram's shocking experiments clearly compliment Zimbardo's study, but instead of studying how people adopt roles, it examines how we submit to authority. His study shows that when people believe they are simply the instrument for carrying out another person's wishes, they no longer see themselves as being responsible for their actions. Once this critical shift of viewpoint has occurred, all of the essential features of obedience follow. Milgram's (1974) agency theory holds that when we receive commands from authority figures, we lose our sense of responsibility because it is diffused (diffusion of responsibility) and we lose our capacity to make our own choices. Essentially, we lose our agency. We enter an agentic-free, state where we become agents of a higher authority, feeling "responsibility to authority" but "no responsibility for the content of our actions that the authority prescribes" (Milgram 1974: 145–146). Clearly, this is the case with soldiers.

Many individuals who have little power in a group assume that they are supposed to carry out the orders of the authority without questioning these orders (Hamilton and Sanders 1999). They no longer believe they are in control of their own actions, and so become willing cogs in the group machine, carrying out the authority's orders without considering their implications or questioning their effects (Hamilton and Sanders 1999; Kelman and Hamilton 1989). One on website devoted to the experiment (http://home.swbell.net/revscat/perilsOfObedience.html), Milgram is quoted as saying:

> This is, perhaps, the most fundamental lesson of our study: ordinary people, simply doing their jobs, and without any particular hostility on their part, can become agents in a terrible destructive process. Moreover, even when the destructive effects of their work become patently clear, and they are asked to carry out actions incompatible with fundamental standards of morality, relatively few people have the resources needed to resist authority.

Later variations of the experiment show that the closer one is to the damage they inflict the less likely they are to comply with authority. When subjects were told to place the hand of the 'learner' on the electric shock plate, conformity rates dropped to just 30 percent. Interestingly, although women showed more distress at having to administer electric shocks, they complied equally with men. Also, when other researchers encourage the subject to apply the shocks, compliance improves.

Latane (1981) analyzes these results through social impact theory, explaining that the impact of power on a target from an authority figure is determined by the strength of influence according to three main factors: First, the strength (or importance) of the influencer; second, the number of influencers; and, third, the immediacy (or closeness) of the influencer. As each of these increase, each will cause the power of influence to increase and subsequently will result in increased conformity. Conversely, decreasing these factors will have the opposite effect. Social impact theory can account for a large body of experimental research on conformity, compliance, and obedience (Latane and Bourgeois 2001), all of which offer useful insights into the explanations for the abuse athletes are subjected to by their coaches.

When it comes to sport, one must ask, if 65 percent of people will administer a lethal dose of electricity simply because some researcher in a white coat tells them to, what will athletes do? How easy is it for a coach, who is imbued with social power, to order athletes to perform while injured, to intentionally foul (injure) others, or to comply with the coach against a plethora of otherwise moral objections (including sexual abuse)? Collectively, the adoption of roles, and the relinquishment of autonomy positions athletes into an agentic-less state of mind, permitting horrific acts to be committed by their coaches or teammates, all in the name of obedience. Brackenridge (2000) argues "authority figures like coaches come to assume dominance and control over athletes, [and] it is clear that these expressions of agency arise from long-term, collective, socio-cultural influences" (p. 5). Crosset (1986) identifies this as a form of a "master-slave" relationship.

For example, Gervis and Dunn (2004) show that of the twelve international-competing youth athletes they studied (aged between 8 and 16), each reported emotionally abusive behaviors from their coaches. They found athletes felt worthless, fearful and humiliated by their coaches, who were found to belittle, humiliate, shout, scapegoat, reject, isolate, ignore and threaten their athletes. All reported belittling and shouting, nine of them reported frequent humiliation, and nine also reported threatening behaviors. Seven reported scapegoating, six reported rejection or being ignored, four reported isolation. As a result, the children (now adults) report feeling stupid, worthless, upset, less confident, humiliated, depressed, fearful and angry.

This occurs because the coach has *too much power*, and because the athletes learn not to contest it. In their study of abused professional athletes, Kelly and Waddington (2006) found that "no matter how abusive or violent the manager's [coach's] behavior may be, his authority was not to be questioned and those who did question it were punished, in this case by being withdrawn from the games" (p. 153). Finally, making the coach's power all the more salient, recall what happened to a prisoner when he contested the guard/coach. He was viewed unfavorably among his prison mates. Accordingly, even when coaches have been abusive, it does not mean their abuse is reported. Brackenridge, Bringer and Bishop (2005: 261) write:

> Abuses of many kinds have been known about for years, but for a variety of reasons have not been labeled as abuse or not dealt with as misdemeanors. The physical demands of training, emotional toughness and a culture of resilience in sports all acted as masks to the suffering that some athletes faced as part of their sporting experience.

Those who stand against authority are perceived as standing against a norm, and this is something Asch shows us is difficult for people to do.

ASCH AND SOCIAL CONFORMITY

Solomon Asch (1951) placed a student into a room with other students who were confederates (individuals who were knowingly playing along with the experiment). All of the students were told to say that, of the three lines presented to them, the shorter line was longest. The test was designed to see how one student (the test subject) would answer when he was asked which line was longer. Asch found that although it was clear which line was longer, 32 percent of the time the respondent would answer according to his peers. Asch argues that this is because people do not want to be out of step with other people. People would rather conform, and say something that they do not believe, than be the one to disagree with a group. I suggest that the obedience of athlete to coach is not only influenced by the process men go through in order to be successful in sport, but also by the behaviors of others in the group/team, and their willingness to obey the coaches' orders. Deutsch and Gerard (1955) propose social influence theory as a way to suggest that athletes obey coaches because when faced with an ambiguous situation, they refer to others for social comparison.

Because of the ruthless and hyper-masculine ethos of so many sports, many athletes not only accept the use of intimidation and violence of their coaches, but many see it as an appropriate "character building" way of socializing players (Kelly and Waddington 2006). Therefore, those athletes who look for social comparison in abusive situations, seeing whole-hearted and often valued acceptance from their teammates (who see it as making them 'real' men or tougher players), will usually conform to the social norm. An individual's need for social acceptance and approval can lead them into compliance with the majority, even in the face of abuse and potential injury. In sports teams, where the need for social acceptance is high (and the coach holds such extensive reward and coercive power), athletes will often conform to the normative behaviors.

The essential effect of conformist desire plays itself out in sports fields across the world. For example, it is easy for one athlete to be blamed for a team's loss, and then have all the other athletes agree to it. More significant to orthodox masculinity, my research on gay athletes (Anderson 2005a) shows that when a heterosexual team captain, or other teammember that retains high masculine capital, says that they have no problem with gay men, the other athletes tend to agree. Conversely, when the individual with the highest masculine capital takes a homophobic stance, others again agree. On one team, the attitudes of the men shifted from homophobic, to gay friendly in one year, and then back to homophobic the next—depending on who the team captain was. This highlights the hierarchical relationship built into sport, and the "follow the leader" nature of athletes.

Unfortunately, the desire not to 'rock the boat' also gives the coach unyielding power. The initially uncomfortable acceptance of minor abuses by coaches often goes unquestioned, less because individuals are influenced not to speak up about them through team complicity. As athletes matriculate through the system the acts of abuse are slowly ratcheted up to be more abusive, coercive and violent, which also become gradually naturalized as just part of the game (Kelly and Waddington 2006). Brackenridge (1995: p.5) writes that the "process involves gradually building trust and pushing back the boundaries of acceptable behavior, slowly violating more and more personal space through verbal familiarity, emotional blackmail and physical touch."

This is possible because coaches are not only bestowed as 'all powerful,' but because they have earned the respect of the players through their previous sporting accomplishments. Coaches encourage the perception of themselves as knowledgeable and infallible by punishing those who question them (Cushion and Jones 2006). Others not directly involved find it difficult to resist a coach because they believe they are doing what they are supposed to. Thus, just as Asch (1951) demonstrated that group members find it difficult to resist because they fear being an outsider to their own group, athletes also find it to resist because they are sporting insiders.

CHAPTER CONCLUSION

The collective nature of athlete's matriculation through sport, and the way in which the cultural and structural environment of sport is used to place an athlete into an agentic-less state, articulates how sport has not only managed to reproduce itself over the years, but how it has managed to resist the impact of more liberalizing broader cultural trends. However, if it can be shown that there exists a competing paradigm within or between groups, it can help athletes see an alternative pathway to constructing their masculinity. If broader social trends become so divergent from what occurs in sport, it may also highlight the barbarism of competitive sporting culture. Inclusive masculinities, I suggest, is such a model.

Inclusive masculinities offer a differing perspective. They provide a different masculinization model: One that enables heterosexual men to see that they do not need to be trapped by the oppressive cult of masculinity. Inclusive masculinities have grown so popular in the broader university culture, that the institution of sport is no longer capable of ignoring them. Accordingly, the next section describes inclusive masculinity theory.

Summary of Part I

In Part I, I described the construction of orthodox masculinity as a turn of the 20th-century invention to resist the gains of women's liberation and to ensure that male youths were socialized into a heteromasculine ideal. I described the policing mechanism of men's social, emotional and physical boundaries as being conducted through homophobia and misogyny but theorized homophobia as being particularly central to the production and stratification of masculinities as an ordered system of valued or subjugated individuals. Homophobic discourse was therefore described as a weapon to deride each other in establishing this hierarchy (Burn 2000). And because femininity is deeply entwined with homosexuality, misogynistic discourse was also described as reproducing intra-masculine difference. Collectively, homohysteria has culturally compelled men to disassociate with femininity, gay men, or any other expression, desire, discourse, or behavior coded as feminine/gay.

However, it was also discussed that orthodox versions of masculinity bring a host of extremely socio-negative outcomes. Not only for women, gay men and heterosexual men who do not fit the dominating archetype, but also to those who do fit the mandates. Men adhering to the principles of orthodox masculinity are limited in their gendered expressions, body language, and emotions. They are limited in the gendered terrains they can work or play within, and they must put social and emotional distance between themselves and other men in order to avoid suspicion of homosexuality.

It was described that orthodox-adhering men also produce a great deal of violence: Violence against themselves, gay men, women, and their teammates. In a culture that esteems orthodox masculinity, men are expected to take violent risks with their physical health, too. They are expected to sacrifice their bodies for the sake of team and/or family, and to resist showing fear or intimidation about these duties.

In short, orthodox masculinity has led to a culture of patriarchal and homophobic, symbolic and actualized violence, while also leading to self-regulation and oppression of those 'in power.' With all of the social harm caused by orthodox masculinities, it is therefore interesting that orthodox versions of masculinity have retained such cultural value over the decades.

In Chapter 3, I questioned how the dominant form of masculinity (the one Connell calls 'hegemonic') manages to reproduce itself, despite all of these socio-negative outcomes. While Connell theorizes this is an effect of men using orthodox masculinity as a way of symbolically justifying and retaining patriarchy, I found this an accurate but nonetheless limited analysis of masculinity's role in reproducing patriarchy. Rather, I suggested that orthodox masculinity is unknowingly and perhaps even unwittingly reproduced with each generation, because nearly all men, regardless of their gender politics, are socialized into the ethos of competitive teamsports. Here, orthodox masculinity has been able to reproduce itself because of the structure upon which it operates. I therefore suggested that, although there are various purposes and outcomes of organized sporting participation for men in Anglo-American cultures, their overarching purpose is to serve as an efficient and resilient mechanism for the political project of promoting orthodox masculinity at the expense of women and gay men.

I explained the resiliency of sport in reproducing orthodoxy through not only its culture, but also its structure. The competitive nature of sport, its decreasing opportunity structure, the lack of oversight and educational attainment required to coach, as well as the manner in which former and failed athletes (who have overconformed to sport's ethos) are employed as coaches, permits sport to remain virtually free from voices of dissent. This structure is made yet more resilient by a culture which is designed to quickly wither at an individual's agency to contest one's coach, and thus the system. Here, I suggested that the structure of sport leads men to enter a nearly agentic-less state, which influences them to conform to the 'role' of the athlete they have had molded to them in popular culture, to obey the 'authority' of their coaches, and fear disconformity among peers. Considering that sport's homophobia either drives gay men away from the institution or denies their voice within it, sport has also been able to resist the gay liberationist efforts achieved in the broader culture.

I suggested that the reproduction of orthodoxy is structurally exacerbated by the gender-segregated framework upon which teamsports are valued. Accordingly, the agency of women, their voices and narratives, are almost completely removed from the coaching and socialization patterns of boys and men. Therefore, from early youth and throughout young adulthood, boys and men are structured into a desire to be associated with heteromasculine dominance by partaking in a sporting space that is used to sculpt their bodies and construct their masculine identities to align with dominant perspectives of masculinist embodiment and expression. Competitive teamsports exacerbate society's gendered values, myths and prejudices about the variations in men and women, while simultaneously constructing men to exhibit, value and reproduce traditional notions of masculinity (Burstyn 1999). Until we gender-integrate sports, men will continue to advantage from patriarchy, even if they individually identify as feminists.

This is because the immense popularity of sport, and its related socio-positive myths, bleeds its ethos into other important institutions, politics, business, the church, education and entertainment. In short, orthodox masculinity is valued in Anglo-American cultures because we value the athlete narrative, the romance of competitive struggle, the notion of 'being a team player,' and the 'work ethic' supposedly embedded into those who are successful in the realm of sport. As long as we believe that the ethics learned in teamsports generalize to other areas of one's life, we will continue to value sport. And, as long as sports are gender-segregated, we will continue to privilege men. Thus, our desire to reproduce orthodox masculinity is less about the conscious and willing reproduction of patriarchy, and more about our desire to morally equip boys with the 'skills they need in life,' through playing sport. This is something Connell does not pay enough attention to in her theorizing about the reproduction of patriarchy.

However, I agree with Connell in suggesting that, as bad as social matters seem to be, things can always change. Connell recently suggested that the changeable notion of hegemonic masculinity means that the current archetype may at some point be replaced by a less oppressive means of being masculine (Connell and Messerschmidt 2005). Of relevance to my work, she also suggests a more holistic approach to the study of power relations is needed, and recognition of the "agency of subordinated groups" (p. 848). I suggest these processes are already occurring. Inclusive masculinities are fast becoming the norm for university aged, white, middle-class men, both inside and outside of sport. Accordingly, in the next section, I theorize the background to how inclusive masculinities operate. The chapters in section 3 then explicate it through empirical evidence.

Part II

Inclusive Masculinity Theory

5   From Homophobia
        to Homohysteria

There are a number of social trends that directly or peripherally impact the creation of inclusive masculinities among university-attending white men. These include a lessening of traditional views and institutional control of sexual behaviors and relationships, something made evident by the lessening of the traditional double standard of girls being "sluts" and guys being "studs" in heterosexual intercourse (Tanenbaum 1999; Wolf 1997), and the growing percentage of those engaging in pre-marital intercourse (Laumann et. al. 1994; Johnson et. al. 2001). Other relevant trends include the growing willingness of men to be dominated in sex (Segal 1994); trends that successfully make men into objects of commoditized sexual desire (Dworkin and Wachs 2009; Heywood and Dworkin 2003; Miller 2001), as well as more fluid gender codes resulting from a merger of gender and sexuality signifiers in consumer culture (Warner 1993). Finally, some evidence shows institutional sexism may also be decreasing among university-aged men (Bryant 2003). But truly central to my theoretical hypothesis for the creation and valuing of inclusive masculinities is the cultural reduction of homohysteria.

Since the early 1990s, both qualitative (Barrett and Pollack 2005; Pascoe 2005) and quantitative (Laumann et. al. 1994; Loftus 2001; Widmer, Treas and Newcomb 2002; Ohlander, Batalova and Treas 2005; Yang 1997) studies have shown a significant decrease in cultural and institutional homophobia within Anglo-American cultures. This is something that myself and others (Harris and Clayton 2007; Pringle and Markula 2005; Southall et. al. 2006) find among teamsport athletes as well. Add this to the emergence of "metrosexual" men in sport, such as England's David Beckham (Cashmore and Parker 2003) and the Welsh rugby player Gavin Henson, and we see more feminized men adopting the more gender-queer genre once only associated with glam rock performers (Harris and Clayton 2007).

The idea that varying degrees of cultural homophobia influence the behaviors of men is not new. For example, Field (1999) observed social groups of 12 year olds at McDonalds in both France and America, finding that American adolescents spent less time leaning against, stroking, kissing and hugging their peers than did the French adolescents. Instead, American youth showed more self-touching and more aggressive verbal and physical behavior. More exhaustive research has been compiled by John Ibson. In *Picturing Men*, Ibson (2002) shows that increasing cultural homophobia influences American heterosexual men to further police their homosocial tactility, while decreasing cultural homophobia has the opposite effect. Ibson's work was highly influential in the creation of inclusive masculinity theory, because it literally illustrates the behavioral part of what I saw occurring in my research.

Ibson does this by describing the history of men's relationships from the 1880's until the 1980s with 5,000 images of men. Ibson does not explain what the photographs mean to us today, but rather what it meant to the subjects at the time the photos were taken. Specifically, Ibson uses the photos to illustrate the changing nature of physical intimacy between men in response to the cultural contextualization of homosexuality in modern society. His book contains images of athletes before the 1920s, as well as friends, servicemen, brothers, collegiate and prep school boys in many settings, lavishly dressed, provocatively undressed, arms wrapped around each other, embracing, lying in piles, sleeping in the same beds, holding hands and sitting on each other's laps in order to show their affection for one another. Viewed through a modern perspective, these images seem homoerotic. In fact, Ibson first thought that he was collecting images of gay men. However, the sheer number of images he found for sale in swap meets and garage sales suggested to him that he was seeing something else.

As explained in the first chapter, the modern homosexual identity was made in the latter part of the 19th century, and it slowly grew more culturally salient as decades passed. Thus, the photographs Ibson collected suggested that the gradual awareness of homosexuality as a static identity (not just an abhorrent behavior) resulted in an equal growth in cultural homophobia. His photographs clearly show that as American culture grew increasingly aware of homosexuality, men began to pry intimacy away from fraternal bonding. This mass awareness of homosexuality, combined with social homophobia increased men's fear of being falsely homosexualized by their behaviors, attitudes emotions or associations. Accordingly, as the awareness of homosexuality grew (in the presence of homophobia), so did the space between men.

This distance between men is clearly illustrated through multiple subsets of Ibson's photographs. Thus, Ibson shows that cultural space has been added between men in many walks of public and private life. However, none is more germane to this book than Ibson's photographs of men's teams.

Ibson uses images of teams to illustrate the evolution of the team portrait, and consequential growing rigidity that athletes displayed through the passing years. For example, prior to the 1920s his photographs show athletes hugging, laying their heads in each other's laps, holding hands, or draping their arms around each other. Soon after, however, teams appeared in the now familiar structure of rows. Men first stand with their hands at their side, and years later their arms are folded across their chests.

Picture Courtesy of Professor John Ibson

I have used Ibson's photographs in lectures on masculinity ever since he published his book. I find them immensely useful because they provide substantial and impactful visual proof regarding the relationship between homohysteria and male intimacy. They help one understand that

Picture Courtesy of Professor John Ibson

Picture Courtesy of Professor John Ibson

homohysteria has greatly limited the expression of gender and intimacy among all men, and that homohysteria may be particularly damaging to the emotional relationships between heterosexual men. However, the progression of Ibson's photographs also made me wonder if we would see a reversal of the straightening-up process, now that cultural homophobia/homohysteria was in decline.

An answer to this question was made salient while watching multiple cheerleading squads pose for their group portraits at a national championship meet, I noticed that the men lined up close together so that the entire team could get into the frame. Team after team approached the stage to line up. Here, men joked with one another, normally pretending to fuck one another and bantering about their mock homosexual behavior. As the men lined up, most stood with their arms at their side, or lapped around each other. This was the pose they *wished* to adopt. However, just before the camera flashed, the men suddenly buffed up, folding their arms across their chests and flexing. Fascinated by the instant masculinizing of their poses, I drew closer and saw the photographer (a male in his 40's) prompting the men to "do like this, guys." He folded his arms across his chest to model the pose. The cameraman had to model for these men what my teammates did 'naturally,' in the 1980s. It was evident that many of the men had not predetermined to project such an image, but faced with his directions, they adjusted their behavior to match more orthodox mannerisms. I later asked the photographer why he prompted them to do this. "They have worked hard for those muscles," he said, "They should show off their masculinity."

When I told the openly gay male captain of the squad I was observing what I saw, he responded, "I'll make sure my friends don't [buff up]." The men from his team stood for the camera, arms lapped around each other. The photographer tried to prompt the men into buffing-up and straightening-up, but they refused. Finally he disparagingly shook his head and snapped the photo. The most important data, however, came just after this team's photograph.

Other teams waiting in line saw the disagreement. Influenced by the agency of the squad I observed, they resisted the cameraman's prompts, too. Not all teams photographed themselves in more affectionate poses; some older coaches sided with the photographer and demanded their players cross their arms. Other coaches desired more affectionate poses. This, it seemed, was a struggle for idealized notions of masculinity and it suggested to me that the stranglehold that orthodox masculinity maintained was beginning to wane. It seemed that these men were more willing to put themselves into poses that older men feared. The power of homohysteria had lessened in this setting. The disordered gender displays were brought about by one astute gay man.

In some ways, gay men might be uniquely positioned to study masculinities. Although I knew I was gay around eight years of age, I did not come out until I was 25. Accordingly, I spent 17 years studying and modeling the behaviors of heteromasculine men in order to pass as straight. And, although I do not believe that the years of depression, suicidal adulation and daily fear of being discovered was 'worth it,' today I recognize that not only did the closet spark my sociological imagination and political activism, but the fact that I grew up during one of the most homohysteric periods in American history, in one of the most homohysteric locales (Orange County, California), also facilitated it.

I use the word homohysteria because the term homophobia does not accurately capture the complications of both how people feel about homosexuals, and whether or not they reasonably thought homosexuals live among them. In examining the first, it is clear that the meaning of what it meant to be a sodomite, a pervert, invert, or homosexual greatly varied from moment to moment in contemporary culture. In some periods it is possible (as Foucault suggests) that homosexuality was simply viewed as a behavior. Certainly Spencer (1995) shows that there are numerous incidents of same-sex behaviors being blamed on temporary demonic possession. Thus, after one was caught having sex with another man, priests would perform an exorcism to pray the demons away, restoring the individual to his 'natural' heterosexual self. In other moments, however, men were understood to be homosexual by static trait, an unwavering sexual orientation. This is certainly the case with Oscar Wilde.

However, fundamental to the creation of a culture of homohysteria is the necessity of public awareness that reasonable and 'normal' people could also be homosexual. I would not describe a culture of homophobia as homohysteric unless people can be thought gay. There are many cultures in which a people know that homosexuality exists but that do not think it exists among their people. For example, in 2007, President Ahmadinejad of Iran said to an American audience, "In Iran we don't have homosexuals like in your country." This cultural belief gives Iranian boys and men more social permission to display gendered behaviors unacceptable in cultures where people are not thought gay. Thus, boys can hold hands in many countries, but not the United States. Homohysteria is characterized by the witch-hunt to expose those who are. When one adds homophobia, to the social understanding that homosexuality exists in great numbers, and that it is not easily identifiable by one's aesthetics, or negated by one's religious affiliation, we have a culture of homohysteria.

I argue that the awareness of homosexuality existing as a static trait, an unchanging sexual orientation, was first thrust into Anglo-American culture through the visibility of the Wilde trials. However, the unusual aesthetic appearance that Wilde represented, and his penchant for aesthetic art and beauty, helped formulate homosexual suspicion only for men who resembled Wilde's flair. This stabilized the stereotype of the homosexual for decades, excusing all others of homosexual suspicion, unless they acted in Wildeian ways. Under this model, James Dean or Rock Hudson are not suspected of maintaining sexual desire for men, while Harvey Fierstein and Stephen Fry are. Quite simply, what this means is that if members of a culture do not believe that homosexuality is possible, there is no need to prove to one's peers that one is not gay. Consequently men are given more freedom of gendered expression.

The public's awareness that homosexuals looked normal (even if still believing that they were not), and that they lived among us, hit an apex in the 1980s. This period ended the heterosexualizing veil that muscularity and masculinity bought. The stereotype of the flamboyant gay man certainly remained, but the public understood that this was just *one* form of homosexuality. This was because 'the gay community' was hit by two substantial socio-political events that raised the general public's exposure to homosexuality. These events impacted not only gay masculinities (Levine 1998), but also men's gendered understanding as a whole.

The first came in the form of a backlash to the gains made by gay men and feminist of the 1960s and the 1970s. The 1980s ushered in a revival of fundamentalist Christianity. At a time in which church attendance began to decline, the advent of cable television brought various ministries into millions of living rooms. Christianity used the hysteria about homosexuality to milk money from callers who could conveniently donate with their credit cards over the phone. Christianity found political purpose in Anita Bryant, Jerry Falwell, Pat Robertson and other monsters of immorality.

Unfortunately, this further helped inspire Christianity to move from the pulpits and into the political arena.

The true propellant for homohysteria however, came in the form of a virus. In the early 1980s AIDS brought such visibility that it solidified in every citizen's mind that homosexuals existed in great numbers. It secured a public awareness that homosexuals lived and worked alongside the normals in *every* social institution. The ubiquitous presence of gay men could no longer be denied, they were dying in normal American families.

The sexual social revolution of the 1970s, with its emphasis on exploring and unleashing once stigmatized sexualities and gendered performances, might best be summed up with a non-sporting example. Instead, disco seems to capture much of the zeitgeist of the time. But as disco began to be replaced by rock, the onslaught of AIDS was disco's requiem. For example, in *The Empire of the Beat* Walter Hughes (1994) poignantly writes, "1970s [disco] songs like 'Don't Leave Me This Way' and 'Never Can Say Good-bye' [became], in the 1980s part of the work of mourning" (p. 156). Songs that once celebrated sexual excess were now being used to cope with unimaginable loss. Bodies that were once virile with heightened sexuality and donned masculinities were now stripped by disease, poxed with Kaposi's sarcoma, and stigmatized as contagion by an ignorant and reluctant government. Now, homosexuality was not only pathologized as a lack of masculinity, but it was associated with viral genocide.

Gay men were stigmatized as being both effeminate and diseased. This, combined with the religious right's crusade to stigmatize homosexuality, meant that Americans were hell bent on having yet another crisis in masculinity (Kimmell 1996). Heterosexual gender roles were to be recalibrated through organizations like the "Promise Keepers," and films like "Rocky." And Freud's explanation of homosexuality as the product of an absent father figure found renewed emphasis. The "men's movement" of the AIDS era was, just as it was during the early part of the 21st century, a way for men to distance themselves from what one was *not to be*. This time, however, Americans (in particular) had more than just a religious reason to 'prevent' homosexuality, it was now epidemiological.

AIDS had an incalculable and unfortunately rarely acknowledged effect on all men's gender expression. Thus, the anxiety over AIDS played a dramatic role in gay men's desire to constitute their masculine subjugation, too. Whereas camp culture once served to show heterosexuals that we (a gay citizenry) were not afraid of them, people living with AIDS were stereotyped as weak, thin, and effeminate. Thus, men's suspicions of other men's serostatus functioned as a form of sexual survival and fostered a corporeal pissing contest among gay men. Such anxieties became reflexive and shaped how men developed and advertised their own bodies for sexual encounters. Now gay men wanted to act hypermacho, too. The sexual economy of the 1980s depended on the theory that the more muscular and young looking a man was, the less likely he was to have HIV/AIDS. This led to the ultra-masculine bodies of the late 1980s and early 1990s. It was a trend that was evident in the heterosexual male community as well. Psychiatrist Harrison Pope shows, for example, that the morphology of the popular American doll, G.I. Joe, evolved since the doll was introduced in 1964. Each new version has since grown larger in muscle mass and muscular definition (Pope, Phillips and Olivardia 2000).

Steroids added to the masculinization of gay and straight cultures. Steroids were first introduced as a necessity for HIV/AIDS patients, but were soon used by many gay and straight men as body enhancers (Halkitis, Green and Wilson 2004). Similarly, with the proliferation of the fitness industry in the 1990s (with gyms and vitamin shops becoming a cornerstone of many urban areas) gay and straight men adopted new workout regimes to ensure muscular physiques (Pope et al. 2000). Ronald Reagan appointed known steroid user, Arnold Schwarzenegger, as his Presidential Physical Fitness Advisor, and a pumped-up Rambo assured us that American muscularity and stoic masculinity would have been sufficient to beat the North Vietnamese, if it were not for those effete politicians running the war from behind their desks.

If AIDS did anything positive for the 'gay community' it started Americans talking about homosexuality from a 'rights' perspective. Then, as the virus later took hold in the heterosexual community, the stigma it brought to those infected slowly began to wane. This brought a further emancipatory call for gays and lesbians. This is not to say that AIDS was not and is still not overly-associated with homosexuality, or that it is not still stigmatized, but today we are at least more nuanced in our understanding that AIDS is not caused *by* homosexuality. As this occurred, social attitudes began to swing back to inclusivity. Accordingly, General Social Survey (GSS) data shows that by 1993 homophobia was in rapid retreat (Loftus 2001).

Unfortunately, the General Social Survey unduly influences participants to over-report homophobia. This is because the question on the survey regarding homosexuality is worded:

> *Is homosexuality always wrong?*
> *Sometimes, wrong?*
> *Occasionally wrong?*
> *Or never wrong?*

Asked face-to-face, by an authority figure, I suggest that it loads the informant's response toward the negative. There is no counter balance, no, *always right, sometimes right, occasionally right, or never right*. Furthermore, it is not clear whether the question is designed to reflect one's views of homosexuality for others, or for one's self. If a heterosexual participant interprets the question, personally, he is likely to state that it is *wrong* to a higher degree. Nonetheless the GSS represents one of social scientists most long term, reliable surveys in the United States, precisely because the way it asks the question has not changed. Thus, it represents the best we have for understanding the changing relationship between homophobia and society. The GSS and its British counterpart, the *British Social Attitudes Survey,* (which asks the same question) provide a reliable, general, measure of shifting cultural attitudes toward homosexuality.

Throughout the 1970s, an average of 70 percent of Americans said that homosexuality was always wrong, but those numbers increased to 77.4 percent in 1988, before dropping ten points when Clinton took office in 1993. That number has slowly but steadily decreased a few percentage points each year, and in 2006, 56.2 percent of Americans thought that homosexuality was always wrong. However, only 42 percent of those between the ages of 18–30 said that homosexuality was always wrong in that same year, and they were matched by 41 percent who said that it was not at all wrong. I would break the variable down by race, education status, and gender too (variables that would be important for understanding inclusive masculinity theory) but this would reduce the sample size as to make it meaningless.

Unfortunately, large-scale qualitative examples concerning the social attitudes of heterosexual male university students specifically are non-existent; as are single institution longitudinal studies. There is, to the best of my knowledge, no quantitative study that might help me accurately describe how decreasing homophobia relates to white, university-attending men. However, Hicks and Lee (2006) suggest that regression models of Gallup Poll survey data determines that sex, age, education, religiosity, positions on gender and racial issues, partisanship and ideology, are all related to anti-gay attitudes.

Attitudes toward homosexuality have been substantially and consistently better in Britain than in the United States. Still, the trend of rising homophobia throughout the 1980s and diminishing homophobia since 1993 remains the same. The British Social Attitude Survey shows that in 1983 (the first year the question was asked) 49.5 percent of the population said that homosexuality was always wrong. However, that number climbed to 63.6 percent in 1987, before dropping to 55.4 percent in 1989. In other words, 1987 or 1988 seems to be the apex of homophobia in both countries. And, just as homophobia has continued to decline ever since this period in the United States, the percentage of British citizens saying that homosexuality is *always wrong* has dropped a few percentage points each year. In 2006, just 23.7 percent of respondents maintained that it was *always wrong.* This, of course, is a startling difference compared to the United States, and it is supported by other quantitative research, too. For example, in 2007 a Pew Global Attitudes Project survey found that when asked *should homosexuality be accepted by society* 49 percent of those in the United States said yes, compared to 71 percent of Britain's citizenry (Sweden was the highest approval rating at 86 percent).

The point is that homohysteria steadily grew in American and British societies as the awareness of homosexuality did. AIDS severely elevated homohysteria because scores of dying gay men proved how ubiquitous gay men were. And, as almost everyone knew that homosexuality now existed, heterosexual men felt compelled to distance themselves from the highly stigmatized homosexual identity. Homohysteria therefore remained at its all-time-high during this period, and gender signs coded as 'feminine' consequently edged toward extinction.

This declining homohysteria of 1993 onwards can also be measured by examining men's idealized bodies. While buffed bodies of the late 80s and early 90s served to show that one was not gay and not effeminate (Pope et al. 2000), things have radically changed since. Part of this was due to AIDS moving into the heterosexual community. For example, Magic Johnson's vehement proclamation that he acquired AIDS through heterosexual intercourse proved that even buff, heterosexual athletes were vulnerable. However, a more significant event came with a movie star.

In 1997, Leonardo Di Caprio was culturally elevated as a sex idol. He was not the first boyish-looking man to achieve fame, but his super-star movie status as sex icon was felt at many levels of society; the way boy band members were perhaps not. His endomorphic body particularly resonated with young women and gay men. His sexualized boyish figure stood in contrast to the sexually esteemed men of the 1980s. DiCaprio, not Stallone, was the icon of this generation. His emergence as an idol marked the beginning for men to be sexualized not through muscle, but the avoidance of fat. This is a trend that gained in strength over the next decade. Filiault (2007) shows that what remains important for men today is not how much muscle they have, but how much fat they have covering that muscle. Straight university men *desire* a thin body today, as opposed to the muscular one of the 1980s. This rapid change is of course likely produced by a number of other social influences including corporate marketing (McNair 2002), but declining homophobia also made this possible.

Di Caprio brought a new masculine narrative to the block. He was straight, but did not appear to care too much to be thought of as such. Some suggested that he was metrosexual. Significantly, the behaviors attached to the label metrosexual are codes that were once exclusively attached to the label *homosexual*.

What is significant to gender scholars however, is that the new age of masculinities studies emerged during the epoch of heightened homohysteria of the 1980s and early 1990s. Embedded in this new sociology of masculinities was the role of homophobia and sport in constructing heteromasculinity. Don Sabo was one of the first to tackle the issue, publishing *Jock: Sports and Male Identity* (1980). R.W. Connell published *Gender and Power* in (1987), where she applied hegemony theory to the study of masculinities. Michael Messner and Don Sabo's highly influential edited volume *Sport, Men and the Gender Order: Critical Feminist Perspectives* was published in 1990, the same year that Brian Pronger published *The Arena of Masculinity: Sports, Homosexuality and the Meaning of Sex.* Messner's next book, *Power at Play: Sports and the Problem with Masculinity*, came out in 1992 and Michael Kimmel's highly influential chapter, "Masculinity as Homophobia: Fear, Shame, and Silence in the Construction of Gender Identity," was published in 1994. Kimmel's influential book, *Manhood in America: A Cultural History*, came out two years later (1996).

These scholars (and others) set the framework from which the new sociology of masculinities developed. As Carrigan, Connell and Lee (1985) point out, men's studies of the 1970s failed to account for the importance of men's heterosexuality in retaining male domination, as well as the importance of gay men's masculinity in undermining it. Messner, Sabo, Kimmel and Connell understood this. Their positioning of the centrality of homophobia to masculinity was understood phenomenologically, too, as the homohysteria during their academically formative years was palpable.

Messner, for example, offers a litany of stories about students' and colleagues' thinking that he was gay for discussing the socio-negative role that homophobia plays in men's lives. When he and Don Sabo first shared a room together at the first North American Society for the Sociology of Sport conference in 1980, rumors abounded that they were gay lovers (despite both being married). Messner says that, "It's clear that for many people, for a good long time, my feminist and pro-gay teaching and writing only made sense to them if it was coming from a gay man—a heterosexual man doing that work did not compute for them." Some even suggested that he 'just didn't know' that he was gay himself. Similarly, Sabo adds, "Most guys I demonstrated with in the 'take back the night' demonstrations of 78 through 80, or who showed up at feminist lectures or rallies in the East Coast were likely to be seen as gay or effeminate." He adds, "Lots of female and male researchers assumed that I was gay throughout the 1980's because I was 'interested in gender' and involved with the men's movement. It was somewhat of a normal occurrence that when somebody found out I was married they would tell me that they were surprised that I wasn't gay." Messner reports the same happening on the West Coast during this time. "The perception of others outside the men's movement was often that if you were involved in a feminist men's group or organization that, 'you must be gay.'"

The extreme homohysteria of the period in which Connell, Messner, Kimmel, Sabo, and others emerged, means that they were aware of the utility of homophobia in polarizing the genders, limiting men's behaviors, and homosexualizing those who dared to be different. And, supporting my hypothesis that homohysteria is in rapid retreat, Messner adds, "I am not so sure that this [homosexualizing] is true anymore." Accordingly, I maintain that in the process of being victimized by homohysteria, these masculinity scholars rightfully assessed the zeitgeist of their time, cementing hegemonic masculinity into the literature.

If homohysteria was not as prevalent during this period, however, one wonders if the model Connell conceptualized to describe the positioning of masculinities in relationship to dominance would include a hegemonic archetype? And/or would it have been as influential in the masculinities literature? Thus, as influential as hegemonic masculinity has been to sport and masculinities literature, the decreasing degree of cultural homohysteria may no longer be appropriate to continually justify its utility (Connell and Messerschmidt 2005). We are in need of new theories that reflect current social trends. The way we honor the forebearers of masculinities studies is by both building upon their works, but also by contesting them.

6 Inclusive Masculinity Theory

Social theorists frequently write about their theories in academically inaccessible language. This permits various people to interpret the theory differently, and perhaps contributes to the life and utility of a theory. As a public sociologist concerned with emancipatory research however, my aim in describing inclusive masculinity theory is the opposite. I desire to explicate the theory in accessible language, so that the reader will understand exactly what I suggest, and what I do not.

The first thing to understand about inclusive masculinity theory is that it emerged from my data, and not the opposite way around. I approached my early research on masculinities using Connell's notion of hegemonic masculinity. This worked particularly well with my work on openly gay male athletes (Anderson 2002). However, in my subsequent research, I found hegemony theory incapable of explaining my data. I began the process of formulating inclusive masculinity theory to describe the emergence of an archetype of masculinity that undermines the principles of orthodox (read hegemonic) masculine values, yet one that is also esteemed among male peers.

For example, I found that the reduction of cultural homophobia in one cheerleading association challenged the dominance that hegemonic masculinity maintained over heterosexual university athletes. Here, openly gay athletes peacefully performed with their heterosexual counterparts, and heterosexual men celebrated men's femininity by dancing erotically and performing otherwise feminized behaviors. Conversely, in a rival association orthodox masculinity was esteemed, and these men did not perform as flamboyantly. And, although there were many gay men in this conservative cheerleading association, they largely remained closeted. Accordingly, I labeled one association as orthodox and the other inclusive, describing how institutional and organizational culture influenced masculine performances and values in each. However, two oppositional masculinities, each with equal influence, co-existing within one culture is not consistent with Connell's theorizing.

Connell suggests that multiple masculinities *do* exist within any organization, institution or culture, but she argues that there will be only one hegemonic archetype of masculinity. In other words, Connell describes hegemonic masculinity as a *hegemonic* process by which only *one* form of institutionalized masculinity is "culturally exalted" above all others (Connell 1995: 77). Then, according to Connell, men are culturally compelled to associate with this one dominant form (i.e. men looking up the hierarchy). This 'looking up' is the *hegemony* in hegemonic masculinity. Again, this was not the case in cheerleading. Even *within* the orthodox institution there were a number of inclusive teams comprised of men who did not value most of the tenets of orthodox masculinity.

Some might be tempted to explain two equally subscribed to and competing forms of masculinity through Connell's notion of protest masculinity. This form of masculinity, she argues, contests the current hegemonic form for dominance. But again, the resolution of this struggle is simply that a new, singular, version of a (hegemonic) dominating masculinity emerges, even if it is a softer archetype. Protest masculinity is valuable for explaining, individual men, or a group of men who opt out of an otherwise hegemonic system, but it fails to adequately capture what occurs with two dominate archetypes, in which neither hegemonically dominates. This is for two reasons.

First, hegemonic masculinity theory did not adequately frame the cheerleading results because neither group felt that they failed to model an ideal type of masculinity. Neither group thought that the version the other aspired to was right, natural, or desirable. The men who ascribed to inclusive masculinity did not aspire to or value orthodox masculinity and those aspiring to orthodox masculinity felt no cultural sway to become more inclusive. Thus, there is no evidence that men were influenced by hegemonic processes. This alone is enough to prove that hegemonic masculinity theory is incapable of capturing what occurred in this setting. In order to use hegemonic masculinity theory one must find examples of hegemony. However, neither group of men felt subordinated or marginalized by the other group. Men did not suffer for failing to meet the other group's mandates. Neither was hegemonic. Connell's theory does not account for this social matrix.

I continued to develop inclusive masculinity theory through the results of subsequent studies of university-attending men: in a fraternity, a rugby team and multiple soccer teams. In each setting, I found that a more inclusive version of masculinity dominated numerically, much more so than in the cheerleading research. But again this dominance did not seem hegemonic; it did not seem to dominate in the way Connell describes the operation of hegemonic masculinity. Furthermore, I am not the only one to describe such findings. Swain (2006a), for example, discusses a notion of personalized masculinity among the pre-adolescents he studies, suggesting that these young men are content to pursue identities not associated with orthodox masculinity.

The final piece to my theory came after conducting a semester-long ethnography with one of my graduate students, Mark McCormack, on a standard British high school. This school sits at the median of England's testing results, drawing students from two sides of a town divided by class. Nonetheless, all boys modeled an inclusive version of masculinity. We found various masculine archetypes co-existing without social struggle (jocks, emos, scholars, artists, etc.), and with no one group dominating. Boys are happy with their group affiliation, and none feel oppressed. Furthermore the public expression of homophobia or homophobic discourse is not acceptable within *any* group. While some elements of orthodox masculinity are valued in some groups (the athletes still value self-sacrifice), the outright expression of homophobia, misogyny, and masculine bravado associated with orthodox masculinity is not acceptable in any group.

Consequently, the temporal-shift in my sequential studies led to the completion of inclusive masculinity theory. I developed it to conceptualize what happens concerning masculinities in three cultural moments of homohysteria (Anderson 2005b, 2008c).

Key to these three phases is the degree of projection of homosexual suspicion and/or labeling of one as homosexual via homophobic discourse. In periods of high homohysteria, homophobia is used to stratify men in deference to a heteromasculine hegemonic mode of dominance (Connell 1987, 1995). The utility of homophobic discourse is made more salient through awareness that, in a homohysteric culture, heterosexual men are culturally incapable of permanently proving their heterosexuality. One's heterosexual capital waxes and wanes depending on the behaviors one exhibits, and the terrains one occupies. Thus heterosexual men (and gay men wishing to remain closeted) must continually attempt to prove and reprove their heteromasculinity through acquiescence to orthodox expectations and behaviors that are coded as heterosexual. As multiple masculinity scholars have shown (cf. Plummer 1999), in periods of high homohysteria, boys and men are compelled to act aggressively, to maintain homophobic attitudes, and they are socially encouraged to raise their masculine capital through sport and muscularity (cf. Pronger 1990).

In periods of high homohysteria, men must also remain emotionally and tactilely distant from one another (Allen 2007), because emotional intimacy and tactility are symbols of femininity and/or homosexuality. Thus, boys and men have traditionally been prohibited from holding hands, softly hugging, caressing, or kissing, in either public or private (Fine 1988; Kaplan 2006). Accordingly, in periods of high homohysteria, men's demonstrations of affection are generally relegated to the public sphere (such as playing sports), and physical intimacy often comes through symbolic acts of violence, such as mock punching and rancorous slapping. Also, unlike studies of today, which find various meanings associated with homophobic discourse (Pascoe 2005), in periods of high homohysteria, homophobic discourse maintains *specific* homosexual meaning.

It is in this zeitgeist that Kimmel suggests homophobia *is* masculinity (1994). The frenzied homohysteric masculine ethos that is esteemed in this cultural moment means that not only is physical femininity among men stigmatized, but anything associated with emotional or personal femininity is looked upon disparagingly, too. This, of course, has serious implications for femphobia, sexism, and the gender order.

It is in this cultural moment that Connell's hegemonic masculinity theory maintains particular utility. In a cultural zeitgeist of excessive homohysteria, homosexuality will be stigmatized, and boys and men will desire to distance themselves from it. Thus, in a highly homohysteric Anglo-American culture, a dominant form of masculinity will exist, and one can predict that it will be predicated in opposition to whatever cultural stereotypes are ascribed to gay men. Men who fail to meet the prescribed or achieved characteristic of whatever that archetype might be nonetheless pledge their allegiance to the dominant form because this association is in itself heterosexualizing and masculinizing. This means that the polarization of masculine and feminine will further separate, and, as Connell suggests, all men will gain in patriarchal privilege.

However, inclusive masculinity theory argues that as cultural homohysteria significantly declines, a hegemonic form of conservative masculinity will lose its dominance, and softer masculinities will exist without the use of social stigma to police them. Thus, two dominant (but not necessarily dominating) forms of masculinity will co-exist, one orthodox and one inclusive. Orthodox masculinity loses its hegemonic influence because there is a critical mass of men who publicly disavow it. Orthodox valuing men remain homophobic, femphobic, emotionally and physically distant from one another. These men necessarily fear transgressing feminized terrains. Conversely, those ascribing to more inclusive versions of masculinity demonstrate emotional and physically homosocial proximity. They begin to blur the lines between masculinity and femininity.

This is permitted because orthodox ascribing men lose the ability to question another's sexuality in order to force them to comply with orthodox masculinities' requisites. Homophobic discourse no longer maintains the homosexualizing effect that it once did, even if it remains the primary weapon of insult. This, I argue, is why some researchers (Burn 2000; Pascoe 2005) find that even though young men say 'that's gay' and 'fag' frequently, they do not unanimously intend for it to be interpreted as homophobic. In this stage, the very meanings of the words and phrases are caught between dueling zeitgeists. This does not mean that the use of homophobic discourse ceases to create frameworks of stigma around homosexuality, but the point remains that the *intent* of this discourse has nonetheless shifted.

In this moment, behaviors and terrains that once homosexualized men, no longer have the same homosexualizing agency. And, once previously stigmatized terrains and behaviors become available to heterosexuals without the need for one to defend their heterosexuality, it opens up yet further social and emotional spaces for heterosexual men to occupy without threat to their publicly perceived heterosexual identities.

In this phase, men ascribing to inclusive masculinity will also show improved social attitudes concerning women. This is a result of multiple processes, including the social permission men maintain to bond with women in non-sexual ways. This is because the mandates of compulsory heterosexuality wane, and once men are permitted to befriend women in platonic ways, the stigma associated with women's narratives and worldly understandings begins to erode. This may have socio-positive implications for men's cultural dominance over women as well.

Finally, inclusive masculinity theory argues that in an Anglo-American culture with severely diminished homohysteria, homophobic discourse, and/or its associated intent to degrade homosexuals, is no longer socially acceptable. In such a setting, the esteemed attributes of men will no longer rely on control and domination of other men; there is no predominance of masculine bullying or harassment and homophobic stigmatization will cease, even if individual men remain personally homophobic. Accordingly, inclusive masculinity theory maintains that, in such a zeitgeist, multiple masculinities will proliferate without hierarchy or hegemony, and men are permitted an expansion of acceptable heteromasculine behaviours. In such a zeitgeist, the gendered behaviors of boys and men will be less differentiated from girls, and the symbolic meaning of soft physical tactility and emotional intimacy between men is consumed within a heteromasculine identity (Ibson 2002).

When there is mass social inclusion of the form of masculinities once traditionally marginalized by hegemonic masculinity, some of the attitudes once esteemed by orthodox masculinity will no longer be valued: homophobia, misogyny, stoicism, and perhaps excessive risk taking. In a culture of diminished homohysteria, boys and men will be free to express emotional intimacy and physical expressions of that relationship with one another. Accordingly, this culture permits an even greater expansion of acceptable heteromasculine behaviors, which results in yet a further blurring of masculine and feminine behaviors and terrains. The differences between masculinity and femininity, men and women, gay and straight, will be harder to distinguish, and masculinity will no longer serve as the primary method of stratifying men. Whereas gender expressions coded as feminine were edged to extinction among men in the 1980s; today they flourish.

Explicating this, my graduate student Mark McCormack and I show that in a British high school, multiple forms of equally esteemed inclusive masculinities exist, even if heterosexism persists. In this culture, there exists a collection of various archetypes, but no singular archetype dominates. Boys are not only free to associate with those of another group, but they are esteemed for maintaining social fluidity. Accordingly, in an Anglo-American culture of diminished homohysteria, those traditionally excluded, dominated, and marginalized should benefit from social inclusion. Mark also shows that individual boys are still socially ranked, but that this occurs through popularity, which is largely determined by charisma.

I desire to be clear; a culture of diminished homohysteria does not necessarily lead to men's utopia. For example, heterosexual men will still maintain hegemonic dominance. Heterosexism is an independent and unrelated variable for the operation of inclusive masculinities. In other words, men can still assume one another heterosexual, while still being inclusive. Some individuals can still dislike homosexual men, but a culture need not be entirely free of homophobia in order to encourage a proliferation of inclusive masculinities. Rather, it is the social unacceptability of the expression of those beliefs that leads to the decreased policing of sexual and gendered boundaries: For inclusive masculinities, a culture must be free of men having to prove their heterosexuality. The driving tenet behind orthodox masculinity is homohysteria, not homophobia. Thus, while a culture of inclusive masculinity indicates a culture of diminishing or diminished homophobia, it does not necessarily mean that all men within that culture will cease to be heterosexist and/or homophobic.

Inclusive masculinities do not guarantee the erosion of patriarchy, either. The existence of hegemonic masculinity was but one of numerous understood cultural mechanisms in which men retain cultural dominance. Thus, a culture of inclusive masculinity is no guarantee for a realignment of the gender order. While decreased sexism is a characteristic of an inclusive culture of masculinities, it does not guarantee social parity for women. Nonetheless, when inclusive masculinities dominate, there should at least be *some* social benefit for women.

Also, categorizing men as ascribing to inclusive masculinities does not mean that these men are completely free from other forms of orthodox sentiment or behaviors. In some of my research, I describe men representing inclusive masculinities as rejecting the domineering, anti-feminine and homophobic behaviors and attitudes of orthodox masculinity, even *if* they maintain the risk-taking, bravado and violence of their sometimes violent sports. Conversely, in other studies I find men eschewing excessive risk. I do not provide a precise formula for determining whether a culture is to be considered inclusive or not. I am not suggesting that all university-attending heterosexual men in my studies have completely redeveloped orthodox masculinity, either. What they have done so far, however, is to make it more inclusive to those once traditionally marginalized, and severely less restrictive of their own gendered practices. Accordingly, the loose indication of a culture of inclusive masculinities is that men look disparagingly at homophobia, they value emotional intimacy and physical tactility, and they are *more* willing to engage in activities or display behaviors that were once stigmatized as feminine. One can assume there will be different versions of inclusive masculinity operating, but I make no claims as to the utility of inclusive masculinity theory in other than Anglo-American cultures. Other researchers will have to utilize the theory to make such determinations.

The implications of inclusive masculinity for the operation of heterosexuality are also varied. In some studies I find that heterosexual men are partaking in certain same-sex sexual behaviors (designed to illicit sexual pleasure) without fear of stigma within their peer culture. Here, these men use their culture of inclusivity to blur the lines between gay and straight. In other studies, I find men unwilling to do such. Nonetheless, I classify both as inclusive masculinities, because neither looks disparagingly at men who *do* engage in same-sex sexual behaviors. Ultimately, however, it seems plausible that as inclusive masculinities spread to groups of other men throughout Anglo-American cultures, it cannot help but influence the redefinition of various sexualities.

Finally, some scholars may find the relationship of inclusive masculinity theory to hegemonic masculinity theory perplexing. This is because inclusive masculinity theory serves as a social-constructionist theory that simultaneously incorporates and challenges Connell's (1987) hegemonic masculinity theory. Both hegemonic masculinity theory and inclusive masculinity theory emphasize the importance of homophobia in the social production of men; however, inclusive masculinity theory accounts for multiple masculinities existing within any one culture, without necessarily having hierarchy or hegemony, something Connell's theory does not. Inclusive masculinity theory maintains that in periods of high homohysteria, one hegemonic form of masculinity will exist, and that it will be predicated in opposition to homosexuality. But as homohysteria lessens, other social processes occur that Connell's theory does not accurately account for. This is not an admonishment of Connell's theorizing, nor do I suggest that Connell's theory no longer maintains utility. It depends on the setting analyzed.

METROSEXUALITY AND INCLUSIVE MASCULINITIES

The men in my studies do not refer to themselves as exhibiting inclusive masculinities. Instead, they sometimes either refer to themselves as metrosexual (particularly between 2001 and 2004), or they give no name to their gendered perspective. Mark Simpson coined the term metrosexual in (1994), but it became popular in 2003 when a global marketing research firm RSCG published findings that heterosexual men were more open to commoditization and sexualization. In his book *The Metrosexual: Gender, Sexuality and Sport*, David Coad (2008) provides an excellent genealogy of the term. Although the term originally referred to Manhattan heterosexual men who wore high-end clothing, it evolved into a definition for heterofemininity among men. For example, Cashmore and Parker (2003) referred to English soccer player David Beckham as metrosexual because:

> Beckham's complex and contradictory identity suggests that there is more room for more than one version of masculine construction (224). He possesses a kind of ambivalence that makes him beguiling to a wide audience. Beckham acknowledges this ambivalence, publicly confirming, for example his awareness of the admiration of the gay community in the UK (222) . . . To this end Beckham's inclusive popularity should be seen as a positive step in terms of the masculine norms which he clearly transcends and the subversive trends and behaviors he explicitly displays (225).

The broadening definition of the term is evident in my various research settings. Some use it to describe increased fluidity in gender. Others use it as a euphemism for bisexuality. Still others use it to describe a heterosexual male who dabbles in same-sex sex. When telling me about their differently gendered perspectives on sex, women, clothing, or just about anything else that varies from orthodox prescriptions, many of the men I interview ask me, 'So does that make me metrosexual?'

Defining the term metrosexual is not my intent. In fact, I like the indefinable nature of the label. This gives it 'queer' power. It provides men who contest orthodox masculinity a label with which to identify. So while I find that metrosexuality means very different things to differing people, I hypothesize that it is this fluidity of the term that makes it so destabilizing to masculine orthodoxy. The label has given men a long-awaited justification for the ability to be associated with femininity, and it has been immensely helpful in decreasing homohysteria. The term metrosexuality permits men to say, "I am not gay, I am metrosexual." It has therefore served as a mediating factor in the manner in which homophobia has traditionally policed gendered boundaries, and this reduces homohysteria.

I recognize the limitations of metrosexuality as an archetype or threat to the hegemonic position of orthodox masculinity. Edwards (2006: 4) has argued that just like the 'new man' literature, metrosexuality is a media invention that is more connected to patterns of consumption than gendered change. But in developing inclusive masculinity theory, I build upon the commoditized foundations of metrosexuality, and also suggest that inclusive masculinities operate in opposition to certain aspects of orthodox masculine values (Harris and Clayton 2007). Men who ascribe to inclusive masculinities might also be metrosexual, but one does not have to dress well to be inclusive. Conversely, it would be difficult to suggest that men who consider themselves metrosexual are also orthodox in their masculine performance. Of course, they are not. Thus, the emergence of metrosexuality compelled us to realize that an alternate masculine narrative existed, at least for those privileged enough to afford it. A decade later, however, the muted definition of metrosexuality (real or imagined) has permitted men of all classes and backgrounds to more freely associate with femininity, with or without identifying as metrosexual.

EVIDENCING MY THEORY

In the next section, I show that inclusive masculinities are sometimes established with, and sometimes established without, the support of organizational and/or institutional cultures. I show that men who subscribe to inclusive masculinities behave in effeminate ways and that they are less defensive about their heterosexuality, all with less (or no) fear of social stigma. Men performing inclusive masculinities participate in tasks traditionally defined as feminine and support women who perform tasks traditionally defined as masculine.

Among the cheerleaders, for example, inclusive masculinities permit men to be tossed into the air (flying), to stand atop the shoulders of others, and even to wear clothing defined as feminine. For the rugby players, inclusive masculinities permit these men to show physical affection for one another, publicly kissing and embracing. For my university student-athletes, inclusive masculinities permit them to dance together, even in the same erotic fashion that they dance with women. And for men in all my studies, inclusive masculinities permit them to emotionally support each other in the face of loss or brutality.

Inclusive masculinities, and the reduction of cultural homohysteria that spawned it, also has a significant impact on the use and meanings associated with homophobic and femphobic discourse. Similarly, the reduction in homophobia and the increased physicality between men has very serious implications for the categorization of what gay and straight behaviors are; and what gay and straight identities are, too. I show that many university men are now kissing each other (on the lips). Just a few years ago this behavior would have been labeled homosexual. But these men have stripped the sexual code from it, so that it is now just a form of affection between two ostensibly heterosexual men.

Finally, I show that the valuing of inclusive masculinities exists among athletes, but not necessarily among their coaches. Not only does this set the stage for strife, but it suggests that it is only a matter of time before the old guard is replaced by a new, more inclusive breed of gatekeepers. In fact, if social matters continue as they are, inclusive masculinities might soon be the normative standard by which we describe all sporting men.

Part III
Inclusive Masculinities

7 Embracing Gay Men

Central to the emergence of inclusive masculinities is the trend of declining cultural homohysteria, which is facilitated by declining homophobia. Accordingly, if inclusive masculinities exist within competitive teamsports, we should expect to see the lived experiences of gay athletes improve. In this chapter, I first outline the findings of my 1999–2004 research on openly gay high school and collegiate athletes. Here, I show a significant variance between what researchers once theorized what would happen to gay athletes in sport, and what their experience actually is after coming out. It highlights the use of individual agency in contesting and reshaping organizational attitudes toward homosexuality.

I next present data collected in 2002, concerning the relationship between heterosexual and gay male teammates in the collegiate sport of cheerleading. Here, I discuss the importance of social proximity in breaking down traditional homophobic sentiment. Straight men in this sport undo their gendered perspectives, learning a more inclusive approach to masculinity building. As with the previous study, while the influence of openly gay men on their teams is significant, this section also highlights the influence of organizational norms of inclusivity in changing long held homophobic sentiment.

I augment these studies with my 2003–2004 findings from the men of a mainstream U.S. fraternity. This data not only finds that the men of this fraternity recruit gay men, but that they even elected an openly gay male to be their chapter president. This fraternity is influenced by multiple factors, including (an institutional mandate to promote inclusivity. I highlight that this policy made it easier for a key member to come out to his fraternity brothers, which then served to further promote inclusivity within the organizational setting.

Finally, I share the results of my 2007 ethnography on an English university's rugby team. Although there are no openly gay players on this team, and although both their institution and their coaches remain highly homophobic, these men nonetheless exhibit inclusive attitudes toward homosexuality. I suggest that (unlike men in these other studies) they learned their inclusive attitudes not from gay men or female teammates, but instead from the broader culture. Accordingly, the various ethnographies I draw upon in this chapter highlight the socializing influences of organizations, institutions, and the broader culture, alongside individual agency in shaping a more inclusive zeitgeist.

HOMOPHOBIA IN SPORT

Researchers who have examined the issue of gays in sports largely agree that organized sports are a highly homophobic institution in both American and British cultures. Messner (1992: 34) writes, "The extent of homophobia in the sports world is staggering. Boys (in sports) learn early that to be gay, to be suspected of being gay, or even to be unable to prove one's heterosexual status is not acceptable." Hekma (1998: 2) writes, "Gay men who are seen as queer and effeminate are granted no space whatsoever in what is generally considered to be a masculine preserve and a macho enterprise." Pronger (1990: 26) adds: "Many of the (gay) men I interviewed said they were uncomfortable with team sports . . . orthodox masculinity is usually an important subtext if not *the* leitmotif" in team sports. But as Griffin (1998) suggests, if gay male athletes who are stigmatized as being feminine can be as strong and competitive as heterosexual male athletes, they may therefore threaten the perceived distinctions between gay men and straight men, and thus the perceived differences between men and women as a whole.

The threat that gay men pose to hegemonic masculinity first comes from the fact that gay men can comply with the gendered script of orthodox masculinity (through their sporting prowess), while also violating the principle rule of masculinity (through their same same-sex desires). For this reason, I suggested in 2002 that gay male athletes may threaten sport's ability to reproduce orthodox masculinity. Basically, gay men expose the falsity of the notion that femininity is weak. It is because of this threat that Pronger (1990) suggests that homophobia presents itself as resistance toward the intrusion of a gay sub-culture within sports. Clarke (1998: 145) agrees, saying that gay males are perceived as mainly "deviant and dangerous participants on the sporting turf," in that they defy culturally defined structures of orthodox masculinity.

Although research on closeted gay male athletes is generally limited (Bryant; 2001; Hekma: 1998; Pronger: 1990), research on male athletes who are publicly out to their ostensibly heterosexual teammates was non-existent until I published a *Gender and Society* article (2002) on 36 openly gay male athletes. In my 2005 book, *In the Game: Gay Athletes and the Cult of Masculinity*, I later expanded this sample to 68. Prior to this, our best understanding of the relationship between the gay male athlete and sport came through interviews with only closeted gay male athletes (Hekma: 1998), from athletes on all-gay teams (Price 2000), or from attitudinal research of heterosexual male athletes toward the possibility of openly gay athletes being on their teams (Wolf Wendel, Toma, and Morphew 2001). Indeed, studying openly gay athletes was not possible in what might be called the first wave of discrimination against gay athletes, because the social sanctions for coming out of the closet were simply too high. Accordingly, despite the fact that Western cultures were rapidly moving away from homophobia (Loftus 2001), in 2001 Wolf Wendel, Toma, and Morphew wrote, "Examining the overall message from these results, we found hostility to gay men and lesbians on nearly all teams and at all the case study sites. Clearly those in inter-collegiate athletics are generally unwilling to confront and accept homosexuality" (470). They suggested that, compared to the liberalization of white attitudes regarding race, attitudes held by heterosexual athletes toward homosexuality were non-progressive. And they attributed this to the lack of experience with, or even knowledge of, openly gay male athletes. The transformative potential of gay athletes in sport was therefore neutralized through overt homophobia and covert mechanisms, like the normalization of homophobic language and the silencing of gay discourse, identity, and behaviors.

And while I will show that matters are improving, there is plenty of evidence to support these claims. Despite the continuance of decreasing cultural homophobia, *openly* gay males are still vastly underrepresented at all levels of sport (Anderson 2002, 2005a). For example, there has only been one openly gay male athlete at my university in the previous four years (a rugby player). Matters are even worse at the professional level.

When examining the ranks of professional teamsports (where tens of thousands of men have matriculated through the various sporting systems), there has *never* been an openly gay professional athlete to emerge from the closets while playing in the United States (in the top four sports), and only one has come out in Britain. Furthermore, there have only been a handful of players who have emerged from the closet after retiring from professional sports. This omission raises the question: is this the product of there *being* so few gay men in professional teamsports or a result of the near-seamless heterosexual hegemony that prevents them from coming out once in sport?

The only way to know the answer, of course, is to know the proportion as a percentage of gay men in the population, and then compare this to what the percentage is in sport. This is a tricky proposition because the presence of cultural homophobia nullifies the possibility of knowing what percentage of the general population is gay (let alone what percentage of athletes are gay). Furthermore, it is impossible to survey people about their same-sex desires if they are compelled to lie about these desires. Accordingly, the only accurate way to answer this question is to examine it once the last vestiges of homophobia have long been erased from our culture. Only when homosexuality is esteemed equally with heterosexuality might we begin to understand the numerical reality and the dynamic dimension of human sexuality. Until then, we can only theorize. And in this theorizing, we can be relatively certain that whatever rates of sexual minorities sociologists come up with, they will remain underestimates. As long as homophobia exits, heterosexuality will always be overly estimated from empirical data.

Further problematizing the demographic understanding of homosexuality is the fact that it is difficult to understand just what it means to be homosexual or heterosexual. Sexuality proves to be an extremely complicated affair that can be described by at least three separate dimensions: sexual behavior (what one does), sexual orientation (what one desires), and sexual identity (how one views one's sexual self). And sexuality scholars rightfully and easily complicate matters to the point that definition is impossible. Therefore, the question of whether gay athletes are overrepresented or underrepresented in teamsports can only be theoretical. The question is too vague, and definitions of sexuality are too fluid. If we can't even agree on what it is to be gay, we certainly can't ascertain what percentage of the population is gay.

These complications aside, we can be readily assured that in youth sports, the percentage of whatever it means to be gay is in statistical equality to whatever the percentage of gay males are in the culture at large. This is because sporting participation has been made a culturally (and sometimes institutional) requisite for boyhood. Therefore, the question of importance is: As athletes advance in the sporting world, does the proportion of gay athletes change? In other words, we know that gays are being assimilated into the culture of athletics at the same age as heterosexuals, but as one matures, how might their sexuality influence whether they drop out of or remain within the institution of sport?

The weight of empirical evidence *suggests* that gay male adult athletes are exceedingly underrepresented in sport. Leigh Steinberg, the sports agent of *Jerry Maguire* fame, believes this to be the case in professional sports because the hostility of men in groups is such that gay athletes in team sports drop out along the way. He contends that it is at the high school level where most males are defining their sexuality, and part of the rite of passage has been hostility towards gays. Supporting this, sociologist Gert Hekma found that once closeted gay men come out in teamsports (in the Netherlands), they no longer need the heterosexualizing façade of sport, dropping out of team sports in favor of individual sports, or dropping out of sports entirely. He also reports that many gay youngsters believe that excelling in sport and being gay are incompatible. Pronger (1990) adds that the mandates of orthodox masculinity found in sport creates a sense of 'not being' for many gay athletes: That they continually feel like an outsider, even if they are on the inside. Pronger suggests that this alienation engenders indifference and/or aversion to sport for young gays. But clearly at least some gay men exist in sport.

Although these are good theories, Pronger (1990) and I suggest that it is also possible that some gay men may be drawn to teamsports precisely *because* of its homophobic and masculinist culture. Gay athletes who are motivated to conceal their sexual identity may actually be attracted to teamsports (or motivated to remain within them) because, as athletes, they are largely protected from gay suspicion.

This is because the presence of muscle and violence in sport is often considered incompatible with homosexuality. The more muscle-bound athletes are, the less likely they are suspected of being gay (increased masculine capital). This buys them insurance against homosexual suspicion. Since football and basketball players are generally more muscular than cross-country runners, these athletes are less likely to have their heterosexuality questioned than those in less macsculinized sports or social arenas. Therefore, if a deeply closeted gay man is both attracted to muscle, and also seeks a veneer from homosexual suspicion, teamsports are a particularly attractive social arena.

Still other laymen might erroneously think that participation in a hypermasculine enterprise will actually change their sexual desires (it doesn't). Supporting the myth that sport actually makes one heterosexual, countless fathers have said to their gay sons that they wonder if it was their 'fault' for not making their sons play more masculine teamsports. Finally, adolescent males who are not consciously aware of their sexuality might find themselves drawn to teamsports without consciously recognizing the homoeroticism of homophilic masculine arenas (Anderson 2005a). Competitive teamsports provide a homoerotic space for gay men. I therefore argue that it is the extreme homophobia (and possibly the extreme homoeroticism) that might initially draw closeted men to teamsport athletics. Teamsports provide the perfect space for athletes to bond with other men, to engage with them on an emotional and a physical level, all of which occurs in a homoerotic and highly sexualized space. The same is true of the U.S. military, and there is certainly no shortage of gay men there.

Moreso, the requirements of competitive training are so demanding that competitive teamsports give closeted gay men an excuse not to date—they simply do not have the time or energy. This was certainly one motivating reason for me to excel at sport. I was able to skip the heterosexist events (dances and parties) because I was resting up for the 'big race' the following morning. Fortunately, there seemed to always be another race to run, freeing me from the awkwardness of heterosexual dating.

It is for the erotic desire of muscles and men with low body fat, the insurance those muscles provide against being thought gay, and the fraternal bonding that those muscles permit, that leads Pronger and I to suggest that the most deeply closeted gay men are the ones drawn to the competitive teamsport arena. Interestingly, it is the presence of muscles that makes gay men (whether athletes or not) *less likely* to chance injury by making sexual advances to another male in sport. Lean and sculpted bodies serve to both intimidate and arouse gay men. This might also explain why homoerotic hazing so often takes place in sporting programs. Athletes frequently report hazing rituals that involve nudity or sexuality. One athlete told me that as part of his initiation ritual, another athlete masturbated, and ejaculated onto a cracker, which he then had to eat. Athletes also tell of being stripped, of having to be slapped in the face by an erect penis, or in more extreme cases, of being sodomized by objects. In 2003, three varsity football players were arrested after hazing junior varsity players by sodomizing them with broomsticks, golf balls and (horrifically) pinecones, in at least three separate occurrences on a Pennsylvania high school football team. One cannot ignore the homoerotic context of many of these violent hazing incidents.

This type of sexualized violence is empirically linked with repressed desire for sex with men. While homophobic attitudes and behaviors have been *assumed* to be associated with rigid moralistic beliefs or sexual ignorance, several psychoanalytic explanations link homophobia to one's own anxiety-based sexual desires. These theories postulate that homophobia is at least a partial result of repressed homosexual urges or as a form of latent homosexuality in which the individual is unaware of or repressing his homosexuality.

Psychoanalysts use the concept of latent homosexuality to explain this emotional malaise, and irrational attitudes displayed by ostensibly heterosexual individuals who feel guilty about their occasional homoerotic interests. Individuals who struggle to deny or repress their impulses may overreact with panic or anger when placed in a situation that heightens their same-sex urges. Homophobia can also be viewed as an intentional response to displace homosexual suspicion. If a man does not want others to know that he is gay, he may act in opposition to homosexuality. In an attempt to be perceived as heterosexual, the closeted individual acts in highly homophobic ways.

I have seen this theory played out multiple times. Once, in a California bar, the man next to me queried me as to whether I thought a particular woman was attractive. When I told him that I was gay, he grew verbally violent. Strangely, he did not move away from me. Instead, he ordered several more drinks and eventually propositioned me. Another time, I saw an inebriated student board a bus, heading back to campus after clubbing. I watched him as he stared at one of my (attractive) male students for much of the ride. He then began calling my student (who was white) a "nigger." I asked my student if he knew him (he did not), or if anything had happened between them, "No. I've never seen him before," he answered. When the bus arrived at the university, a hundred students spilled out, and the student in question began to physically attack my student. I restrained him, and after the hubbub ended, I was left with the assailant alone. I asked him why he attacked him, and when he gave no reasonable answer I said, "You found yourself attracted to him, didn't you?" He answered, "I'm not a fag." I replied, "Don't say it like it's a bad thing, I'm gay." The boy said, "That's gross." To which I responded, "You don't really think that." Within a minute he told me, "I think maybe I am gay." This is an example of a pattern I have witnessed so many times, that I am quite nearly ready to say that any university-aged man who exhibits homophobic attitudes *is* concealing same-sex desires. Perhaps this is the real reason my athlete was beaten in 1995.

Empirically testing this theory, researchers at the University of Georgia (Adams, Wright and Lohr 1996) surveyed heterosexual men for their attitudes toward homosexuality. They strategically selected men who represented either extremely homophobic or extremely gay friendly attitudes (leaving out those in the middle) and attached erectometers to their penises before showing them gay pornography. The men identified as highly homophobic demonstrated significantly more sexual arousal than the gay friendly group. Interestingly, when the highly homophobic group was asked about their level of arousal, their ratings of erection and arousal to homosexual stimuli were not significantly different from the gay friendly men, suggesting that they consciously or unconsciously denied their arousal.

COMING OUT IN SPORT

Given the homophobia theorized to still exist within sporting culture, one would hardly expect gay athletes to report positive experiences after coming out to their teams. But my extensive research into openly gay high school and university athletes shows just the opposite. For example, Ryan typifies some of the positive experiences my informants report. A 19-year-old first year student at a private university in Southern California, he came out to his crew team in a rather public manner. "The whole school knows about me, so from the first day of practice the team also knew about me" he said. Ryan, like the other athletes in my study, said that he had no difficulty with teammates. There was no homophobic taunting, and certainly none of the symbolic and literal violence that I faced when coming out in sport.

When I probed for situations that might make homophobia more salient, Ryan said, "I thought the real test would be when we were out on the road, when we had to share a bed. That was when it would come down to it." When the bedding configuration placed three athletes in a room with two beds, the rowers did not want Ryan to have one of the beds alone. They feared that not sharing a bed with him would send a message that they were homophobic. "We talked about it for a while, and we just pushed the two beds together and made one big one. That way nobody felt bad."

Perhaps not all of the athletes I interviewed felt as supported as Ryan, but most were unexpectedly pleased with their coming out experience, even those who played American football. I asked all of the informants, "If you could do it all over again, what, if anything, would you do differently?" to which almost all responded that they would have come out earlier. One athlete said, "It was so much easier than I thought. Now I look back and wonder why the hell I didn't do it sooner." Another said, "I forgot what I was supposed to be so worried about after I came out."

But some of these informants over-generalized how well things were for them. For many, coming out highlights the reduction of cultural homophobia, but it also highlights the persistence of heterosexism. For example, Gabriel initially spoke of his coming out in glowing terms. He and two other of his fellow distance runners came out all on the same day, and Gabriel praised his coach for creating a supportive environment for them. However, because Gabriel attended a private Christian school, the team decided to keep their identities concealed from the rest of the school. This was justified because the school had kicked one of its students out the previous year simply for saying that he was gay. Highlighting how homophobia of the institution still controlled his life, Gabriel talked about his state finals 1600-meter relay race, and how he and his teammates enacted their agency to contest their subordination:

> My friend (also openly gay) and I were approached by our other two (heterosexual) teammates, right before the final race. They reached into their bag and pulled out two pairs of gay pride socks and said that they wanted us to wear them. We were really touched. And then they pulled out two more pairs and said that they were going to wear them in support of us.

Gabriel's experience was perceived as being positive to him. Together, he and his teammates symbolically stood against the school's homophobic policies. The glory of the story is unquestionable. Although I have repeated it many times now, it still brings tingles to my spine. But as enjoyable as those tingles are, there is a problem that they conceal. The athletes had to keep their identities secret in the first place. Gabriel's story, in fact, typifies how gay athletes normally relay their experiences to me.

Gay athletes first began by speaking of their experience as a general positive, praising their teammates, and talking about how accepted they felt by them. However, when I inquire about their richer experiences, a different story often (though not always) emerges. While these are not the stories of outright violence that many would predict, they remain stories of (often) extreme heterosexism, silencing, and sometimes the use of homophobic discourse. Nonetheless, athletes remain in high spirits about their coming out, and they are unbothered or even unaware as to the high degree of heterosexism and homophobic discourse around them. I explain these results through reverse-relative depravation theory.

Whereas sociologists usually discuss people who compare themselves to those who have it better via relative deprivation theory (Davies 1962; Tilly 1978) these athletes seem to compare themselves to those who had it worse, something I call reverse-relative deprivation. They do not actually have examples of those who fared worse after coming out; instead they compare their experience to their worst-imagined fears. Fear, of course, is the hallmark of the closet. Gay athletes and gay men in general fear all types of things: losing friends, respect, and even emotional (and sometimes financial) support of their families, should they come out. Yet, to this day, I have never known an athlete who regretted coming out of the closet. This suggests a wider pattern of fear-based control that keeps men closeted.

Thus, one way that orthodox masculinity can adapt to include gay men, without compromising much of the institutional values, is to permit gay men to play, but deny their existence and mute their voices. As an openly gay tennis player, Tim exemplifies how one is both able to challenge orthodox masculinity while simultaneously reproducing it. I asked him if he was treated any different after coming out. "No," he replied. "They didn't really treat me as gay, if that's what you mean. In fact, they didn't even mention it really. They just treated me like one of the guys." I then asked him if his teammates continued to include him in locker-room talk about women. "Yeah, they ask me like who I think is hot and stuff." When I questioned if his teammates ever asked what guys he thought attractive; he replied, "Hell no. They'd never do that. They don't want to hear that kind of stuff." Recall that a culture of inclusive masculinities does not necessarily imply one of decreased heterosexism. Heterosexism is an independent variable to homohysteria.

I suggest that Tim lives with a segmented identity. His teammates know he is gay, but they continue to treat him (at some level) as if he were not. Perhaps his teammates think they are doing what is best for Tim; and perhaps Tim thinks it is what is best, too. Without interviewing his teammates I cannot be sure what the motivations are. But the situation is one of 'don't ask, don't tell.' Silencing gay men's identities and politically avoiding discussions of their teammates' sexuality is, in some ways, a compromise between tenets of orthodox masculinity. The combined effect of silencing of gay identities and promoting heterosexuality serves to venerate heterosexuality and marginalize homosexuality (Butler 1990; Connell 1995; Messner and Sabo 1990; Pronger 1990). Tim is allowed to *be* gay but he is not permitted to *act* gay. Ken, an NCAA champion track runner, illustrates this policy when he says, "Even to this day, people know, but people just won't say it. . . . It's like they just can't talk about it."

Gay athletes often fail to recognize that their identities are partially denied within their sporting spaces. Highlighting the hegemony of orthodox masculinity, they frequently take part in their own oppression by self-silencing and partaking in heterosexual dialogue. Of course the athletes don't see it this way. This is the operation of hegemony in heterosexism. Victimized by hegemony, many (but not all) athletes avoid discourse about homosexuality. Frank said, "Sport is not the appropriate place for such discussions" and another openly gay athlete said, "The gay thing was never talked about . . . end of story."

SHIFTING NARRATIVES

Because I have been interviewing openly gay athletes (formally and informally) since 1998, I have seen a shift in the way athletes tell their stories. Collectively, what can be said from their experiences is that even though sport is still a macho enterprise, openly gay athletes *increasingly* exist within sporting spaces (even among football and basketball teams). Many of these athletes conform to all other mandates of orthodox masculinity, but increasingly many do not. Increasingly, they suggest that their heterosexual teammates also do not.

More recent stories of athletes to emerge from the closet, I argue, threaten the ability of sports to seamlessly reproduce orthodox masculinity. In doing so, they may help open the doors to increased acceptance of subjugated masculinities and perhaps even the acceptance of female athleticism.

While the culture of sport may not yet permit the creation of a formidable gay sub-culture, gay athletes are beginning to contest sport as a site of orthodox masculine reproduction. Their ability to perform on the pitch challenges orthodox notions of what it means to be 'a man.' This highlights that hegemony in the athletic arena is not seamless. Gay men are increasingly accepted within the belly of masculine sports.

Also, when I first published about gay men in 2002, I found that virtually every openly gay athlete I could locate was not only good, but he was truly outstanding. Of my sample of just 36 openly gay men, I had four national champions (representing various sports). But by the time I published my updated research on gay athletes in 2005, I was able to locate dozens of lesser quality athletes. Although these are small numbers, they are also significant. The coming out of lesser athletes cannot be attributed to others blazing the path for them; these represent individuals who made individual decisions to come out to their teams without having other openly gay athletes to lay the groundwork. If 32 of 36 were extraordinary prior to 2000, but only 8 out of 22 were extraordinary after 2003, it highlights that individuals felt more confident in coming out due to a wider-spread phenomenon. Similarly, whereas I had a difficult time locating gay men to interview in the early parts of 2000, today they are much more accessible, there is even a public registry for them on Outsports.com.

If I am right, and decreased homohysteria is the hallmark of inclusive masculinities, we should see a similar tolerance and acceptance of diversity occurring throughout multiple sectors of sport and society. Supporting this, a February 27, 2006 Sports Illustrated magazine poll of 1,401 professional teamsport athletes also shows that the majority (and 80 percent of those in the National Hockey League) would welcome a gay teammate, today. In the rest of this chapter, I pull from various studies to show how university-aged heterosexual men *are* embracing homosexuality. Interestingly, I show that there is more division of attitudes toward gay men in the feminized sport of cheerleading than I find in the masculinized sport of rugby. There are perhaps a number of reasons for this. First, rugby players do not live within a culture of homosexual suspicion, so they may feel less need to distance themselves from gay men. But this might also reflect the fact that I conducted the cheerleading ethnography in 2002 and 2003, and the rugby ethnography in 2006 and 2007. These few years may not seem like an extended period of time for tracking other social issues, but on the issue of homophobia particularly (among youth) there seems to be measurable improvement each year.

LEARNING INCLUSIVE MASCULINITIES IN CHEERLEADING

With their competition finished, dinner eaten, and the movie over, I walked back to the hotel with a group of seven men from a cheerleading team that I will call the Troubadours. Howie said, "Time for some drinking games. I've invited over the guys from [names university]." I knew Howie was sharing a bed with one of his openly gay teammates, so I asked if he was worried that the cheerleaders from the other team might think that he was gay because of this, "No. Why would I?" he responded. He then added, "Or why would I care if they thought I was?"

Like all of the men I strategically sampled in my cheerleading studies, Howie once played high school football. "It's just what the guys did," he tells me. "I absolutely loved high school football. Have you ever stuck somebody?" he asks. "It's amazing, an incredible feeling of power." I then asked him if he felt that type of masculine power in cheerleading. He fumbled with an answer before saying, "It's not the same . . . I hold people in the air, and we do amazing things, but it's not the same rush you get when you stick someone." However, Howie's discussion of holding women in the air, understates what occurs in co-ed university cheerleading competitions.

Cheerleading has long evolved from simply "cheering" other athletic teams to victory. Today, cheerleading squads compete directly against each other in complex performances, where athletes dance, cheer, stunt, and tumble to rhythmically synchronized, high-energy music. Higher, faster, and more complicated are the hallmarks of successful squads, and these qualities demand cheerleaders (of both sexes) be more than peppy supporters, they must also be courageous gymnasts that perform complicated and dangerous stunts.

Despite the transition of cheerleading from the sidelines to main stage however, the sport has largely maintained its cultural ascription of femininity (Adams and Bettis 2003; Davis 1990). Hanson (1995) writes, "The overriding contemporary perception that cheerleader equals girl is reinforced by popular culture which defines it strictly in feminized terms" (p. 116). Adams and Bettis (2003) have, for example, shown that young female athletes from other sports often participate in cheerleading because it, "offered them a space to revel in what they called being a girlie girl"

(p. 84) to counter stereotypes of their athleticism in other more "masculinized" sports.

Conversely, sentiments regarding men who cheer *within* the sport maintain that these men are anything but "girlie girls." They are self-promoted as real men, daring, heterosexual, and strong enough to hold a girl (or two) above their heads, yet agile enough to perform complex gymnastic routines. In an interesting twist on the feminized nature of this sport, many cheerleaders (of both sexes) maintain that *certain* tasks or positions within the sport are *actually* highly masculinized activities (Adams and Bettis 2003; Davis 1990; Hanson 1995). They have simply been culturally misread.

Carving out a task as masculine is a mutually agreed upon script between heterosexual men and women in cheerleading. It helps heterosexual men raise their masculine capital and ward off homosexual suspicion. This is not a new sociological finding (Davis 1990). What is new however is that the presence of gay men in marginalized terrain has not previously been shown to influence a significant number of heterosexual men to challenge orthodox masculinity.

Previous investigations of heterosexual men in feminized occupational and/or recreational terrain find that orthodox masculinity retains its hegemonic position and heterosexual men in these spaces claim them to be erroneously feminine. Women's role in maintaining this script is significant, because they perform the exact same activities in the women's division of cheerleading as men do in co-ed cheerleading, yet female cheerleaders are not masculinized for holding women above their heads.

Ironically, one type of athlete—the American football player—is almost perfectly adapted to learning the complexities of competitive cheerleading, even if they have been previously socialized to objectify female cheerleaders and stigmatize male cheerleaders. Football players normally possess strong bodies and are highly trained in the rigors of athletics. They are socialized into valuing personal sacrifice and taking considerable gambles with their health, something deemed necessary if one is to learn the complex gymnastic skills required of cheerleading. But because football players have been socialized into a highly sexist and homophobic arena, and because cheerleading is a culturally defined feminine activity, recruiting football players to cheer is difficult. Male *and* female cheerleaders therefore use a variety of methods, including the sexualizing of female cheerleaders to recruit them.

For example, Howie's journey from high school football player, which yielded him one of the highest degrees of masculine capital in North American school systems, to university cheerleader, is obviously not simple. Accordingly, men in cheerleading have developed a grand narrative that they pass to other men; making it hard to know what their motivation was at the time they made their decisions to join the sport. Because I came to my data after their transition, I can only speculate, but their narrative goes as follows: Men who drop out, are forced out, or otherwise do not make their college football teams find themselves reeling over their detachment from much of the power and prestige that they once enjoyed—something sport psychologists call the "disengagement effect" (Greendorfer 1992). This, of course, makes sense. Messner (1987) writes, "Many retired athletes retain a powerful drive to re-establish the important relationship with the crowd that served as the primary basis for their identity for so long" (p. 204). Under such conditions, athletes normally report a desire to be part of a team again, and it makes sense that athletes who once maintained high masculine capital would also feel the greatest loss upon disengaging from that status. Indeed, this is something that most all of the heterosexual ex-football players express.

While having lunch with a group of male cheerleaders I asked, "How many of you would rather be on the football team instead?" Indicating a fondness for the retention of cultural power, all six men resoundingly answered, "I would." Richie said, "Yeah, I wish I could have made the football team, I really miss football." Howie agreed, saying, "I wasn't going to make any other team, so cheerleading was a way of getting back into the game, well, as close as I could anyhow." When I asked informants what, specifically, they missed about football, responses indicated that they near unanimously missed the highly masculinized identity that once brought them cultural power. One athlete said, "As a football player it all revolves around you. You walk the hallways and everybody knows who you are." Richie confirmed, "On the playing field everybody is looking at you, thousands of fans are cheering for you, and when you stick some guy and knock him on his ass in front of all those people, it feels so good." His teammate Andrew remarked, "When you are a football player, everybody at school knows who you are, but as a cheerleader we're not only less recognized, but sometimes we're made fun of."

Much of the stigma of being a male cheerleader revolves around the stereotype of male cheerleaders being gay. This is a popular and persistent perception throughout North America, and it was evident in discussions with virtually all male cheerleaders. Richie said, "As a football player all the girls wanted me. I was very popular. Now, nobody knows who I am, and if they do, they think I'm gay because I cheer." One heterosexual cheerleader even aggressively "defended" his sport when I asked him about the stereotype of male cheerleaders being gay. "It's absolutely not true!" he said. "I hate that stereotype. All it does is scare away men who might want to cheer. There are fewer gay cheerleaders than there are [gay] football players."

In this aspect, ex-football players turned cheerleaders occupy a transitional space in the production of masculinity; where they once occupied the pinnacle of masculine stratification, their chosen activity of cheerleading substantially reduces their masculine capital. While they still embody the symbols of high masculine capital—their cheerleading has not decreased their muscular strength, economic status, heterosexuality or aesthetic appeal—these men find that their cultural masculine capital has diminished because they now play within culturally feminized and homosexualized terrain. Signaling their desire to associate with the cultural power they once possessed, it is common to see college cheerleaders at cheerleading competitions wearing hats, caps, sweatshirts and T-shirts of their ex-high school or college football teams, even though all teams have their own cheerleading regalia.

The identification with the status of a football player may serve a number of purposes. First, it sends a message that these men once achieved high masculine capital in another arena, and perhaps this makes their transgression less substantial in the current arena. But identifying with the football player image may also serve as a public proclamation of heterosexuality. Unlike football players, who are inundated with heterosexual presumption, the sexualities of male cheerleaders are highly suspect. Thus, most of these men maintain an affiliation with what I call "the football player inside" as a way of publicly expressing their masculine and heterosexual identity. While in many ways some cheerleaders' behaviors are consistent with findings of other marginalized men who display masculine bravado when actually in a state of decreased power (Majors 1990), in this transitional space these men find that it takes more than just "acting" hyper-masculine in order to resolve the dissonance, it also takes a well-crafted narrative of their attraction to cheerleading as a product of heterosexual desires.

The reasons that heterosexual men use to justify their cheerleading are consistent with orthodox scripts of heterosexual masculinity. These men, particularly in a culture of gay suspicion, are over-the-top about how heterosexual they are. It is therefore highly relevant that they do not also use the other tool men have available to them to prove their heterosexuality— homophobia. While individually and collectively these men use sexually objectifying *heterosexual* discourse and exclusionary *heterosexist* discourse, the use of overt homophobia is rare (practically non-existent in the Inclusive Cheerleading Association). Since male cheerleaders are publicly perceived as gay, one might expect a stronger homophobic sentiment to counter this assumption. This was not the case.

Consistent with what we might expect from football athletes (Anderson 2002; Griffin 1998; Messner 1992; 1995), most of the informants reported to me that the form of masculinity they exhibited as a football player included overt homophobia. "I used to hate fags," Don, a player from a southern school told me. "I guess I just didn't understand why a guy would want to do that sort of stuff." Andrew said, "Yeah, most of my teammates used to just hate gays, I mean what football player doesn't?" He continued, "To be honest with you, I used to be homophobic. I used to be one of the guys calling the cheerleaders on my high school team fags. Now, I'm on the other side. I mean, I'm not gay, but others sometimes think I am because I cheer."

These excerpts reflect the culture of cheerleading in whole. Heterosexual men's attitudes reflect the fact that while most of these informants once considered themselves homophobic, they learned to undo their homophobia after joining cheerleading. The experience was so common that whenever an informant would start a sentence with, "To be honest with you . . ."I could usually predict that he would follow with, "I used to be homophobic."

While this transition was difficult to see in observations (mostly because I had come on to the team after the attitude shift), interview data suggests that this transition may have been made possible for a number of reasons. First, gay male cheerleaders seem to have strong support from heterosexual female cheerleaders. For example, Dan said, "Oh yeah, you learn not to be homophobic real quick. I mean you can't be. The women and coaches in cheer would never stand for that." But in cheerleading heterosexual men are also likely to befriend at least one gay male teammate. While slouched across his hotel room bed, Jeffrey, a fourth-year cheerleader and captain of his Midwestern team, said:

> I grew up in a town of 2,000. I never met a gay person. In my town, you were just taught to hate them, even though we didn't know who it was we were supposed to hate. So I did. I mean I just hated the idea that someone could be gay, until I met Jamie [an openly gay member of his team]. I mean, I used to call guys fags all the time, but I'd never call him that. He was a real cool guy, and now I think that gay people are just really cool people.

Institutional support also helps shape a new understanding of homosexuality among ex-football players. Cheerleading competitions are not run by a central organizing body like the NCAA; rather there exist hundreds of cheerleading associations. These associations amount to corporations because they organize and market commercial cheerleading camps, instruction and competitions for profit. Because the world of cheerleading is not structured by one central organization, I split my research evenly among the two primary and dominating organizational bodies of the cheerleading world. In general, one cheerleading corporation subscribes to the belief that men (even gay men) should disassociate from femininity, while the other encourages (more) feminine expression among its men. I call these associations the *Orthodox* and the *Inclusive* Cheerleading Associations. For example, one association encourages men to erotically dance by providing extra points on their performances, while the other association penalizes men for this. Accordingly, one association incorporates femininity into the sport, and the other rules it out. Still, there is not total uniformity in thought among all the coaches, participants, and organizers in either institution.

Strong support for homosexuality especially comes from the *Inclusive Cheerleading Association*, where it was common to find many heterosexual male cheerleaders reporting having no difficulties whatsoever with gay men. Most said they appreciated and respected them. Indeed, many heterosexual cheerleaders in this organization were not afraid to be thought gay. Of course not all cheerleaders reported changing their homophobic ascriptions. At the end of a sixty-minute interview with an athlete from a southern school I asked, "So do you have any gay athletes on your team?" He responded, "Thank God, no. And I hope we never do." "Why is that," I asked. "They give us a bad name. People think we're all a bunch of fags already."

I also found that attitudes toward homosexuality among cheerleaders varied predictably depending on geographical, cultural, and institutional factors. The most homophobic teams, for example, were clearly teams from the American South (even though there were a number of gay-friendly teams from the South as well). Still, other informants presented ambiguous or nuanced perspectives regarding homosexuality. Like Goffman's front stage/back stage (1959), I was able to see contradictions and nuances in their understandings and expressions of masculinity and sexuality.

For example, after an hour of drinking games with Jeff, who early proclaimed he was homophobic, and his teammates, one of the heterosexual men said, "Hey guys, do you want to see if coach will drive us to a club?" Jeff responded, "You guys know of any around here?" To which his best friend, Steve, answered, "There is Gold Diggers, the Slush House, and then of course there is the Phoenix, it's a gay club." Jeff interrupted, "Let's go there," and the others agreed. When I asked why they would rather go to a gay club than a straight one, Jeff answered, "The vibe is better, the music is better, and there are still good-looking women, so why wouldn't we want to go there?" When I then asked, "Aren't you worried about being thought gay?" each of the five heterosexual men shook their heads *no* and Jeff said (in an irritated voice), "Get over this thinking we're afraid to be thought gay stuff."

Jeff rounded up more teammates from other rooms, piled into two vans, and headed for the club. Once there, heterosexual men danced with both women *and* gay men, two heterosexual men even 'freaked' each other (a term used by these men to describe two people dancing with their groins together), and they freaked me as well.

While there was not a universal position on homosexuality among men in cheerleading, a great number of these men had few inhibitions about homosexuality. Their attitudes ran from tolerant to celebratory. Typical comments included, "I don't care what people think of me" to "Why is it necessary to have a label?" One male cheerleader even said, "I used to go to gay clubs all the time, and then I actually got a job at a gay club. I got hit on all the time. It was flattering." Still another said, "Why should I care? Why should people care if I'm straight?"

I suggest these altered (and varying) constructions of masculinity occur because collegiate cheerleading places ex-football players into a state of what Turner (1967) calls *liminality*: a space characterized by ambiguity, openness, and indeterminacy. I call collegiate cheerleading *a transitional heteromasculine space* because these are the characteristics that describe the space (for men). The transition from football to cheerleading involves a change to the informants' social status and their perceived masculine and heterosexual capital. Men in cheerleading then report befriending gay men in collegiate cheerleading, where they (often for the first time) learn of their sexual and gendered narratives. I suggest this then influences them to reconstruct homosexuality to be compatible with masculinity.

EMBRACING GAY FRATERNITY BROTHERS

For several years I taught a large Masculinities class at the University of California, Irvine. Here, I was lecturing on the role of fraternities in reproducing orthodox masculinity, telling my students that research on fraternities near-unanimously attributes them to an organizational and institutional culture of extreme homophobia (Sanday 1990; Windmeyer and Freeman 1998). "Not our Fraternity," Jairo protested. "What do you mean?" I asked of the boy who proudly wore Sig Ep on his sweatshirt. "Our fraternity is nothing like you describe." "Perhaps it's not," I responded. "But I can only tell you what the research says." Jairo, however, would not let the issue go. "Then why don't you do research on our fraternity?" I stood before four-hundred students, absolutely stunned. Initially, I thought Jairo's invitation was just a defensive mechanism, designed to ward off my fraternity-bashing lecture. So I asked, "Is it possible that you're just a bit defensive because it's your fraternity." Jairo raised his voice so that all in the room could hear, "Well, I am the President. But I am also gay."

Jairo came to see me in my office the next day. He brought with him the official documents of his fraternity. Jairo and I discussed the possibility of me doing research on his fraternity and, after Institutional Review Board approval, along with confirmation by his fraternity members (and with consent of the national chapter), I conducted a two-year-long ethnography on the men of his fraternity. It's a relationship that I maintain today.

The organizational culture of this chapter of the fraternity does not aspire to the traditional tenets of orthodox masculinity. After all, in addition to representing the same racial diversity as the university's student population, *they had a gay president*. Wright (1996) suggests that when this type of diversity does occur in the fraternal setting, it generally indicates a lower fraternal social status. This, however, was not the case: Sigma Phi Epsilon is among the largest and most successful fraternities on campus. It is also one of the oldest fraternal orders in the nation. Exemplifying this, during the research period, this fraternity was awarded for possessing the highest collective grade point average *and* they were also awarded *fraternity of the year* by vote of the university sororities. More important to this research, they were also ranked first in inter-fraternal athletic competitions. Thus, the men of the UC Irvine chapter of Sig Ep, not only represent a highly diverse fraternity, but they also maintain high social prestige within the Greek system.

It is possible that this fraternity's organizational culture of inclusivity is partially influenced through a top-down institutional perspective. In addition to being the first to pass a national bylaw forbidding discrimination based on sexuality, the National Chapter also encourages a softer and more inclusive form of masculinity among its members, something they call being "a balanced man." Part of this directive includes discussions of homosexuality.

Jon, the chapter president succeeding Jairo said, "We try to distance ourselves from the *Animal House* stereotype . . . we seek a variety of men, including gay men . . . we are not looking for the typical frat boy." When asked whether they *actively* seek gay men or whether they just accept those who come out, he responded, "Well we don't put a poster up saying that we are seeking gay men . . . but it is part of our recruitment discussion. So when guys come to our table [during the week in which students pledge fraternities] we let them know that we are seeking diversity, and we specifically mention sexual orientation."

Jon explains that seeking a diversity of members is part of the balanced man program. In order to be considered a balanced man chapter, each Sig Ep chapter must institute a program of coursework and activities, all designed to construct a different form of masculinity among its members. These members must promote inclusive attitudes toward both sexual and racial diversity, and they must also promote the treatment of women with dignity. Alex further explained the balanced man concept:

> It is really about respect. It's about being a gentleman, polite, and respectful. Not just respectful toward one another, but toward women, gay men, Christians and atheists . . . But a large part of it has to do with not being a stereotypical frat boy, too. We expect our brothers not to partake in that macho jock mentality. We want to stand out as being intellectual and athletic, but also as being kind and respectful.

Along with the institutional influence to include gay men, there is considerable organizational effort to also promote dialogue about homosexuality. Chapter leaders are encouraged to engage their members in formal discussions on the issue, and this particular chapter discusses the issue quite regularly.

The organizational efforts toward inclusivity of homosexuality began at least two years prior to this research, when Brian came out as the fraternity's first openly gay member. Jairo, who was closeted at the time, said that there were multiple discussions of this and that, "some of the members even wanted to keep him out. But the fraternity voted on the issue, and the overwhelming majority welcomed him." He added, "Most of the members were cool with it anyhow, but of the few who weren't, either they changed their views or they left the fraternity."

Mike is one of the guys who changed his views. "I used to hate gays, but now I think that's stupid. Brian was a senior my first year here and I had a lot of discussion with him. Now I think it's cool having gay guys around." His roommate Ben added, "I never had a problem with gays, but a couple of the older guys did when I first joined the fraternity [four years earlier], some of them used to just hate gays. But you don't find that here anymore."

Discussions about homosexuality were abundant with these men. My husband was encouraged to attend all social events, and there existed a political climate which challenged heterosexism. Many of the brothers even challenged the polarization of sexual binaries. Nate said, "I don't get it. Why do we have to be gay or straight? Why can't we just be?" Trevor added, "Or why can't we be somewhere between. I don't really believe anyone is a hundred percent anything." Alex agreed, saying, "I think we are all bisexual to some degree," and Andrew said, "Gay, straight, whatever, I really don't care."

In the four years since I ended my ethnography with the fraternity, I have been in contact with old and new members. The number of gay men in the fraternity has waxed and waned over the years. And at the time of this writing, there are currently three of 62 members who are out. These members tell me that their fraternity remains resolute in promoting their version of 'a balanced man' masculinity, and they tell me that there are increasing numbers of openly gay men in other fraternities on campus, too. Inclusive masculinities, it would seem, is spreading within the fraternal setting.

RUGBY PLAYERS LEARNING INCLUSIVITY THROUGH THE BROADER CULTURE

Although rugby exits as a minor sport in the United States, it is positioned alongside soccer as a leading definer of masculinity in both youth and university-aged men's cultures in the United Kingdom (Harris and Clayton 2007; Cashmore and Parker 2003). Within British and many other Western cultures, university rugby players are known for promoting and valorizing masculinist acts of hooliganism, alcohol abuse and hazing, as well as perpetuating masculinist bravado and risk-taking (c.f., Donnelly and Young 1988). Grundlingh (1994: 197) describes rugby as the "ultimate man-maker," inculcating characteristics of courage, self-control and stamina, alongside a deeply ingrained culture of homophobia.

As with other teamsport athletes, rugby players are also thought to project their masculine attributes at the expense of marginalized and subordinated men (Dunning and Sheard 1979), principally, gay men (Price and Parker 2003). Coaches, administrators and fans are thought to lend institutional and cultural support to the promotion of rugby men to their exalted peer status (Light and Kirk 2000), so that the playing pitch serves as a figurative "proving ground" (Muir and Seitz 2004) or "training field" (Schacht

1996: 562) for a socially conservative hegemonic embodiment of masculine behaviors and attitudes.

But just as my fraternity ethnography began when I was challenged to investigate an alternate way of doing fraternal bonding, I was also prompted to conduct research on a rugby team because I was told they did not meet the definition of orthodox masculinity. One of my students, told me that his team-mates were "all rather cool with gays." It was a conversation that ended in his formal recording of notes, and my interviewing rugby men, some of their female fans, and men not affiliated with sport at my university in England.

I was not the only one to be dubious of the gay friendly nature of this team. "Of course they are a bunch of homophobes," Sam, a third-year male student told me. "That's how they can do all that gay stuff as part of the sport." When I asked another non-athlete at the university if he thought the members of the first rugby team were homophobic he said, "I wouldn't doubt it. If you are going to find homophobia anywhere, it's going to be there." However, a triangulation of data between our notes, interviews, and experiences with members of the team, show that these rugby players are actually very accepting of homosexuality.

I asked Graham why he thought others perceive his teammates as homo-phobes. He laughed, "We probably used to be," [referring to the traditional culture of rugby], "but sexuality shouldn't really matter to anyone," he said. "There are still people stuck in the past, I guess. But that isn't the way I see it. I have absolutely no problems with gay men." When asked if he would mind having an openly gay player on the team he said, "Maybe my coach would, but I wouldn't." His answer reflects the myriad of gay affir-mative responses to questions designed to probe for homophobia among the players interviewed on this rugby team. "I wouldn't give a shit," one responded. "Not in the slightest." Another said, "Seriously what kind of people do you think we are?"

My participant observations concur with recorded notes. Often, on Wednesday nights, I go clubbing at the university's dance club. Here, I socialize with a number of men from this team. Frequently, they buy me drinks, players come to talk with me, and occasionally they dance up on me. Often, when the men leave the fraternity to attend an after party, I am invited. These, of course, are not the actions of homophobic men.

An equally strong measure of their inclusivity came at a home game. Here, all of the men on the sidelines sat on the bench in front of student-filled arena waiting to be called into the game. During the middle of the game, I walked on to the field into the 'player only' arena, so that I might say hello to a few of the athletes. Here, in full view of thousands of men I was greeted with hugs. When I then said goodbye to one player before the match was over, he smiled and squeezed my ass.

What is interesting about these men, however, is how they came to their inclusive perspective. Although there is now, at the time there were no openly gay men on this team, and they were not modeled to it by organizational or institutional culture. More so, their coaches represent men devoted to orthodox notions of masculinity. Accordingly, the heuristic utility of inclusive and orthodox masculinity is made salient when comparing these men's attitudes and behaviors to that of their coaches. Here, a distinctive variance exists in the two groups' masculinity-making process. My student's observations show that the team's coaches' use homophobic and misogynistic discourse with regular frequency.

"Don't be a fucking poof," a coach screamed after a player failed to properly complete a play. And when another player told his coach that he didn't think he should practice because of an ankle injury, the coach said, "For God's sake, what are you gay?" Graham said, "He calls players 'poofs' when they are injured and he frequently says, 'You're fucking gay,' just to put a player down." Interviews with other athletes confirm that they perceive their coaches' homophobic and misogynistic comments as intended to hurt, degrade and objectify, all in a failed attempt motivate the players to pursue and value physical risk and pain. "I can see why he does it," Graham said, referring to their homophobic and misogynistic banter. "That's his generation. But it doesn't work for us. It doesn't make us jump up and perform better. It doesn't make me think, 'oh, no. I'm not a real man, I need to play harder.' It just makes me think he's a fucking idiot."

Collectively, the athletes despise their coaches' masculinity building approach, and they are fairly adamant to relate that they are opposed to their coaches' behaviors and beliefs. Still, it is interesting to note that they do not actively contest their coaches. "No. You don't say anything," Graham said. "That would be a sure way to sit on the bench." When asked why that should matter, he says, "You have to remember that most of us are trying to make the next level. Or earn more money. You don't prove yourself on the bench." This illustrates the type of uncontested authority I showed coaches maintain in Chapters 3 and 4.

However, athletes do support and encourage each other to 'shake off' the abuse. Ollie said, "Yeah, he says those things all the time. And no, I don't like it or appreciate it, but it doesn't, you know, get to me." He continued, "First, I can't be bothered to care too much about what a jerk like him thinks. So you just ignore him, really." Mark added, "But the other guys are there for you when the coach screams this shit at you. They give you a hug and say, 'don't listen to him, he's a jerk.'"

In addition to using homophobic and misogynistic language against the players, the coaches occasionally try to relate to their players through a failed attempt at bantering with them. Graham explains, "Occasionally he uses it [homophobic discourse] in what he thinks is good humor, to try to be one of the boys. To banter with us about being gay the way we do. But it is just bad most of the time." Alex said, "No. They don't banter like we do. They don't relate to us like they might think they do . . . He [the Head Coach] talks about gay people in ugly and disparaging ways." Mark agrees, "Yeah, like I'll say to a mate, you're gay, and that will bring us closer, but he does it differently. He said, 'That guy's gay,' and it's a totally different thing."

Once, when discussing the fact that Mark has a gay roommate, the coach went off about how "fucking gross" it must be to see the roommate bring a guy home. And once, when some of the players were discussing me (I'm well known on campus), the head coach (who has never met me) said, "That guy is just fucking gay. Gay. Gay. Gay." Neither of these coaches is affiliated with the university today.

This ethnography not only shows that the form of masculinity these men desire and construct is fundamentally inclusive, but it also shows that these players are constructing this inclusive perspective despite the masculinity they have modeled to them by their coaches. I suggest that the coaches' reliance upon orthodox tactics of homophobic intimidation and masculine subordination reflects their socialization into an orthodox sporting ethos, one that holds increasingly less weight with these younger men. Athletes and coaches on this team therefore share a discursive field in which variations in language and belief systems are (mostly covertly) contested. Instead of direct confrontation, however, these athletes utilized their agency through protested silence and changing the meaning associated with discourse. They do not speak the language of their coaches, maintain the same attitudes, or even perform on the pitch as they coaches desire. Instead, they bond in *opposition* to the gendered understandings that their coaches maintain, offering each other emotional comfort and shoring up their version of inclusive masculinity against their coaches' gendered perspectives.

This study also adds to work on inclusive masculinities because previous investigations show that men who perform inclusive masculinities have either benefited from strong institutional support (such as they did in cheerleading), or they have been influenced by the agency of a gay member after coming out (such as they did with Jairo in the fraternity). But members of this team have no exposure to openly gay athletes or gay men of high masculine capital, nor do they have institutional support for their inclusive gendered perspective. Thus, unique to this study, rather than social change occurring from the larger sporting social structure, or being institutionalized as part of a micro-culture through formal leadership, these men highlight the power of collective agency (Foucault 1984; Taylor 1999). I theorize that they do so as a result of the influence of the growing inclusivity toward homosexuality in their university's culture more broadly. It appears that this is a case in which the dominant society's more inclusive attitudes influence sporting men's gendered accounts, instead of it being the other way around (Connell 1987; Messner 1992).

8 Rethinking Misogyny and Anti-Femininity

The previous chapter discussed how the cultural reduction of homophobia and homohysteria has led to the embracing of one's gay teammates and friends. However, a reduction in homohysteria also has an impact on gender relations. This is because homohysteria and anti-femininity are intricately related, as antifemininity codes one as 'not gay.' If men are less concerned with being thought gay, there should be a resultant reduction in antifemininity. However, if men are less antifeminine, it should also impact positively upon their views of women. Thus, one might expect to see a decrease in both antifemininity and misogyny as homohysteria declines. This reduction might even have an effect on the men's dominance over women more broadly, eroding at patriarchy. This occurs because once heterosexual men are freed from the burden of having to reprove their heterosexuality, once they no longer care if others think they are gay, they maintain more liberty to investigate and embrace once-tabooed social spaces, behaviors and ideas.

I am certainly not trying to credit all of the advancements in reduced cultural sexism and femphobia to a reduction of cultural homohysteria. University-aged men may think differently today about women and femininity for a variety of reasons. Nor am I trying to say that men who ascribe to inclusive masculinities do not continue to also reproduce sexism to some degree. Instead, I suggest that the type of sexism the men in my various studies represent is less than that of men in the generation preceding them. It has less negative consequences.

In this chapter, I first examine how once highly misogynistic heterosexual men learn to undo their sexism after being introduced to the narratives of women as teammates and team captains. Here, these men report rapidly changing their views on women, women's athleticism, sexualities and leadership capabilities. I next examine what happens in a fraternity in which gender integration occurs not through formal structure but instead organizational alliances with sororities. Here, men learn to not only rely on women as friends, but they value their input into their personal and fraternity matters.

Finally, I show that a reduction in sexism is also possible without gender-integration. I highlight the lack of sexism among a group of men traditionally known for being highly sexist—rugby players. But I do not find that they maintain the same quality of relationship with women as men in cheerleading do. Accordingly, in the chapter conclusions, I reiterate that because these results show that gender-integration leads to a reduction in sexism and femphobia, we should reconsider the gender-integrated structure upon which sport is built.

THREE CHEERS FOR MEN WHO CHEER

I found that the cheerleaders in my study were less concerned about associating with things culturally coded as feminine than they were as football players. Men who subscribed to inclusive masculinities were particularly less concerned with the expression of femininity among other men. In fact, discussions of what behaviors were considered feminine or masculine often suggested a great deal of thought and critical thinking as to the nature of gender performance in the sport. Many men participated in role-reversal activities, otherwise stigmatized by men in the orthodox group of cheerleaders. For example, some men in the inclusive group agreed that certain behaviors were socially understood to be feminine but they displayed irreverence for such essentialist thinking. Other men questioned the usefulness of categorizing things as gendered in the first place. Much of their gendered understandings were attributable to institutional influences, and nowhere was this more apparent than in dancing.

Men in the Inclusive Cheerleading Association perform differently than those in the Orthodox Cheerleading Association, who retain the traditional element of cheering (yelling) as part of their regimes. They therefore stunt and dance, but stop to cheer things like, "Go, Team, Win!" The Inclusive Cheerleading Association does not however make this component of their performances mandatory; in fact they look down upon it. Instead, they have more complicated dance routines. Conversely, the Orthodox Cheerleading Association penalizes men for dancing or performing in "effeminate" ways. They do this by reducing team points if men dance in ways coded as feminine. In contrast, the Inclusive Cheerleading Association *awards* points for this type of performance. Thus, unlike men in the Orthodox Cheerleading Association, men in the Inclusive Cheerleading Association dance in the same fashion as the women, often performing the exact same routine. The Inclusive Cheerleading Assertion's competitions are widely recognized as being more dynamic, artistic and physically daring than the Orthodox Cheerleading Association's routines, which are described as being closer to the core of traditional cheerleading.

Men in the Inclusive Cheerleading Association participate in other feminized activities, too. For example, while it remains taboo to see men fly (being thrown into the air) in the orthodox group, at the Inclusive Cheerleading Association's national championships, I saw several teams do exactly that, throw (usually small and thin men) high into the air where they were safely caught in the arms of fellow men. One squad even *concluded* their routine by having a man fly over a two-person high pyramid, landing in the arms of four other men. Where this action would result in strong disapproval in the Orthodox Cheerleading Association, in the Inclusive Cheerleading Association it was met with thunderous applause.

This example shows how the structure of a sport might also influence acceptable gendered behaviors within a sport. Because the Inclusive Cheerleading Association awards points for originality, the increased demand of competition (which must always be higher, better and faster) necessitates that the envelope increasingly be pushed. This persuades men to do what only women once did. The encouragement of men to break traditional gender roles (for the sake of performance) then appears to rub off on to their gendered understandings of the world more broadly. Interviews with men in the Inclusive Cheerleading Association indicate that they are much more critical in questioning what is socially coded as masculine or feminine, and why. Further highlighting the difference between these associations, men from one inclusive squad wore shirts that were sleeveless and zipped up the back, the fashion of women's cheerleading outfits. A gay cheerleader from another squad told me, "Did you see the team from [gives location], I couldn't believe it, they were wearing women's tops! That's even pushing matters for me."

Whereas Davis (1990) suggests that men in cheerleading once used to defend their masculinity by sculpting out a masculine subculture, and masculinizing certain tasks within the sport of cheerleading, I found that half of male cheerleaders today willingly embrace the feminized roles they used to flatly avoid. For example, Max, a heterosexual cheerleader, practiced with another male teammate for nearly half an hour, trying to put a woman into the air with perfect form. This is consistent with the gendered expectations of men in cheerleading that Davis (1990) discusses: Men lift women and women do not lift men. After growing bored however Max said, "My turn." The athletes switched positions, and Max stood atop the hands of one male and one female. According to those with an orthodox understanding of masculinity, this position is something men simply do not do. Max, however, was unconcerned. He willingly embraced the coded femininity of such tasks. In this respect, he highlights how men in this group are less concerned about performing consistently with some of the tenets of traditional masculinity, challenging the bifurcation of gender in the process.

This is not to suggest that men completely redefined their sexist notions, however. Virtually all of the informants in my cheerleading research viewed men as maintaining an athletic advantage over women. Their involvement in cheerleading—where they were exposed to women's athleticism—did little to change this view. Still, about 70 percent of the informants said they had no idea that women could be *this* athletic. This struck me as strange, considering most had seen women cheering on their football sidelines in high school. "Yeah, you see them doing some of this stuff on the sidelines," Max said, "but you don't really get an idea of just how physically tough it is until you try it." Tony agreed, "I never really thought about how hard it must be to do what they do. Not until I tried it."

Accordingly, most of the cheerleaders maintain that they never really had their preconceptions about the inferiority of female athleticism challenged. Like Max, Jim said that he used to believe that women were physically incapable of competing with men. He said, "I used to think women were weak, but now I know that's not true." David added, "I never thought women were so athletic before. I hated women's sports. But these women are *athletes*. They do stuff I'd never do, and I bet there are a lot of sports women can do better in." Brad summed up much of the sentiment:

> I didn't appreciate women as athletes before. [In high school] I heard that another school had a girl on their [football] team and I thought that was wrong. My teammates and I were talking about it, and we all agreed that a woman just couldn't handle what we could. Now I see that women can handle a lot and they aren't as fragile as I thought they were.

Participant observations show why these men have improved their views on women's athletic abilities. In cheerleading, men see women performing highly dangerous feats that require the same strength, balance, and fearlessness that they claim masculinizes them (Davis 1990). And even though men do most of the heavy lifting in the co-ed division of cheerleading, they need only watch the all-women's division to see the same stunts performed by women.

Furthermore, virtually all of the men expressed a new-found appreciation for the leadership qualities and coaching abilities that women exhibit in cheerleading. Perhaps this is because virtually all of the collegiate female cheerleaders competed in high school, and this gives them considerable knowledge of the sport. Watching David, a wide-eyed new recruit, trying to learn a complicated and dangerous stunt illustrated this. David listened to Emily's directions, asked for clarification, and relaxed at her encouragement. Immediately after landing the stunt, he turned to hug her, beaming with self-pride. He then awaited her congratulations and smiled again upon receiving it. It makes sense that men listen to women in cheerleading, when one is contemplating flying through the air, performing a back flip or holding a person above one's head, listening to the experts prevents injuries.

Finally, data from interviews and participant observations also indicate that many of these men rethought their misogynistic attitudes, particularly regarding women as sex-objects. The data clearly shows that when these same men become familiar with the experiences of women (in the gender-integrated sport of cheerleading), almost all adopt a new gender strategy that looks more positively upon women (none downgraded their position). Relying on retrospective reports, about half of the men said they maintained misogynistic attitudes before joining cheerleading, mostly in that they hyper-sexualized women and desired to socially exclude them (cf. Muir and Seitz 2004). Yet most (not all) of these men maintain that cheerleading helped them undo this thinking. Dan enthusiastically said, "Oh, we totally learn to respect women, I mean they [teammates] are like our sisters." Ronnie confirmed, "Yeah, I never really understood women too much before, but my teammates are a family to me. I have grown real close to them, and now I can often see things from their perspective." Ryan said:

> In high school it was all about the cheerleaders making signs for our games or baking us cookies. I mean, we hung out with them at parties, but it was nothing like what occurs here [in cheerleading]. We didn't travel with them or have team dinners and stuff. I never really had female friends in high school . . . I never really got to know them like I do now.

These results suggest that the sex-segregation in Ryan's high school effectively denied him the opportunity to see women as equal members in responsibility for the outcome of a game. I asked Ryan if his high school social network of friends was also comprised of mostly men. "Yeah, my teammates. That's really all I socialized with." Conversely, in collegiate cheerleading, Ryan was able to make friends with women in ways he was not able to in high school. Will concurred, "I've never before had best-friends that weren't men. But now, some of my best friends are women."

I also explored this theme with 12 group interviews. Here, the cheerleaders and several coaches were asked about the social interaction between men and women. Collectively, both men and women, coaches and athletes, near-unanimously maintained that cohesion occurs between the sexes. Jill (a player) said, "The men in cheerleading learn a new respect for women in this sport. They learn that not only are we good athletes, but we are smart athletes and competent leaders, too." Highlighting how gender-integration might also change women's views of men, Lindsay (a coach) said: "These guys have given me a new understanding of men, and they aren't all that bad." Another female coach added:

> Oh yeah, they become like family. I mean they spend so much time together, they change in the same locker rooms sometimes, and they just get real comfortable, even with bodily issues. I can't imagine a more cohesive group of athletes than you find in cheerleading.

Data from the cheerleading research clearly indicates that there exists a significant socio-positive attitudinal shift regarding men's attitudes toward women. Informants near-unanimously maintained that they enhanced their beliefs about the athleticism of women; all but a handful reported that they had learned to see women as more than sex objects. Finally, *all* of the athletes report having learned to respect and value women as friends, teammates and competent leaders in the sport of cheerleading. Thus, in the sex-integrated sport of collegiate cheerleading, even sexist and misogynistic men were able to witness the athleticism of women, befriend them in ways that they were previously unable to, and to learn of their sexual and gendered narratives—humanizing them in the process. And while not all men were equally affected by their experience in cheerleading, and while some of this change may occur because of the liberalizing attitudes of university life in general (Ohlander, Batalova and Treas 2005), I attribute much of their reconstruction to the gender-integrated sport of cheerleading. When men are forced to play with women, they are also forced to travel and train together. Accordingly, men are likely to have conversations with women about sex, gender, sport and life—the kind of conversations they were often unable to have in a homo-social culture such as football. In these conversations, informants not only hear the multiple narratives of women, but they also see them as worthy and competent athletes, teammates, coaches and leaders. In cheerleading, even men who were once highly sexist were able to socialize and develop cohesion with women as participants of equal agency and responsibility for team performance and outcomes—something that works against gender stereotyping. Coupled with a more inclusive institutional and organizational setting, these men were now able to undo much of their separatist and sexist thinking.

The findings contrast with research showing that the integration of men and women does not always deter gender stereotyping (Jackson and Warren 2000; Harvey and Stables 1984). I therefore suggest that teamsports may be uniquely effective in reducing gender stereotypes because they necessitate that men and women work together for the accomplishment of victory. It makes sense that men relying on women to obtain their athletic goals look more favorably upon them, compared to when they compete directly against them. Conversely, it is also possible that these results are influenced by the feminized nature of cheerleading, and the process these men go through to realign their masculinity with this feminized terrain. Either way, these findings indicate that the gender-integrated nature of cheerleading may help *disrupt* the reproduction of orthodox masculinity among men who have participated in gender-segregated teamsports. These results question how much of men's anti-feminine, sexist and misogynistic attitudes might be prevented if teamsports were structurally gender-integrated across all sports and among all age cohorts.

DEVELOPING A SENSE OF BROTHERS
AND SISTERS IN FRATERNITY LIFE

The men in cheerleading were not the only ones to view women as sisters. Previous investigations of masculine construction among fraternal organizations near-monolithically find that men in fraternities revere orthodox masculinity (Boswell and Spade 1996) and that they attempt to approximate it through distancing themselves from subordinate men. Serving as either a product or indicator of this socially elite form of masculinity, American fraternity members have therefore been individually equated with emphasizing the tenets of orthodox masculinity, and American fraternal organizations have been described as reproducing orthodox masculinity through an institutionalized, gender-segregated, racially-segregated, sexist, and highly homophobic culture (Martin and Hummer 1989; Ross 1999; Sanday 1990). Indeed the organizational culture of fraternities in America (fraternities do not exist in Britain) parallels the structure and culture of sports.

Therefore, men who participate in fraternities have been so endowed with masculine and heterosexual capital that, just as with competitive teamsport athletes, the sociological literature often attributes to them an organizational culture conducive of sexual assault against women (Boeringer 1996, 1999). Sanday (1990) suggests that the type of masculinity exhibited in fraternities is almost monolithically based upon sexual aggression toward women. She maintains that brotherhood is constructed in opposition to femininity, as women's bodies are used to construct and unite men as highly virile, heterosexual, and masculine. Wright (1996: 33) agrees, saying that, "sexual aggression so permeates the language, lifestyle, and morals of fraternity members, [that] fraternity houses have become a virtual breeding ground for men indoctrinated into the ways of sexism and sexual harassment." Wright adds that the Greek system fosters stereotypical views of male dominance and female submissiveness, so that women solely represent objects to be sexually conquered. Regarding the sexual threat that fraternity organizations pose to women however, Boswell and Spade (1996), warn against over-generalizing, clarifying that there exists stratification from high- to low-risk settings. This research found very little sexism, and no evidence of sexual threat to women.

Indicating the strength of association between masculinity and misogynistic attitudes within the fraternal system at this California university, informants from other fraternities demonstrated the pervasive use of misogynistic discourse among most fraternity brothers. In this case, the socio-negative discourse mostly comes through the terms *bitch* and *slut*. However, the chapter of the Sig Ep Fraternity I studied was not like this. Allen said, "We don't look at women in the same manner [men of] other fraternities do. You'll notice that we treat them with respect. They are just part of the group." Mike agreed, "Women are some of my best friends. Like Melissa. She is in my room all the time. She's like my best friend." Jon added, " . . . it's not appropriate to use that type of terminology, and the use of it simply won't be tolerated." Steve agreed, "There is a strong belief that we are to treat women well. There is actually peer pressure this way. In fact, if you don't treat women well, I mean if you even do something perceived as mean-spirited, you can be brought to standards" [a judicial hearing]. When asked whether this included misogynistic discourse, Steve responded, "Of course. In fact, we had a brother brought to standards because he called a girl a bitch." Observations largely support this claim. Hardly ever (three times within the two-year study) were the casual use of the terms *bitch*, *slut*, and *dyke* used in reference to women.

Also, many strong non-sexual relationships were formed between Sig Ep members and women. A number of individual women embedded themselves into the social networks and cliques of this fraternity. Gender integration also occurred through organizational pairing and gender-integrated dances, and events with sororities. Accordingly, many female friends of the fraternity belonged to sororities, but others did not. Many attended social events, and several spent the night in the fraternity with regular occurrence. And as far as could be discerned, these relationships remained non-sexual.

It was not uncommon to walk the fraternity's hallways and see, through an open door, women (usually fully dressed) sleeping on a bed (usually on top of the covers) in one of the members' rooms. These female friends were granted considerable access to the fraternity and, when interviewed, expressed that they had no fear of being sexually victimized. One said, "Come on, they are Sig Ep." Whether the decision to sleep in a fraternity house is wise or not, the event establishes a level of comfort they maintain with these men—something influenced by the positive treatment they have received from them.

It should be noted however that these men have not redefined all aspects of orthodox masculinity. After returning from a dance at 2:30 in the morning, Dan called out, "Don't go in there, Tim is in there and he hasn't been with a woman in a few months." Tim, who had met Kate at a club, brought her back to his room. The next day he received comments like, "Tim, in the room with the door closed" and "Tim, I see your all smiles today." However, the discourse lacked the hyper-macho tone of symbolic rape or sexual objectification. None asked, "Did you fuck her?" "Nail her?" or "Score?" Essentially, they asked the same question, using less misogynistic discourse. Also, not all members pursued sex. Two of the men publicly proclaimed their desire to remain virgins. While one of the brothers identified as being bound to Christian morality on the issue, Chris expressed that his lack of heterosexual sex was a result of a low sex drive, self-identifying as asexual. "I just don't care much for sex. I have like no sex drive." When asked if his brothers made fun of him for this, he responded, "Not really. I guess maybe every great now and then. But it's not like they really care." Thus, unlike previous research, which generalizes all fraternity men to be hyper-heterosexual, there is no homogenous view of heterosexual activity among these fraternal brothers—even though many men were socially esteemed for having heterosexual sex.

These results do not suggest that there are *no* misogynistic or antifeminine attitudes among the men in this group. Nor is this to suggest that this fraternity does not help reproduce patriarchy, after all, it does remain a formally gender-segregated institution. Many of the men do sexually objectify women in constructing their heterosexual identities, but they also align themselves politically with sexual equality.

RUGBY PLAYERS AS "NICE GUYS"

The reputation of rugby players as conducting a form of masculinity acted through the sexual objectification of women has been described as resilient within rugby cultures. Accordingly, rugby players have been shown to psychologically and sometimes physically dominate women. This is partially because heterosexuality is deeply implicated with masculinity. For example, Hughson (2000: 13) writes, "The surest way of proving heterosexuality to one's male peers is through the sexual conquest of women." Thus, pulling, fucking and the broadcasting of one's heterosexual activities have been central tenets in establishing one as representing orthodox masculinity. Schacht (1996), for example, shows that when sexually attractive women walked by the rugby team he studied, players were expected to stop practice and yell sexually harassing comments at them. He also found that rugby players sang traditional rugby songs concerning fucking women. Furthermore Schacht shows that during post-competition celebrations the players selected a woman (telling her that she was to be honored as their "queen") and then sexually degraded and harassed her, until she cried.

What is unique about my findings is that none of this was happening on the university rugby team that my graduate student and I studied. For example, when Nicky was asked about how these rugby players treat women, she replied, "Everyone in general thinks that they must be really arrogant womanizers. But they are not! Take John for example. He has been with his girlfriend for a few years. And you will never see him even approach a woman in a pub. You will never hear him say anything degrading about women." She added, "Some of the guys try to pull women, of course, but they don't do it in a way that's any different than the way any other guys do it. And if they get rejected, they don't give her shit for it, they just move on." Jemma agreed, "Not these guys. These guys are different. Maybe you won't believe me, but they are gentlemen. Real top men."

Beth maintained that the university's rugby players get an unfair rap. "They are big, and that intimidates people" she said. "I think when they walk into a pub people are scared by their size, and judge them before they get to know them. But most of them are just sweet guys." When asked if these men look to pull and have sex with women, she answered, "Of course. It's not like they are a bunch of virgins. They want to get laid as much as the next guy, but they don't make a big deal of it. It's not like sex is a big deal or anything." And when asked about use of misogynistic discourse she said, "You won't hear it. You just will not."

These women's perspectives are confirmed by the yearlong observations, too. Here, my co-researcher found that the term "bitch" was occasionally used between men, but it (or other misogynistic discourse) was not directed at women. This is the case in all but two recorded exceptions. In one, Joe said, "That chick's a slut." However, Joe's proclamation failed to raise comment, agreement, or any indication that it bonded his teammates. The same was true of the second comment, where Dan called a woman "a bitch." Furthermore, both of these men are marginalized from the core of the team. They are not respected teammates.

Field notes do, however, document quite a bit of sexual discussion *about* women. Phrases like "she's fit" are heard frequently. But this exemplifies the difficulty in interpreting discourse. Certainly readers will have varying opinions about whether this language is misogynistic or not, and what type of culture it promotes concerning women. However, what is important here is the contrast I find compared to older studies of university rugby players (Grazian 2007; Muir and Seitz 2004; Schacht 1996). Unlike rugby players in these other studies, these men do not regularly partake in calling women "bitches," "sluts" or "whores." Furthermore, there is no ritualistic degrading of women through songs or post-performance celebrations. There is no yelling at them from the pitch, either.

Furthermore, interviews show that many of these young men express the same difficulties in dating that one might expect of any group of university-aged men. Several of the players maintained long-term girlfriends, and they suggest that their social lives are largely taken up by these relationships.

Collectively, the data from the participant observations, combined with interviews of the men and their female friends, suggests that men of this rugby first team expresses less misogyny and decreased objectification compared to other studies of men in rugby. Still, I am hard pressed to say that these men, or men in any other gender-segregated group, do not promote patriarchy. Indeed, the very act of playing for a gender-segregated team implicates them with it. It is noteworthy however, that while sexism has occurred in sport through ingrained (unintentional) patriarchal values and intentional objectification, these men do not intentionally seek to objectify and/or degrade women as part of their masculinized identities.

The heuristic utility of inclusive and orthodox masculinity is made salient when comparing these men's attitudes and behaviors to that of their coaches. Here, again, a distinctive variance exists between how the players construct their masculinity compared to their coaches. The coaches use a good deal of misogynistic talk in their attempt to "relate" to their athletes. Mark said, "He's always talking about women as bitches, and saying stuff like, 'hey, did you nail that bitch last night?' and stuff like that. He really steps over the line, even about guys' girlfriends." David said, "I don't think it's a good situation when a coach is giving out harsh girlfriend banter!" Graham clarified, "Their banter isn't the same as our banter. It's mean. It's like they try to use our way of relating to each other, but then they twist it to insult." He adds, "It's really derogatory. It's more bullying than bantering.

Illustrating this, Tom recalls a time in which one of the coaches questioned his girlfriend's faithfulness in front of the team, describing in detail how he believed that she was being "violated" by a number of men while he was away on holiday. "I just couldn't believe it," he said. "He was talking about how guys were fucking her raw. This is my girlfriend he's talking about. And this man is our coach? Someone we're supposed to want to respect? I just want to fucking kill him."

Accordingly, this research not only shows that the form of masculinity these men desire and construct is fundamentally more inclusive than what the literature says about rugby players, but it shows that these players are constructing this inclusive perspective despite the masculinity they have modeled to them by their coaches (who are no lnoger affiliated with the university). I therefore suggest that the coaches' reliance upon orthodox tactics of homophobic intimidation and masculine subordination reflect their masculine socialization into a sporting ethos that holds increasingly less weight with these younger men. Athletes and coaches on this team share a discursive field in which variations in language and belief systems are covertly (and sometimes overtly) contested.

This is noteworthy because athletes (as discussed in Chapters 3 and 4) normally conform to coaches' gendered perspectives: This increases players' favor among their coaches, and helps them with their athletic matriculation. In other words, athletes normally fear cultural and institutional punishment for failing to meet the mandates of the coach. This is the nature of competitive hierarchies of sporting careers (Hughes and Coakley 1991). As such, these men's concern for remaining part of the team, and their learned obedience to authority, limits their willingness to directly contest their coaches. Instead of direct confrontation, athletes utilize their agency through silence and changing the meaning associated with homophobic and misogynistic discourse. They bond in *opposition* to the gendered understandings that their coaches maintain, offering each other emotional comfort and shoring up their version of masculinity against their coaches' gendered perspectives. This is not the type of masculinity their rugby forefathers valued.

CONTESTING GENDERED BINARIES
THROUGH GENDER-INTEGRATION

Results of the aforementioned ethnographic investigations lead me to some general conclusions concerning the gender-segregated arena of sport. Here, I suggest that the extreme regimentation and inordinate amount of time required to excel at sport often deprives men of experiences outside of the athletic arena, where they might otherwise be introduced to the sexual/gendered narratives of women or gay men. Instead, in the homosocial world of men's teamsports, males are socialized into an ethos in which women are valued as sexual objects, devalued as athletes, and masculinity is predicated in opposition to femininity. This is made more possible because there are no women or openly gay men to contest these narrow understandings. But it is also made possible because coaches are recruited from a pool of ex-athletes who matriculated through the same system. Essentially, I argued in part one that because teamsports are near compulsory for youth, young boys are indoctrinated into a masculinized, homophobic and sexist gender regime from early childhood—an institution they cannot easily escape. Even if boys are fortunate enough to enter a gender-integrated sports team when young, by the time they reach high school, gender-segregation is the norm.

Additionally, the demands of competitive sport often consume such quantities of time that it also structures men into off-the-field social networks of teammates—positioning them into a near-total masculine institution. Bereft of alternative gender narratives, and desiring social promotion among their peers, boys and men are more willing to subject their agency to orthodox masculinity, which remains predicated in anti-feminine, sexist and (frequently) misogynistic thinking. In this aspect, segregation on the field is complicated by the effect of a near-total institution off the field.

But in addition to providing a model for how orthodox masculinity is reproduced among teamsport athletes, I also suggest how this process might be interrupted. Data from my research on male cheerleaders and fraternities, clearly shows that when men become familiar with the experiences of women, almost all adopt a new gender strategy that looks more favorably upon them. I suggest that in gender-integrated sports, the time constraints of training and travel structures athletes into mixed-sex social networks, at least part of the time. Here, men are likely to have conversations with women about sex, gender, sport and life—the kind of conversations they were often unable to have in a homosocial culture. I find that, in partaking in these conversations, men not only prevail themselves to hearing the multiple narratives of women, but they also learn to view women as worthy and competent athletes, teammates, coaches and leaders.

I therefore suggest that gender-integrating teamsports may be the required crack in the system to help undo patriarchy. Gender-integrating participants on sports teams is more valuable than gender-integrating men and women in other masculinized terrains (like firefighting or the police force) because virtually all boys play organized sports. Thus, I maintain that gender-integrating sports should be a starting point for an "opposing [gender] strategy" (Foucault 1984: 101) that erodes at patriarchy.

I do not however wish to claim that gender-integration is a panacea for the sexual, social, ethical, and gender-related problems associated with men's sports, men's teamsports are far too intertwined with other masculinist systems and institutions for that. Furthermore, I do not analyze how gender-desegregating teamsports might negatively impact on female athletes, particularly considering that women have been shown to be sub-ordinated by men within other integrated terrains (Britton and Williams 1995; Reskin and Roos 1990). Nor do I know how gender-integration might impact upon the number of socio-positive attributes that Sabo and his colleagues (2004) correlate with women's sporting participation.

However, there is another reason for further investigating my gender-integration proposition. Where the dominant ideology maintains that gender-segregation is valuable to women because it shelters women from men's violence in sport, I question whether violence against women off the field might instead be promoted through sporting-segregation. We know that male teamsport athletes have elevated rates of violence against women compared to non-athletes and non-teamsport athletes (Kreager 2007). Accordingly, if gender-segregation in sport is even *partially* responsible for men's violence against women, then the socio-positive results of what I found in the sport of cheerleading should serve as a call for further aca-demic inquiry into the effects of gender-integrating other/all sports.

Still, the notion of gender-integrating sport (and changing the rules of sport to facilitate this) is met with great resistance. Whenever I speak about the subject, I find opposition. For example, I recently debated the issue with athletes in a class in New York. The class (comprised of equal numbers of men and women) was wholly resistant to the idea of gender integration. Men had a plethora of reasons and rationales why women should not play with men: 1) they might get hurt at the hands of overly muscled men; 2) they might not want to play on men's teams; 3) it would be impossible to change the structure of sports to permit this as the purists of sport would never permit such. When I then pointed out that 1) a 100-pound male can try out and play rugby for a man's team, but a 300-pound woman cannot; 2) women should have the choice to play with men; and that 3) those who control sport are more likely to change the structures and rules when they see financial profit (think of the three point line and shot clock in basket-ball), they did not yield. Instead they came up with a host of new reasons why women 'simply' should not be allowed to play with men.

Interestingly, not a single woman spoke during the entire hour. Although I begged and pleaded with them, "Women, how can you let these men say this about you? Where are your voices? Why are you so complacent to the men's complaints?" Not one of them spoke up. In the end, it helps us realize that this is not only a problem of men trying to protect their sacred terrain, but it is a problem of women having been so subordinated, and being so complacent with what they have been given, that they fail to enact their agency to bring about gender parity.

So why do most people protest the gender integration of sport? More important is the question of why it is socially permissible to say that women should not play on men's teams, but it is not permissible to say that gays should not play on straights teams, or that blacks should not play on white teams? Exemplifying this, when I ask my students how many think that black men have an advantage over white men in the hundred-meter dash, every student raises their hand. "So why not then have a black men's 100-meter race, and a white men's 100-meter race?" The students object to my proposition, "That would be racist." So why, I ask, is it not sexist to suggest that woman should have their own finals?

After all, it is quite possible that gay men may be better served better by being formally excluded from heterosexual men's sports, instead being given their own sporting spaces. It is also possible that black athletes might benefit from playing on racially segregated teamsports. Therefore (according to this logic) they should be provided their own space. But each of these suggestions is readily met with charges of homophobia and racism. This of course is the power of patriarchy: It prevents even women from seeing their own oppression.

Whatever one's theoretical position on gender-integrating sports, empirically, my work on the cheerleaders and fraternities shows that the more contact men have with women, the more men upgrade their perspectives on them. It is for these reasons that I desire scholars to further investigate the effect of gender integration in sport.

9 Reconstructing Heterosexuality

Heterosexual masculinity is traditionally achieved by boasting of one's heterosexuality, repudiating homosexual sex, and by ostensibly having never lusted after someone of the same sex. Thus, according to this orthodox model, the only way to be considered heterosexual is to avoid any same-sex sexual behavior and never to admit same-sex sexual desire. The perfect integration of one's sexual orientation, sexual identity and sexual behaviors is something Messner (2004, p. 422) describes as being "100 percent straight." The ironic problem for heterosexual men is however that, in a culture dominated by and for heterosexual men, homohysteria makes it impossible to definitively prove that they *are* heterosexual. This is a result of the impossibility of proving a negative.

Just how does one prove that one is *not* gay? Just because one is married, or masculine, or even in the military; just because one plays sports, or talks endlessly about one's sexual desires for women, does not guarantee one freedom from homosexual suspicion. Tom Cruise serves the perfect example. He is an attractive, athletic male who dates/marries some of our culture's most esteemed women. By all attributes he epitomizes Connell's notion of hegemonic masculinity. Furthermore, there is no evidence of him desiring same-sex sex, yet he is nonetheless inundated with homosexual suspicion.

It is the very fact that gay men are first 'in the closet' before coming out that makes this possible. Homohysteria makes it possible for *all* men to be thought in the closet. It only then takes one slip from heterosexualized behaviors or terrains for an individual to be culturally homosexualized. Thus, one can talk endlessly about how good looking women are, but one errant comment about a male and all of one's publicly perceived heterosexual capital is lost.

Thus, sociologically speaking, heterosexuality is unprovable because homosexuality is stigmatized. The operation of stigma prevents people from admitting to socially stigmatized identities (Goffman 1963). Accordingly, men (gay or straight) wishing to avoid homosexual stigma must attempt to prove and reprove their heterosexuality.

Borrowing from Harris's (1964) one-drop theory of race, in which a dominant white culture once viewed anyone with even a portion of black genetic ancestry as wholly black, I suggest (Anderson 2008a) that one same-sex sexual experience is socially equated with a homosexual orientation in Anglo-American cultures. I call this the "one time rule of homosexuality," describing how this serves as a cultural mechanism to conflate the complex issues of gender, sexual orientations, sexual desires, sexual identities and the social construction of sexual acts themselves into the polarized identities of simply, 'gay and straight'—simultaneously re-inscribing heterosexual power and privilege.

Furthermore, Schwartz (1995: 12) points out that the inverse of this rule does not seem to apply to heterosexual men. "We have demonized the power of homosexuality so that we assume it to be the greater truth of our sexual self—as if one drop of homosexuality tells the truth of self while one drop of heterosexuality in a homosexual life means nothing." This one-way application of the one-time rule has traditionally created a double jeopardy for men who reveal that they have experience with any form of socially coded same-sex sexual behaviors, as it both excludes them from achieving the requisites of heterosexuality and diminishes their masculine capital. Accordingly, with few exceptions (cf. Klein 1993; Reis 1961), the rule seems to be that for heterosexual men in Anglo-American cultures, socially perceived heterosexuality is conditioned upon gender exclusive heterosexual behaviors.

Curry (1991) adds that it is simply not enough for heterosexuals to avoid gay sex and say that they are not gay. He posits that they must also behave in *vehemently* homophobic ways if they desire to cast off homosexual suspicion. Thus, proving one's heterosexuality also occurs through denouncing tolerance of those who desire same-sex sex. This is how (many) heterosexuals overtly police their dominance, and this is how homohysteria has been used toward the continual maintenance of a heterosexual identity. Accordingly, I sometimes call the orthodox version of heteromasculinity, *defensive heterosexuality*, because it is predicated in defense/opposition of what one is not. This constructs an artificial binary to all men's sexual identities.

MAINTAINING HETEROMASCULINITY DESPITE HAVING SAME-SEX SEX

In my research on gay athletes in the late 1990s and early 2000s, I found a number of gay athletes had sexual experiences with their heterosexual teammates. But these accounts specifically detailed that heterosexual men who invited them to partake in sexual activity were explicitly concerned with anonymity in these behaviors. One athlete tells me that while sleeping in the same bed with a teammate, the heterosexual teammate slowly positioned himself closer to the gay teammate, crossing a leg onto his. As the night progressed, the straight athlete began to wiggle atop the gay athlete, grinding crotches until the heterosexual athlete achieved orgasm through his underwear. No words were exchanged, and the heterosexual teammate forever distanced himself from the gay teammate.

Another gay athlete said that he had a long conversation with one of his teammates about sex, and that in the early hours of the morning, his teammate said he would be willing to try receiving oral sex. So the gay athlete gave the straight athlete oral sex. The heterosexual athlete achieved orgasm, and then he " . . . freaked out and even threatened to beat me up if I told anyone." The two men returned to their friendship as normal the following day, but neither spoke of the incident again.

These incidents, and the dozens of similar situations I have heard from gay athletes over the years, support orthodox notions of heteromasculinity being predicated in exclusive opposite-sex sexual behaviors. The simple act of having sex with another man jeopardizes the publicly perceived heterosexual identity that these men strongly desire to maintain. Accordingly, after the individuals have some form of same-sex sex, the heterosexual demands silence—sometimes these demands are enforced with threats of physical violence. This not only polarizes sexual identities as either being gay or straight, but it supports the one-time rule of homosexuality and heterosexual dominance.

KISSING AWAY THE 'ONE-TIME RULE'

The men of a UK soccer team who were subject of a study do not, however, follow such strict protocol for their same-sex sexual behaviors. They contest orthodox notions of heterosexual masculinity in a very unique way: They engage in prolonged, public, kissing. Twenty of the twenty-two players, that my graduate student Adrian Adams and I interviewed, said that they have (sometimes frequently) engaged in provocative displays of same-sex kissing as part of their homosocial banter. For example, Jon said that, "I kissed a guy with tongues for about three or four seconds." And when asked about this type of behavior with a teammate he said, "I've kissed about three other lads in that way." Grant recalls a time when he unexpectedly saw one of his best mates in a club. "I came running over to him and pulled him. Like properly," he said. When asked what 'properly' meant, he answered, "Like a proper pull . . . tongues and everything." When asked about the duration of the kissing, he answered, "Maybe ten seconds." Similarly, Chris said, "I've kissed over ten of my lad mates; and made out with some, too." Yet all of these men identify as heterosexual.

The most common venue for these heterosexual men's same-sex kissing occurs at dance clubs during nights out. Here, informants are normally under the influence of alcohol. This is consistent with literature that shows that men use alcohol in their homosocial bonding (Peralta 2007; West 2001). One informant said, "Kissing happens on nights out, yeah. It happens all the time." Pat clarified that they kiss each other as part of their fraternal celebration of having a good time. Accordingly, their kissing normally occurs in exuberant moments. However, informants are clear to indicate that they do not consider this a sexual act. Instead, their prolonged kissing is described as homosocial banter.

KC said that he has one teammate who gets particularly 'kissy' when he's drunk. "I kiss him quite often," he laughed. When KC is asked if he considers this 'making out,' he answered, "No. Not really. I mean, you can call it that if you want. I don't care. But it's not a sexual thing. I don't know how to explain it. It just is." Other men we interview concur, that they see this as simultaneously sexual and non-sexual. Pat says, "No. It's not sexual. You just do it for fun." But he understands that others might interpret his behaviors as sexual. "Of course. Yeah, two guys with their tongues in each other's mouths. But I guess it just doesn't matter." Matt clarified, "When I do it, I don't see it as making out. But I can see how others might."

Like the other heterosexual men we interview, KC said that he is not erotically attracted to the men he kisses. Conversely, when asked if he is 'turned off' or 'grossed out' from kissing, he indicated that he was not. Pete concurred. "No. It's not gross. Not at all. It's sexual but not sexual." Matt agreed, "No. It's not sexual. Even if you're pulling another guy (kissing) it's just something you do for banter, or to show him you love him. But it's not sexual. Not at all." It is because of this juxtaposition of private meanings contrasting with traditionally understood public coding of two men kissing that I call this type of behavior semi-sexual. It can be (but is not always) coded as sexual. Regardless of how it is interpreted, the men insist that it is not erotic (although there is no objective way of measuring this).

This type of kissing behavior is compatible with research that shows that men in Anglo-American cultures have long used joking (something these informants call banter) through the use of semi-arbitrary, ambivalent language and behaviors as a way to produce homosocial intimacy (Emerson 1969). In many ways, it is no different than the mock homosexual experience that heterosexual male athletes (and men in other homo-social institutions) engage in to not only bond, but to ironically show that they are heterosexual (Schroeder 2002). Thus, key to this form of intimacy, and relevant to this work, is that the men we interviewed expressed a shared understanding that they are not erotically attracted to the men they kiss, but that they are emotionally close to them. Privately, they kiss other men as a way to facilitate their emotional intimacy. Publicly, labeling their actions as banter *helps* ensure that they distance themselves from the eroticism associated with kissing. Highlighting this, prolonged kissing is sometimes (but not always) performed in an exaggerated manner. Here the intention is to, ironically, draw heterosexualizing attention. Thus, this type of public kissing serves as a juxtaposition of a semi-public performance with a semi-private meaning.

It is this type of shared meaning that permits prolonged kissing within a semi-public sphere to remain acceptable within a heterosexual framework, regardless of whether those outside their cadre understand the non-sexual

Two heterosexual men embrace in public.

meaning behind their behaviors. Highlighting this, Jon said, "Did you see those two rugby players pulling in [names dance club on campus]. They were really going at it." When asked whether the men were gay or straight, he answered, "Dunno."

Still, these men recognize that they are performing a behavior that was once coded as homosexual, and might still be to others (just not their friends). They recognize that their kissing is a sexual behavior, whether or not there is desire associated with it. When Matt, Pete, and Grant are asked if performing the same kiss on a woman would be sexual, they concur that it would. Matt said, "Well, if she's fit, then yeah. Of course." Grant added, "But that's because I'm attracted to women. I'm not attracted to guys." Chris said that kissing a guy is, "a bit different. Normally they've got a bit of a beard and that's sometimes a bit rough. But apart from the stubble it feels the same as kissing a girl." He clarified, however, that while it feels the same as kissing a girl in one aspect, "it is not the same as kissing a girl." He said that, whether it is in celebration, out of affection, or performed as banter, kissing other men is strictly non-sexual. When he is asked to further clarify he said, "I mean it is sexual, but it's not sexy [read erotic]."

Whether those outside their team understand their behaviors as sexual or not is hard to say. There is considerable evidence that others are engaging in the same behaviors. This means that these men receive no public stigma and they are not policed by others. Jonathan said, "I couldn't really tell you that I have had a bad reaction from other people. I don't see why anybody would either." Like the other informants, when Grant, is asked if he's ever been accused of being gay, or received gay epithets for publicly kissing another guy, he answered, "Not at all. And if I did, it just wouldn't really bother me." However, this type of kissing is also likely to be acceptable because these men's university peers are unconcerned with gay men kissing in their shared space (Peterson and Anderson 2009).

This type of kissing almost always occurs when intoxicated. When asked about whether alcohol is necessary for creating a social environment conducive for men to engage in prolonged kissing, Grant said. "Yeah, I guess we kiss more often that way when we're drunk. But that's because we're out having a good time. Obviously you are going to do it more when you're out having fun." Ian added, "But it's not like you wake up the next day going, 'What did I do?' You don't regret it or anything." He said, "Look on Facebook, you'll see that we don't regret it" (referring to the almost ubiquitous phenomenon of heterosexual men placing photos of them kissing other men on Facebook).

Pete clarified the need for alcohol in kissing other men with humor, "I kiss guys when drunk," he said. "But I have to be *real* lashed [drunk] to work up the guts to try and pull women." Pete is also clear to indicate that when he kisses a mate, it is not *because* he is drunk. "Alcohol might make it easier for some guys, I guess. But I don't think that's why guys kiss." He adds, "I can tell you why I kiss my friends. I kiss them because I love them." He is not the only one to frame his actions with homosocial affection.

ORTHODOX CHEERLEADERS CHALLENGES TO THE 'ONE-TIME-RULE'

Asking about same-sex sexual interactions was *particularly* easy in the research on cheerleading. This is because cheerleaders attend days-long competitions, which provided for a number of hotel room conversations. Here, both gay and straight men integrate and in total, 40 percent of the 49 self-identified heterosexual men I asked said that they once engaged in or continue to engage in some form of same-sex sex; even if they are not immediately forthcoming with the information.

For example, when Tim introduced me to his Orthodox Cheerleading Association teammate, Jeff, he half-jokingly said, "Jeff is the homophobic one on the team." I shook Jeff's hand and asked why that was. "I have no problems with gay men," he said. "I just don't understand why some have to prance around like little girls. Being masculine isn't about who you sleep with. It's about how you act. Your verbal inflection doesn't got to be a flamer." Jeff said that his coach and one of his teammates are both gay, "But, you don't see them acting like that."

Jeff expressed anger over one particular cheerleader, Carson, who is known for both the quality of his stunting (he holds two individual national championship titles) *and* his flamboyancy. However, the following evening we ran into Carson at an intra-squad cheerleading party. And, after a few drinks Jeff asked, "Who wants to take a body shot off me?" Flamboyantly jumping up and down Carson shouted, "I do! I do!" The room erupted with laughter as the individual with the least heteromasculine capital volunteered to perform a sexually-charged drinking game on the man with the most. Jeff smiled, motioning Carson to come closer. "Go for it," he said as he removed his shirt and lay down on a hotel room bed. Carson pinned Jeff's hips to the bed, poured alcohol into his naval, and erotically licked it up; running his tongue considerably lower than Jeff's naval—all to the cheers of onlookers.

The way Jeff allowed Carson to perform a sexually charged drinking game on his body was surprising, particularly concerning his view that gay men should "act masculine." I wondered, *was allowing another man to lick his body also consistent with masculinity?* When I later asked about this Jeff answered, "I bet there are lots of things about me that would surprise you." He continued, "One time, me and [teammate] Trevor had a threesome with a girl. Yeah, well, I actually had a threesome with [teammate] Drew, too." Jeff also "made out" with his teammate, Ian, and once, "jacked him off a bit." I followed up with open-ended probes to confirm theses assertions and found there has been a regular sexual combination of two men and one woman among five of his nine heterosexual male teammates.

Although Jeff indicated these behaviors were not simply a matter of two men separately engaging in heterosexual sex with the same woman, he publicly defined himself as heterosexual. "I'm not attracted to them [men]. It's just that there has to be something worth it. Like, this one girl said she'd fuck us if we both made out. So the ends justified the means. We call it a good cause. There has to be a good cause." Similarly, when I asked Jeff's teammate Patrick, if he had sexual experience with men, he replied, "No. Not yet. But I will. It's just that there has got to be a reward. If I have to kiss another guy in order to fuck a chick, then yeah it's worth it. It's a good cause."

Illustrating the malleability of the good cause scenario Jeff, Patrick and three other heterosexual teammates and I went to a gay club, where Patrick met Lauren. She agreed to take him back to her apartment for sex. In the dance club's restroom Patrick told me, "Maybe I'll see if they [Jeff and Lauren] want to have a threesome." Thus, Patrick, who earlier stated there must be a "good cause" in order to have a threesome, and had already secured heterosexual sex for the night, overlooked this good cause antecedent and propositioned Lauren for a threesome (to which she agreed). When I asked Patrick what specific interaction would take place with Jeff he said, "Well, for the most part it would be about getting it on with her, but like we might do some stuff together, too." Patrick said he would also allow himself to receive oral sex but was not sure if he would give oral sex to Jeff. He then smiled and said, "It depends on what she wants."

The good cause scenario underscores that it is desire for another man which is problematized, not the sex itself. The good cause scenario retains the subjectivity of heterosexual desire, hence the need for a woman's sexual presence (and her request for their same-sex sexual behaviors). This seems to help Jeff and his teammates negate suspicion of homosexuality, so the good cause scenario therefore becomes the mantra for acceptable same-sex practices, even if the guidelines are not followed. Accordingly, Jeff and his teammates are able to manage their same-sex sexual behaviors within a heterosexual framework, avoiding discussion of a gay or bisexual identity. They can partake in limited forms of same-sex sex as long as it takes place in pursuit of or in the presence of heterosexual desires, the good cause scenario.

Jeff and Patrick also report being *so* heterosexual that they are capable of engaging in same-sex sex without threatening their social identities as heterosexual (Klein 1993; Reis 1961). This is similar to how boys with high masculine capital are given more permission to associate with femininity compared to boys lacking masculine capital (McGuffey and Rich 1999).

When discussing this type of sex with informants of another orthodox team, Stuart said, "I've done that." "Yeah, switches and trains," Kevin confirmed. When I asked what switches and trains were Kevin answered, "Switching is when each guy is fucking a girl and then they switch and fuck the other girl. Trains are when a line of guys wait to tag-team a girl." Stuart elaborated, "You just sort of stand around waiting to fuck her. Hell, I even got my leg shot [ejaculated] on once!" When I asked Stuart if this bothered him he laughed, "No. It was kind of an assumed risk." And when I asked why he liked threesomes he responded, "Hell, if you're gon'na hit up a chick, it's cool to have another guy there to talk about it." This misogynistic language, where women's bodies become the receptacle of men's heterosexualizing discourse, is similar to what Curry (1991) describes as normal occurrences in men's locker rooms, and it was difficult for me to hear this type of sex talk because it is also consistent with research on groups of men bonding over the sexual abuse of a woman's body (Martin and Hummer 1989). Accordingly, this violent discourse may be viewed as an attempt to regain cultural power—an effort to remasculinize themselves at the expense of women—and it can therefore be argued that these sexual activities are less of an expansion of heterosexual boundaries and more of an expansion of misogynistic practices. However, it would be problematic to apply *only* this framework to the situation.

Stuart's phrase, "Hell, I even got my leg shot on," made me question, *how could he get ejaculate on himself if he was waiting behind another guy for his turn at the "switches and trains?"* He answered, "Well, my friend was fucking her and I was making out with him while he was doing it."

Similarly, when I asked Stuart's teammate, Tim, if he had done anything sexual with men he answered, "Yeah, sure. Why not? I made out with a guy once and I would let a guy blow me. I'm not gay but I think all guys wonder what it would be like. And I bet guys do it better anyhow."

"GETTEN SOME IS GETTEN SOME:" THE RECONSTRUCTION OF HETEROSEXUALITY

Not all of the cheerleaders view the expression of femininity among men as unprofessional or undesirable. And not all of the self-identified heterosexual cheerleaders feared letting their occasional desire for same-sex sex be publicly known. Inclusive cheerleaders have created an acceptable pathway for disclosing homosexual experiences.

I found this inclusive perspective influenced the permissiveness of heterosexual men's same-sex sex differently to the orthodox men in several ways. First, I was struck by the comparative ease with which many of these men discussed their same-sex sexual practices. Upon learning that I was gay, four men immediately informed me that they once had gay sex. Second, a woman's presence was not required for these men to engage in same-sex sex. None of the men from the two inclusive teams thought so. Pete said that he, Sam, and another (now graduated) heterosexual teammate once shared a room with Aaron (an openly gay cheerleader). "We let Aaron give the three of us a blow job," he told me without hesitation, and then added, "And we're not the only ones who've done stuff with guys." He then listed the names of others who engaged in same-sex sex.

When I asked Sam's teammate, Tom, if a woman's presence was necessary for same-sex sex (as it was with the orthodox cheerleaders) he said it might be a "bonus" but it was not *required*. His friend, Joe, added, "Hey, getten some is getten some." And when I asked if they were afraid others might think they were gay because of their same-sex sex, Tom clarified, "Just because one has gay sex, doesn't mean one is gay." Carson, who is gay, (half-jokingly) said, "Honey, I've sucked more straight dick than gay. It's almost to the point that when a guy tells me he is straight, I just wan'na say, 'yeah, you're straight—straight to bed.' "

The difference between these accounts and other accounts of straight athletes who have sex with men is that my informants are more willing to engage in these behaviors without anonymity, something I attribute to a lessening of traditional sexual mores and the decreasing levels of cultural homohysteria found among men of this cohort. However I also recognize that this can be interpreted as appropriating gay men as sexual objects, an approach similar to the orthodox men sexualizing women to reclaim masculine power.

Informants of the other inclusive cheerleading team I researched also viewed same-sex sex as compatible with heterosexuality. Mike expressed several times that he had kissed and received oral sex from men. Still, he said, "I don't perceive myself as gay. I like women far too much for that." When I asked Mike if he identifies as bisexual he said, "Not really. I mean, you can call me that if you want. I'm not into labels and I don't think anybody is 100 percent anything, but I consider myself straight. I'm just not a homophobe." His teammate, Rob, added, "Yeah, I let a guy give me a blow job once and I don't think that makes me gay."

None of these men discussed "good cause" scenarios or "switches and trains," as men from the orthodox association did. In fact, several outwardly questioned the polarization of sexual identity categories. When I asked Jonathan if he thought gay men could be masculine he said, "Of course. Masculinity has nothing to do with sexuality. I have really flamboyant friends who are straight, too." And when I asked if he thought men who have sex with men are gay he said, "Not really, no. They can be, but don't have to be. And gay men can have sex with women, too. It doesn't mean they're straight."

I asked the same types of questions of the orthodox men, and while it is difficult to quantify the variance (because not all were asked the exact same questions), I generally found fewer of these men saw matters the way that the inclusive men did. While men in the orthodox group almost unanimously agreed that gay men can act masculine, they still code the expression of femininity among men as a sign of homosexuality. Similarly, they were more likely to assume a man gay for passively receiving oral sex from another man (when away from the sexual presence of a woman) than men of the inclusive group.

For men of the orthodox group, same-sex sex is largely seen as a way of sharing "conquests" with "brothers," mutually reassuring each other of their heterosexual desirability. It is also a way to get and give pleasure from men, although the subjective desire for men remains stigmatized. For men of the inclusive group, same-sex sex is largely viewed as an acceptable form of sexual recreation without threat to one's heterosexual identity, as long as their interactions are also limited to kissing, oral sex, and mutual masturbation.

Interestingly, none of the men in either group used the label of bisexuality to describe their sexual identities. I suggest this reflects either a defensive measure to protect themselves from higher rates of bi/homophobia outside of cheerleading culture, or a growing binary of sexual categorization among men in this age cohort more broadly. Answering this question is difficult because I did not specifically ask these men why. Also, just because informants indicate they once received oral sex from another man or engaged in occasional kissing or mutual masturbation with other men does not mean they are radically reconstructing what it means to be heterosexual. There is a near-total absence of voluntary discussion about either active or passive anal sex among informants. The negative responses I received about this (from men in all groups) suggest that the changing definition of heterosexuality is still predicated in the avoidance of anal sex. Perhaps future research will address whether North American and Western European men are displaying evidence of a model of sexuality determined more by sexual activity/passivity, rather than the sex of one's partner (Carrier 1971, 1995). For these men, rather than behaviors being indicative of identity, *identity* is privileged over behaviors or desires. In other words, these men are permitted to maintain a publicly perceived heterosexual identity simply by proclaiming a heterosexual identity, even if their behaviors point to bisexual desires. Thus, behaviors and desires are less important than they once used to be, as the one-time rule has diminished in this setting.

CONCLUSION

Although I did not present the same type of rich data regarding same-sex sexual experiences with the fraternity members or rugby players as I did with the cheerleaders and soccer players, attitudinal data collected in these ethnographies supports my contention that there is a diminishment of the one-time rule of homosexuality among university-attending men. It seems that whereas men's publicly perceived sexual identities were once easily jeopardized in a homohysteric culture, today men maintain more freedom to explore certain forms of same-sex sexual behaviors without threat to their publicly perceived heterosexual identities. Where men's public identities were dependent on an alignment with 100 percent sexual behaviors and desires, this no longer seems to be the case.

Some of the acceptability of same-sexual contact between men might have come through the media. Highlighting the reduction of the one-time rule of homosexuality, recall how shocked I was to see Carson licking alcohol from Jeff's naval in 2003? Yet, on the most popular British kids television show, in 2007 (TMI) I was stunned to see the male presenters (in their early 20's) trying to prove that they were better friends than the two young female contestants. To do this, each team had to complete a challenge, which involved doing something coded as "disgusting." The girls were to retrieve a sweet from a jar of maggots, while one of the male presenters had to lick liquid out of the other's bellybutton. Remarkably, this was not what was considered gross. Instead, it was that he had to lick hot chili sauce. *This* is what that the audience groaned about when the game was announced.

Similarly, the British television show that carries the most cultural currency with teenagers is *Skins*. This show frequently portrays straight high school boys behaving in ways that would likely shock men of older generations. On one episode, the leading heterosexual character decided to give his best gay male friend a blow job. There was no justification for it. Nor was his heterosexuality questioned. It was, rather, just something to do while on holiday. In another episode, he kisses his best heterosexual friend (who he often shares a bed with) saying, "I love you. You are my best friend." This is not the type of heterosexual masculinity my peers exhibited when I was in high school!

The Internet has also been influential in breaking down homophobic gender binaries and boundaries. Networking website like Facebook and MySpace specifically ask for one's sexual orientation, which is listed alongside the other markers of relationship status, age and gender. This *asking* has broken down barriers of what was once considered private information for men of my generation. Today's youth can also easily find who the openly gay boys or men are at their school or university by simply clicking their computer's mouse. Accordingly, the Internet has brought sexuality out of the domain of secrets and silence. In the process of transforming from an act of perversity to one of endearment, the same-sex kiss has also reshaped traditional notions of men's sex and sexuality. This, I argue, has influenced men to rethink the form of masculinity passed down to them by their forefathers. Essentially, the one-drop rule of homosexuality has been betrayed by a kiss.

Whatever history or antecedents one draws upon to explain the transmogrification of these once tabooed behaviors into heterosexual compatibility, whatever hypothesis one determines to explain this historical evolution, the empirical findings highlight that the meanings associated with the same-sex kiss and other forms of same-sex sex has significantly shifted. This, I suggest, has sent university-attending youth into attempting to prove that they are not homophobic. Thus, unlike men of my generation, who tried to prove they were 'good boys' by being homophobic, today desire to prove that they are good boys by being gay-friendly. As inclusive masculinity grows in this (or other settings) we should see a further reformulation of the rules and understandings of what it means to be heterosexual, bisexual or gay.

10 Conclusions

The data presented in this book illustrates a competing category of masculinities to orthodox masculinities. I show that inclusive masculinities are gaining cultural, institutional and organizational power among white, middle-class, university-attending heterosexual men. Most of the men studied are distancing themselves from the corporeal pissing contest of muscularity, hyper-heterosexuality and masculinity that I grew up with during the mid 1980s.

The data from the ethnographic studies of heterosexual men in both feminized and masculinized spaces is also supported by several other ethnographic investigations of university-attending white men: Studies that my graduate students and I have conducted that are not formally discussed in this book but nonetheless have influenced my conclusions. After researching fraternity men, football and soccer players, cheerleaders, rugby men and a host of other groups of university attending men, on both sides of the Atlantic, the evidence suggests that inclusive masculinities are increasingly dominating university settings, and that the homophobia, misogyny, violence and homosocial separation associated with orthodox masculinity is increasingly unfashionable.

I find that various versions of inclusive masculinity numerically dominate all of these settings, on both sides of the Atlantic (with the exception of cheerleading, where men are split). I find inclusive masculinities dominate among the men of a soccer team studied at a small, Catholic university in the American Midwest, as well as of soccer players among a major East-Coast university, and a major British university. I find inclusive masculinities dominate among cheerleaders of a traditionally conservative University in the American South, a major Midwestern university, two west coast cheerleading teams, and that it is at least somewhat evident in another conservative university in the American South. Inclusive masculinities dominate among the men of a California fraternity and the men of an English university's rugby team. Inclusive masculinities have also been found to dominate among the boys attending a British high school. Finally, individual gay athletes discuss the inclusive masculinities of some of their teammates from high schools and universities throughout the United States.

Collectively, this research suggests that we at least need to be measured in our claims when we generalize about the orthodox nature of university athletes or university-attending men in Anglo-American cultures.

I do not however claim that inclusive masculinities are completely free of oppression and subordination. Inclusive masculinities are not to be mistaken as a gender-utopia. Men categorized as belonging to one archetype of a set of inclusive masculinities might still be heterosexist; they might still sexually objectify women; and they might still value excessive risk taking; and they might still use homophobic discourse (without intent to wound). Furthermore, I have not analyzed race, class or other important variables of social stratification alongside inclusive masculinities. So generalizations are limited.

My research on mostly white, university-attending athletes and fraternity members also highlights the inability of Connell's model to capture the complexity of competing masculinities. Therefore, we not only need a renewed emphasis on studying the multiple masculinities and their various demographical intersections, but I suggest that we need a new theoretical model of explaining and exploring how men construct their masculinities in contemporary times. I propose inclusive masculinity theory as that model.

This is because, although Connell's hegemonic masculinity theory has served as the most prolific and perhaps the most helpful heurism to understand the relationship between men and their masculinities, it retains less utility in a culture of diminishing or diminished homohysteria. Connell's model is unable to capture the proliferation of men's femininity and parity among masculinities that occurs in these settings. Results from this research show that heterosexual men exhibiting various forms of inclusive masculinity are not complicit to or subordinated by any singular version of masculinity. These men are not looking up to another form of hegemonic masculinity, or desiring to be associated with any one dominant archetype. And because these men are not building their masculinity in reference to a singular hegemonic version, they are not performing protest masculinity either.

Inclusive masculinity theory helps explain what happens to the behaviors of straight men when homohysteria no longer works as a stigmatizing weapon and boundary policing tool. Inclusive masculinity theory therefore serves as a valuable heurism for understanding what happens when the geeks, nerds, fags and otherwise feminized men not only rise up, but more important, it helps explicate a changing gender order when those who ruled with orthodox masculinity willfully abandon the tools that helped them maintain privilege. Inclusive masculinity theory not only describes these men as being situated across a masculinity horizon rather than masculinity stratification, but it also explains how this flattening out process has occurred.

I am not the first to critique Connell's model along the lines of being incapable of capturing a richer complexity of masculinities; there is a long tradition of doing so (cf. Connell and Messerschmidt 2005). Harris and

Clayton (2007), write, "Where, for example, might we locate metrosexual men in Connell's gender order? Many of their commonly understood characteristics may be related to gay masculinities, and thus, categorized within Connells' framework as 'subordinated' practice . . . In this sense, metrosexual men may be located within the hegemonic group." Miller et al. (2005) adds that queerness has become un-problematically adopted by middle-class, professional men. If they are not protesting hegemonic masculinity, and they do not feel stigmatized by it, what are they?

Inclusive masculinity theory accounts for these critiques because it suggests that as cultural homohysteria decreases, masculinities are increasingly situated upon a horizontal, not a vertical position. One way of mapping this is to position orthodox-acting men on the far right and inclusive masculinity on the left. For men who aspire to either version of masculinity, they may feel content, they may even feel morally superior to those on the other end of the continuum, but nonetheless neither retains hegemonic dominance.

If one were capable of locating and interviewing all university men in Anglo-American cultures, I suggest we would see a dominance of men concentrated on the right side of the spectrum throughout the 1980s, but since 1993, and perhaps at an ever-increasing rate, they are shifting left. Viewing masculinities on this spectrum makes more sense than viewing masculinities as a hierarchy. But this only works in a culture of decreased homohysteria. This is because in a culture of decreased homohysteria those on the right (orthodox) are not the only one's thought heterosexual. Thus, even if orthodox masculinity retains some cultural power, it would be hard to argue that it is culturally hegemonic. It would also be difficult to maintain that those aligned with inclusive masculinities maintain more social privilege than those exhibiting orthodox masculinities.

My data indicates that in the process of inclusive masculinities proliferating, gender itself, as a constructed binary of opposites, may be somewhat eroding. I argue that the efforts of the first, second, and now third wave of feminism, combined with the gay liberationists and gay assimilationist efforts of the past four decades, are slowly withering at the gender binary. Increasingly, gender is the business of decreasing polarization for university-attending men.

This is particularly true for gender *between and among* men. This has socio-positive implications for the tolerance of gay men as well. Many of the long-held codes, behaviors and other symbols of what separates masculine men from feminized men (who were therefore homosexualized) are blurring, making behaviors and attitudes increasingly problematic to describe as masculine, feminine, and thus gay or straight. Yesterday's rules no longer seem to apply. I have an increasingly difficult time trying to select 'gay' students from 'straight' students through cultural markers of fashion and presentation. The codes of gay, are increasingly adopted by heterosexuals, and therefore become meaningless as symbols of sexuality.

While I can say that men in this research are increasingly associating with once-feminized and therefore stigmatized terrain, I cannot say whether this is because they are increasingly less afraid of social stigma. It's not necessarily that today's university aged men no longer care if they are stigmatized. Perhaps they are equally as compelled to display acceptable gender behaviors as men of my generation. However, if this is the case, I am just not sure what behaviors are associated with stigma. Research conducted by one of my graduate students (McCormack 2009) suggests that British high school boys do not know themselves. Accordingly, piece by piece, since the apex of homohysteria in 1988, orthodox masculinity and its emphasis on heteromasculinity has been eroding. Increasingly, men's femininity grew acceptable, and this paved the way for others to chip away at remaining stigma. While the project may not be complete, the trend is clear, heterofemininity is increasingly acceptable in men.

LEVELS OF ANALYSIS

The influence of this change is multiple and varied. Accordingly, I borrow from Foucault (1984) to explain the construction of inclusive masculinities. Foucault suggests that power must be understood as the multiplicity of force relations emanating from individuals, organizations and institutions. In this manner, individuals are not merely subject to institutional perspectives on masculinity; they are active in shaping the institutional perspective through complacency or protest. Accordingly, various levels of influence have helped construct inclusive masculinities as valued and esteemed in the cultures studied.

I have, throughout this book, examined for institutional, organizational and individual agency in shaping masculinity. I have not, however, researched the dominant culture. This is because understanding the influence of culture in general is largely the work of large-scale quantitative investigations. However, the influence of the broader culture is perhaps deductively addressed with my rugby research. This is because, unlike the men in the other ethnographies, I could not detect a strong institutional, organizational, or individual agent in shaping their inclusive culture. Certainly the institution of rugby has been established as valuing orthodox masculinity, and the two coaches on this team certainly maintained a reverence for orthodox masculinity. Furthermore, there were no openly gay men to contest orthodox masculinity, or straight men with particularly outspoken inclusive views. Thus, I suggest that the influence that has helped construct these men as inclusive must be the wider culture of decreased homohysteria; one that exists among university-aged men at this university more broadly.

But I do not think that one necessarily needs quantitative data to experience how the wider culture has greatly reduced its degree of homohysteria in recent years. Perhaps an equally valid measure of decreasing cultural homophobia comes from lived experience. For example, I continuously return home to tell my partner just how amazed I am that boys are dancing together (Peterson and Anderson 2009). I am delighted to see that men's clothing have consumed once-feminized styles as fashionable: The adoption of pink, cardigan sweaters, skinny jeans and one-strapped bags. I am delighted that men can now use facial moisturizers and other skin care products. I am thrilled that heterosexual men can now go on 'man dates.' Most of all, I myself remain in near disbelief myself when I see two heterosexual men kiss. These examples are not anecdotal because they are prolific and repeatedly observable in youth culture (although, for now, kissing remains a British behavior). This is not the case of making a rule from one example. These examples are perhaps even a *better* indicator of the changing relationship between homohysteria and masculinity in the broader culture. This is because they reflect not the survey research of attitudinal data, but how attitudes influence the *lived* experience.

My research also makes it clear, however, that the *institution* of sport still somewhat values orthodox masculinity. I found the broader culture and organizational culture more influential in constructing inclusive masculinities than the institution of sport itself. Thus, I still call the institution of sport "a cult of masculinity." In fact, socio-positive changes I find do not appear to be driven by changing institutional norms at all. Sport, as an all encompassing institution, remains not only highly masculinized and gender-segregated, but it has remained over-representative of heterosexual men, and continues to be governed by orthodox-valuing men.

However, just because the *institution* remains homophobic, does not mean that individual organizations do not strike a more inclusive standpoint. The best example of organizational contestation in reformulating representations of institutionalized masculinity comes from one of my cheerleading squads, the Troubadours. Unlike the rigid masculinity I observed on teams from throughout the Orthodox Cheerleading Association, the coaches and players of this Orthodox Cheerleading Association have taken a political stand against their institution's conservativism.

Finally, highlighting that not all of the attitudes regarding homosexuality and masculinity are a result of simple top-down modeling, and supporting agency in contesting institutional norms, my research shows the influence that many individuals had on changing their teammates perspectives on homophobia and masculinity. For example, Jairo used his agency to change the homophobic culture of his fraternity, making it one of the most gay-friendly places for men on campus. And Carson dared to be flamboyant in the orthodox cheerleading association, changing orthodox-acting men's attitudes (like Jeff's) at the same time.

Of course, I also met individuals using their agency to reproduce orthodox masculinity. Unfortunately, many of these men were coaches. Nowhere was this more evident than when it came to the coaches of the rugby team. The lack of direct confrontation that the rugby athletes had with their coaches over their varied perspectives on homosexuality and masculinity is attributable to the agency that the coaches maintain. As representatives of an institution and leaders of an organization, their ability to punish those who failed to meet the mandates was evident. Nonetheless, it was not enough to stop the collective agency of the many players on the team. In fact, after the season concluded, these players petitioned for and had their coach fired. Thus, unique to my ethnographies, rather than social change occurring from the larger social structure, or being institutionalized as part of a micro-culture through formal leadership, these men highlight the power of individual and collective agency (Foucault 1984; Taylor 1999), even in opposition of a larger institutional culture.

I conclude this discussion of the multiplicity of power by suggesting that even though the institution of sport was founded for and remains structured around the production of orthodox masculinity, it is not immune from the agency of individuals, groups, or the broader culture. The rugby men eventually were able to use their collective agency to stand against their coaches. This, then, is a case in which the dominant society has influenced sporting men's gendered accounts, instead of it being the other way around. So while the results of these ethnographies make it clear that the institution of sport resists inclusive masculinities, it is unable to resist the power of individuals empowered by the broader culture. It might even suggest that the power of sport to influence non-sporting men is dissipating.

PATRIARCHY

When I first theorized about inclusive masculinities in 2001, my dissertation advisor said, "So if they don't base masculinity in opposition to femininity, what do they base it in?" She asked this question because masculinity and femininity have traditionally been defined in relation to each other. She was schooled in the world that gender must be represented in oppositional terms. My answer was, "I don't know." I would be hard-pressed to suggest that inclusive masculinities are predicated in hegemonic influence of inclusivity, or increased social, physical and emotional bonding. These are just not attributes that one views as right, natural, or that one aspires to regardless of whether they fit the category or not. Rather, it seems that inclusivity and the ability to homosocially bond is simply the byproduct of decreasing homohysteria. So, perhaps the answer lies in the ways in which men continue to reproduce patriarchy without simultaneously valuing orthodox masculinity, as Connell suggests is the purpose of hegemonic masculinity.

But I do not think that men who are aligned with inclusive masculinities help reproduce patriarchy in the same way that Connell suggests hegemonic masculinity accomplishes. The men in my studies seem to erode at sexism, which *should* at least help wither at patriarchy. Thus, inclusive masculinities should open a new arena in gender politics. One distinguished by the fact that within masculinities, it is somewhat indistinguishable—an indeterminacy that is rather queer. Still, patriarchy will not go away.

This is because gender remains more than just about differences between men and women; it is also about domination and subordination. Accordingly, while inclusive masculinities are not built around any of the traditional variables of masculinity, it may remain vital to have one trait that might help keep men's dominant social status—maleness. Masculinity, as Connell says, (1995: 71) may simply define " . . . a place in gender relations." For this reason I continue to speak of masculinity as an ascription for men.

I contend that another influential aspect of patriarchal reproduction comes through the socialization of nearly all boys into a sporting culture of orthodox masculinity. Here masculine traits, behaviors and experiences are coded by masculine gatekeepers as valuable in other social institutions. Thus, men's patriarchy is supported through the gender-segregated structure upon which sport is esteemed. In this aspect, gender-segregation and the social networks of masculine homophily it builds, will continue to promote patriarchy until sport is gender-integrated.

CONCLUSION

In the beginning of this book, I argued that the development of an inclusive form of masculinity is at least partially the byproduct of the decreasing levels of cultural homohysteria. I said that if orthodox masculinity is based on a relationally dichotomous system which is policed by homophobia, it follows that as homophobia decreases the gender system will correspondingly shift. This inclusive form of masculinity should then allow heterosexual men to both engage in behaviors and permit them to occupy arenas that were previously associated with homosexuality without threat to their heterosexual masculinity. At the end of this book, I hope you agree: We *are* seeing a shift toward inclusive masculinities, *at least* among university-attending white men. And if it is occurring among a group of once highly orthodox-ascribing men (teamsport athletes and fraternity members alike) it is certainly possible that we are seeing the beginning stages of the de-gendering of institutions more broadly.

I look long and hard at the men in my studies, trying to distinguish the privileged from the marginalized. This, however, is an increasingly difficult task. It no longer seems that men's athleticism, the size of their muscles, the amount they can drink, or how 'bad ass' they are, matters to them. Gay men easily socialize with straight men, and athletes with non-athletes. The scenario reminds me of the influential 1985 movie *The Breakfast Club*, which brought three men (one jock, one geek, and one rebel) together with two women (a princess and a female Goth) into high school detention. Their varied archetypes had previously prevented them from socializing with members of other groups, thus they could not learn to appreciate each other's difference. However, after a day in detention, they walked out still different, but nonetheless equally esteemed.

I understand that some may have difficulty trusting that today's youth are rapidly shaking off the masculinist orthodox burden of their forefathers. After all, we have been talking about the horrors of orthodox masculinity for a quarter century now. Still, others may think that I am overly stating the data, or being overly optimistic about what is occurring. Accordingly, I highlight that similar findings are reported by other researchers (Heasley 2005; Kaplan 2006; Markula and Pringle 2005; McCormack 2009; Swain 2006b). However, I suggest that what I describe in this book is also somewhat immediately verifiable through talking with university students about masculinity, observing the way they dress, the way they relate to each other, and what they think about homosexuality. One can easily see how today men are permitted to carry one-strapped bags. One can easily see the sexualization of men's bodies in advertising. One can see the increasing demands that men dress sharp. One can see that items, colors, and behaviors once heavily associated with the purchasing power of women, have been marketed to men. In fact, in 2007 the proprietors of the pink Japanese cartoon cat 'Hello Kitty,' reported that they would soon be selling men's clothes, too. A Hello Kitty spokesman summarized inclusive masculinities well, saying, "That generation feels no embarrassment about wearing Hello Kitty."

Of course, the best data will come from socializing with youth on their terms and in their social spaces. On too many occasions academics sit in their ivory towers proclaiming what is or is not happening from a distance. We are stamped with a version of youth's social world from which we experienced, and we add to this what research *traditionally* reports in order to calibrate our understandings of sex and gender. Accordingly, we look for data to confirm our view, this is something known as confirmation bias. For example, despite all measures indicating that homophobia is in retreat, some academics hold onto one example of a homophobic attack to support an argument that times are not improving. This, of course, is poor sociology. Exemplifying this with masculinities, I had a passionate argument with a valued colleague who decried that men at our university were absolutely not inclusive. I settled the debate by asking for his class roster, locating dozens of his male students on Facebook, and showing him the photos of his male students kissing other men. Because he did not see this happening within his context with his students (the classroom and walking around the university), he could not imagine it was occurring in other contexts.

Accordingly, I appeal to graduate students and young scholars, those who possess enough adolescent capital and those who can freely associate with youth without feeling out of place: Investigate the intersection of inclusive masculinities in other arenas. Examine what is occurring among youth of color, those from impoverished areas, and those with no college education. Help paint a broader, more accurate picture of what it means to be multiple types of young men, in a rapidly changing culture.

Appendix 1
Methods: Gay Male Athletes Research

Finding informants for this research was difficult as few gay male athletes come out to the community and fewer still come out to their athletic teams. This scarcity is exacerbated by the fact that once an athlete does come out of the closet he is more likely to drop out of sport because he may no longer feel that he needs the false representation of heterosexuality that being an athlete provides (Hekma 1998). I located 42 informants, of whom 26 were openly gay on their teams, through a variety of means. The majority of informants came to me through the use of the Internet after I posted queries on gay websites and list-serves. I also obtained informants by keeping e-mails that gay athletes sent to me after I published an article on gay athletes in the August (1999) issue of *XY Magazine*, a national magazine designed for gay youth.

Athletes were represented from the following sports: bowling (1), cheerleading (1), crew (3), cross country (8), diving (3), fencing (1), football (6), hockey (1), rodeo (1), rugby (1), soccer (6), speed skating (1), swimming (4), tennis (2), track (12), volleyball (2), waterpolo (3), wrestling (3). Although 26 of the 42 informants were openly gay on their respective teams, openly gay athletes were represented in all of the sports mentioned with the exception of water polo. The number of teams represented above (59) is larger than the number of athletes in my sample (42) because some informants participated in more than one sport. Their ages ranged from 18 to 25 years.

The sample included athletes from both contact and non-contact sports, and from all regions of North America. Race was not accounted for because there was not enough variation in the sample as all informants identified as white except one. The sample may have been weighted toward cross country and track athletes because of interest these athletes may have had in the fact that the researcher is an openly gay cross country and track coach. The athletes' names have been changed in order to protect their identity, and the taped interviews are locked to restrict access to all but the principal investigator.

Criteria for inclusion for informants were: (1) athletes had to have participated on high school or college athletic team(s) during the past two years; (2) subjects had to have been aware of their homosexual orientation at the time they played; and (3) they must have competed in the sport for at least one full season. Bisexual and heterosexual athletes were excluded. The remaining sixteen athletes considered themselves "closeted" on their teams, in that they believed that their teammates were unaware of their homosexual orientation. In order to expand my sample I used data from eight in-depth interviews that were published in *Jocks: The Stories of America's Gay Male Athletes* by Dan Woog (1998). Although Woog is not an academic researcher, he is a respected and valuable contributor to the field through his journalistic interest in the subject.

I conducted the interviews mostly by phone. Although I came into the interviews with some preconceptions about what it would be like to be an openly gay athlete on a high school or college team, my intention was to hear the experiences of the athletes and to let the theory develop from the data. To facilitate this, the athletes were questioned in detail about their socialization into sport, why they chose their sport, what their experiences were as a gay athlete, what those experiences meant to them, and how they dealt with homophobia in sport. The interviews were loosely structured, but I maintained a set of topics to use as a guideline. The taped interviews ranged from 40 to 90 minutes in length. Each tape was then transcribed and the data were coded using an emerging set of themes.

Appendix 2
Methods: Heterosexual Male Cheerleaders Research

This research uses in-depth interviews and participant observations to examine how heterosexual men in collegiate cheerleading construct masculinity through micro and macro social processes. Because cheerleading is commonly understood to be a feminized terrain, this research also examines the relationship between hegemonic processes of masculine dominance and individual agency (Dilorio 1989; Glaser and Strauss 1967) in the social construction of gendered identities.

The informants are 68 self-identified heterosexual men who used to play high school football but became collegiate cheerleaders because they were unable to make their university football teams. While a self-selection process cannot be ruled out (i.e., it is possible that men most affected by the masculinization process of football do not become cheerleaders), most of the informants reported that upon entering cheerleading, they held orthodox notions of masculinity, including sexist views and overt homophobia. The men, between 18 and 23 years of age, come from diverse regions from throughout the United States, but 80 percent of the informants are white, middle-class men, so generalizations can only be made for this group.

My orientation into the culture of collegiate cheerleading began with informal discussions with friends who were collegiate male cheerleaders and through the analysis of cheerleading Web pages. Next, twelve collegiate male cheerleaders were contacted for interviews by using the member profile search on America Online, which provides a search engine for accessing the stated interests of AOL's 33 million subscribers. After communicating with these cheerleaders through instant messaging, I asked them for in-depth, taped, telephone interviews. Snowball and theoretical sampling techniques (Corbin and Strauss 1990) were used with these initial informants to obtain an additional 12 interviews. The 44 other informant interviews were obtained randomly at cheerleading competitions by asking potential informants if they were willing to participate in academic research. In total, 68 interviews with self-identified heterosexual male cheerleaders were transcribed and coded.

The interviewer began by asking informants to discuss their life history in sports and the process by which they came into cheerleading. Informants were then asked about their views on homosexuality and feminine expression among men as well as their perceptions of women's athleticism and leadership qualities. They were also asked to discuss how they maintained a heterosexual identity in cheerleading and how their identity, or identity management techniques, might vary from when they were in football. In addition to these coded and transcribed interviews, twelve informal group interviews (60 to 120 minutes) were conducted on coed cheerleading teams throughout the United States, some of which included women, coaches, and gay men. Men in these groups were asked about their relationships with women and gay men and about the gendered underpinnings of cheerleading.

In addition to these interviews, 300 hours of participant observation were conducted on four selected coed teams. These teams were solicited in advance of a major competition, and each agreed to be observed and interviewed over three- to four-day competitions, but observations also took place at practices in their home states and while they socialized away from the athletic arena. Field notes (with either a microrecorder or a pocket-sized memo pad) were recorded outside their direct presence. The teams' willingness to be observed was due in part to the author's experience as a coach. Knowledge of kinesiology and sport psychology enabled me to speak their language and help with their athletic endeavors. During the analysis of this research, I maintained relationships with several heterosexual male cheerleaders (from both cheerleading institutions), who were used as key informants for understanding the complexities of cheerleading rules, maneuvers, and cultural practices.

Categorizing informants as belonging to one form of masculinity or the other was based largely on an informant's perceptions of how men and women should act and what tasks men should or should not perform within the sport of cheerleading. Categorization was also influenced by the informant's views on homosexuality and feminine-acting men. For example, athletes who expressed dislike of gay men or held antifeminine or misogynistic attitudes were grouped as orthodox cheerleaders, while those expressing support for gay men and femininity among men were classified as inclusive. Thus, men who stigmatized the performance of certain roles within coed cheerleading as strictly feminine (such as erotic dancing or being thrown into the air) were classified as orthodox, and men who comfortably performed these feminine-coded roles were grouped as inclusive.

It is important to understand that there are two major competing associations that control the world of cheerleading. This research, however, analyzes these associations only as far as they relate to collegiate cheerleading. This is not an analysis of high school or professional cheerleading. Each cheerleading association is a profit-oriented corporation that markets cheerleading instruction, merchandise and training camps. At the collegiate level, each of these two associations maintains near-equal university membership, and each organizes a series of competitions leading to a national meet that draws hundreds of college teams. To protect their identity, the names of these associations have been changed in this article to the Inclusive Cheerleading Association and the Orthodox Cheerleading Association. Since these two cheerleading associations maintain different institutionalized perspectives on gender (in collegiate cheerleading), data collection was evenly split between them.

It is also important to understand that the given names of the two cheerleading associations are intentionally conflated with the categorized forms of masculine expression found in this study. This is primarily for simplicity but also because, as one might expect, the informants of each association largely reflect the institutional creed of their governing body. Men who belonged to the Orthodox Cheerleading Association largely displayed and valued the tenets of orthodox masculinity, while the men in the Inclusive Cheerleading Association largely displayed and valued the tenets of inclusive masculinity. During the coding of the research, however, men were classified as belonging to one group of men or the other, independent of their organizational (university) or cheerleading association affiliation.

Appendix 3
Methods: Fraternity Research

Data collection comes from two years of participant/observation on 67 heterosexual and one homosexual member of Sig Ep (a national fraternity) located at a university which maintains a population of 19,000 undergraduate students. Of these students, 53 percent are Asian, 31 percent are white, and 12 percent are Latino. There are 31 fraternities on this campus, all with men raging between the ages of 18 and 23. Because of the costs associated with fraternity membership, most come from middle- to upper-class backgrounds, making a class analysis difficult. Furthermore, this research only provides an in-depth analysis of Sig Ep, at this particularly university, so generalizations cannot be made for other chapters of this, or other fraternal orders.

The type of total access gained to Sig Ep is not common. It came as a result of a formal invitation to serve as the fraternity's faculty mentor. In order to help facilitate my status as an insider, the chapter president determined that it was best for me to partake in initiation procedures and rituals alongside the class of new recruits. As with these other recruits, this initiation did not include demeaning or degrading hazing rituals. After this ten-week imitation period, all fraternity activities were open to me, including formal meetings, athletic contests, parties and rituals.

Notes were taken both during and immediately following visits, which occurred at all hours and in multiple locations. While the members of the fraternity knew that their faculty advisor was also conducting research, care was taken not to make notes in their presence. I believe this strategy helped enable the fraternity members to forget that their faculty mentor was also conducting research.

Data is also drawn from 18 qualitative interviews strategically selected for racial diversity from this chapter. Interviews generally occurred over private meals or in members' rooms. They generally began by asking informants to discuss their history in the fraternity and their views of its organizational culture regarding sexuality and gender issues. Informants were also asked about their perceptions of the sexual and gendered views held by other fraternity members on this and other campuses. These in-depth, loosely-structured, one- to two-hour interviews were transcribed verbatim by research assistants. They were then coded for content, and emerging themes were organized into conceptual and thematic categories (Goetz and LeCompte 1981). In order to improve reliability, researcher triangulation was used on ten percent of the transcription coding, and a key informant checked several drafts of the paper.

A strategically selected sample of 10 other fraternity members was also obtained. Four of these interviews were conducted on closeted gay male fraternity members within the same university, but within different fraternity chapters. Another four interviews were conducted on heterosexual members of other fraternity members within the same university. Two were then conducted on heterosexual Sig Ep members from other universities.

Appendix 4
Methods: Rugby Research

My co-author and I represent unique investigators to this research. This is because one is a student-athlete rugby player, while the other is a gay sociologist who is quite critical of men's teamsports. Together we adopt a triangulated approach toward understanding the gendered perspectives of the 24 men on this elite rugby team (Emmerson, Fretz and Shaw 1995). We collect data through the second author's year-long participant observation, and two sets of semi-structured interviews, conducted by each researcher.

The team is a fairly homogenous group of men, aged 18 to 22. They are drawn from England, Scotland, Wales and Ireland. All of the members are students at the university, and most come from middle- to upper-class backgrounds. All but one of the players are white, and all of the players identify as heterosexual. This, therefore, is a select population of privileged white men—so generalizations about the findings are limited accordingly.

This research began with the second author conducting 10 months of participant observation. This portion of the research was conducted by the second author because he was already a member of this team. We did not include the primary author on participant observations, as we felt the presence of an openly gay academic might severely alter the men's behaviors. Thus, the primary author had no contact whatsoever with the men until the interviews began in the final two months of the academic year.

As part of his participant observation, the second author recorded data not only on the pitch, but in several other social settings. Here, care was taken not to make field notes in the presence of teammates. Instead, all note-taking was left to immediate recall (Emmerson, Fretz and Shaw 1995; Spradley 1970). We recognize that the second author's familiarity with his teammates, and his love for the sport of rugby, potentially bias him toward promoting the socio-positive aspects of the data. Conversely, the primary author is likely to be biased in the other direction—he is contemptuous of men's teamsports. Thus, we highlight that the notes on these participant observations were coded and categorized thematically by both researchers. Here, the primary researcher discussed the second researcher's field notes and perceptions of his teammates' behaviors. We each then coded and compared a portion of the field notes, until our coding of categorical behaviors concurred with one another (Emerson, Fretz and Shaw 1995). We continued with this constant comparative method until the tenth month of the study, when we augmented the research with player interviews. These interviews came near the end of the academic year (primarily in the eleventh month), after the second author had collected his field notes. We requested interviews from all of the players, making appointments with and interviewing as many as we could schedule during the allotted time. We managed 18 player interviews before having to move to the final stage of the project.

In the final month of data collection we selected six women for interview request, targeting them because they had appeared at two or more social events with players of the teams. Importantly, these were not girlfriends of the players. What we mean here is that they were social friends without romantic ties. These informants were interviewed about their understandings and relationships with men of this team. Thus, we discussed with them how they perceived the rugby men's attitudes toward, women, gay men, risk and violence.

In order help balance potential bias, each researcher conducted half of the semi-structured in-depth interviews. And in order to assure consistency of investigative topics, we used an interview schedule. We did not however direct the informants into an ordered discussion. Instead, each researcher used his interview skills to sway the conversation back to the pre-determined topics. Interviews lasted between 20 and 60 minutes, and most averaged about 40 minutes. These interviews were also transcribed and coded using a constant comparative method; analyzing the data as it emerged (Bakeman and Gottman 1997). Thus, emerging themes were then organized into conceptual and thematic categories (Goetz and LeCompte 1981; Strauss and Corbin 1994) and cross-checked by each researcher.

There are only two coaches on the team. These are professional coaches, drawing a living wage from their occupation. One is in his late-30s and the other his early-40s. Both hail from middle-class backgrounds, and both played rugby for a number of years. Accordingly, the coaches match the demographics of the players (class and socialization into the sport) with the notable difference that they are from a different generation. An attempt was made to interview the coaches. One refused, however; citing that he wasn't interested in a study about masculinity. The other missed repeated appointments. After his fourth failed attempt, we took his pattern as a desire to avoid the interview and ceased trying.

Finally, although our aim in approaching this work is to incorporate what Altheide and Johnson (1994: 489) refer to as "validity-as-reflexive-accounting" (through our strict coding procedures), we recognize that multiple meanings, indeed multiple truths, may nevertheless exist. We therefore try to capture the core meanings and contradictions of rugby players' experiences by examining their *actions* alongside and against their *language*.

Appendix 5
Methods: Kissing Research

The objective of this research is to examine how heterosexual male English football (soccer) players construct heterosexuality compared to how British men traditionally establish heterosexuality. This is accomplished by examining the frequency, locations, types, and meanings of same-sex kissing between the players of this highly ranked British university.

The informants are 22 self-identified heterosexual undergraduate men between 18 and 23 years of age. They hail from diverse regions throughout Britain, and most of the students represent middle- to upper-class backgrounds. All but seven of our informants are white. And most of the students come from middle to upper-class backgrounds.

The interviews were conducted as semi-structured, in-depth interviews (ranging between 20 and 70 minutes). We began these interviews by asking informants to describe (in their own words) what their attitude towards homosexuality is. Although this does not give us an exacting measure of homophobia (as informants may be inclined to underestimate their homophobia), it nonetheless provides a general measure. We next asked if they had ever kissed another man.

If the informant had kissed another man (on the lips), we asked how he kissed him (pursed lips, how long it lasted, and whether or not he used his tongue). We also asked about the location of the kiss and why it happened. Those that were more willing to discuss their kissing were asked what it is emotionally like kissing men, what it means to them intellectually. We also asked who got kissed, and what criteria were used in judging the recipients of a same-sex kiss.

We discussed with informants their perceptions about why they thought men could kiss today, and how they viewed homosexual men also kissing in public. We also discussed with informants how they might attempt to portray an image of heterosexuality after kissing, and whether or not they thought they were homosexualized by their peers for kissing men. We discussed with them why they thought men were able to kiss at this university, and whether or not they thought their friends from home, or fathers would approve. Also, we discussed with them the use of alcohol in their kissing. However, it is important to note that that we do not investigate or count kissing that took place as part of a hazing ritual—which traditionally involves humiliation, degradation and abusive behaviors (Neuwer 2004). The order of discussion in these long interviews varied, as did the exact wording used. Furthermore, the amount of time allotted to each question varied depending upon the flow of conversation with each informant. Thus, not all questions were asked of each informant.

We used a constant-comparative method of open and axial coding for all data, and each researcher coded half of each data set. We compared 10 percent of our coding for inter-rater reliability. However, we approached this research from a constructivist/interpretive perspective. Thus there may be multiple interpretations of the findings, and other researchers may come to differing conclusions regarding the data. The validity of this research should be judged by the rich descriptions provided (Davies 1999).

References

Acker, J. (1990). Hierarchies, jobs, bodies: A theory of gendered organizations. *Gender & Society, 4*, 139–158.

Adams, A. (2008). "A bunch of fucking tarts:" Masculinity challenging discourse in football. Underfraduate Dissertation, University of Bath, England.

Adams, N., & Bettis, P. (2003). Commanding the room in short skirts: Cheering as the embodiment of ideal girlhood. *Gender & Society, 17*, 73ñ91.

Adams, L.W., Wright, Jr. & Lohr, B.A. (1996). Is homophobia associated with homosexual arousal? *Journal of Abnormal Psychology, 105*(3), 440–445.

Adler, P., & Adler, P. (1998). *Peer power: Preadolescent culture and identity.* New Brunswick, NJ: Rutgers University Press.

Allen, L. (2007). Sensitive and real macho all at the same time: Young heterosexual men and romance. *Men and Masculinities 10*(2): 137–152.

Altheide, D. L., & Johnson, J. M. (1994). Criteria for assessing interpretive validity in qualitative research. In N.K. Denzein & Y.S. Lincoln (Eds.),Handbook of Qualitative Research. Thousand Oaks, CA: Sage.

Anderson, E. (2000). *Trailblazing: America's first openly gay high school coach.* Fountain Valley, CA: Identity Press.

Anderson, E. (2002). Openly gay athletes: Contesting hegemonic masculinity in a homophobic environment. *Gender & Society, 16*(6), 860–877.

Anderson, E. (2004). *Masculine identities of male nurses and cheerleaders: Declining homophobia and the emergence of inclusive masculinities.* PhD Dissertation, University of California Irvine.

Anderson, E. (2005a). *In the game: Gay athletes and the cult of masculinity.* Albany, NY: State University of New York Press.

Anderson, E. (2005b). Orthodox and inclusive masculinities: Competing masculinities among heterosexual men in a feminized terrain. *Sociological Perspectives, 48*, 337–355.

Anderson, E. (2008a). Inclusive masculinities in a fraternal setting. *Men and Masculinities, 10*(5), 604–620.

Anderson, E. (2008b). "Being masculine is not about who you sleep with . . .": Heterosexual athletes contesting masculinity and the one-time rule of homosexuality *Sex Roles*(1–2), 104–115.

Anderson, E. (2008c). "I used to think women were weak": Orthodox masculinity, gender segregation, and sport. *Sociological Forum 23*(2), 257–280.

Anderson, E. (2009). The masculinization of sport and its stakeholders. *Sport Magement Review*, 12, 3–4.

Anderson, E. & McCormack, M. (forthcoming). Intersectionality, critical race theory and American sporting oppression: Examining black and gay male athletes. *Journal of Homosexuality.*

Asch, S. (1951). Effects of group pressure upon the modification and distortion of judgments. In H. Guetzkow (Ed.), *Groups, leadership and men* (177–190). Pittsburgh: Carnegie Press.

Bakeman, R., & Gottman, J. M. (1997). *Observing interaction: An introduction to sequential analysis.* Cambridge: Cambridge University Press.

Barnett, S. & Thomson, K. (1996). Portraying sex: The limits of tolerance. In R. Jowell et al. (Eds.), *British Social Attitudes, the 13ᵗʰ Report.* Dartmouth: Aldershot.

Barrett, D., & Pollack, L. (2005). Whose gay community? Social class, sexual self-expression, and gay community involvement. *The Sociological Quarterly, 46,* 437–456.

Becker, G. (1964). *Human capital.* Chicago: University of Chicago Press.

Bernhardt, P.C., Dabbs, J.M., Jr., Fielden, J.A. & Lutter, C.D. (1998). Testosterone changes during vicarious experiences of winning and losing among fans at sporting events. *Physiology and Behavior, 65*(1), 59–62.

Bissinger, H.G. (1990). *Friday night lights: A town, a team, and a dream.* Boston: Addison-Wesley.

Blass, T. (2000). *Obedience to authority: Current perspectives on the Milgram Paradigm.* Lawrence Elbraum Associates, New York.

Boeringer, S.B. (1996). Influence of fraternity membership, athletics and male living arrangements on sexual aggression. *Violence Against Women 2,* 134–147.

Boeringer, S.B. (1999). Associations of rape-supportive attitudes with fraternal and athletic participation, *Violence Against Women 5,* 81–90.

Boswell, A., & Spade, S.Z. (1996). Fraternities and collegiate rape culture: Why are some fraternities more dangerous places for women? *Gender & Society 10*(2), 133–147.

Bourdieu, P. (1984). *Distinction: A social critique of the judgment of taste.* Cambridge, MA: Harvard.

Bourdieu, P. (2001). *Masculine domination.* Stanford, CA: Stanford University Press.

Bowker, L.H. (1998). *Masculinities and violence.* Thousand Oaks, CA: Sage.

Brackenridge, C.H. (1995). Think global, act global: The future of international women's sport. *Journal of the International Council for Health, Physical Education, Recreation and Dance. 31*(4), 7–11.

Brackenridge, C.H. (2000). Harassment, sexual abuse, and safety of the female athlete. *Clinics in Sports Medicine, 19*(2), 187–198.

Brackenridge, C.H., Bringer, J.D., & Bishopp, D. (2005). Managing cases of abuse in sport. *Child Abuse Review. 14*(4), 259–274.

Brannon, R. (1976). "The male sex role-and what it's done for us lately." In R. Brannon & D. David (Eds.), *The Forty-Nine Percent Majority.* 1–40. Reading, MA: Addison-Wesley.

Britton, D.M. & Williams, C. (1995). Don't ask, don't tell, don't pursue: Military policy and the construction of heterosexual masculinity. *Journal of Homosexuality, 30*(1), 1–21.

Bryant, M. (2001). Gay male athletes and the role of organized team and contact sports. Unpublished Master's Thesis, Seattle Pacific University.

Bryant, A. (2003). Changes in attitudes toward women's roles: Predicting gender-role traditionalism among college students. *Sex Roles, 48*(3/4),131–142.

Bryson, L. (1987). Sport and the maintenance of masculine hegemony. *Women's Studies International Forum. 10,* 349–360.

Burn, S. M. (2000). Heterosexuals' use of "fag" and "queer" to deride one another: A contributor to heterosexism and stigma. *Journal of Homosexuality, 40,* 1–11.

Burstyn, V. (1999). *The rites of men: Manhood, politics and the culture of sport.* Toronto: University of Toronto Press.

Burton Nelson, M. (1994). *The stronger women get the more men love football.* New York: Avon Books.

Butler, J. (1990). *Gender trouble: Feminism and the subversion of identity.* New York: Routledge.

Butterfield, S.A. & Loovis, E.M. (1994). Influence of age, sex, balance, and sport participation in development of kicking by children in grades K-8. *Perceptual and Motor Skills, 79,* 121–138.

Cancian, F.M. (1987). *Love in America: Gender and self-development.* Cambridge: Cambridge University Press.

Carlson, D., Scott, L., Planty, M. & Thompson, J. (2005). *What is the status of high school athletes 8 years after graduation?* Report released by the National Center for Educational Statistics, United States Department of Education.

Carrier, J. M. (1971). Participants in urban male homosexual encounters. *Archives of Sexual Behavior, 1,* 279–291.

Carrier, J. M. (1995). *De los outros: Intimacy and homosexuality among Mexican men.* New York: Columbia University Press.

Carrigan, T., Connell, R.W., & Lee, J. (1985). Toward a new sociology of masculinity. *Theory and Society. 14,* 551–604.

Carter, N. (2006). *The football manager: A history.* London: Routledge.

Cashmore, E., & Parker, A. (2003). One David Beckham: Celebrity, masculinity, and the soccerati. *Sociology of Sport Journal, 20,* 214–231.

Cense, M. & Brackenridge, C.H. (2001). Temporal and developmental risk factors for sexual harassment and abuse in sport. *European Physical Education Review. 7*(1), 61–79.

Chodorow, N. (1978). *The reproduction of mothering.* Berkeley: University of California Press.

Clarke, G. (1998). Queering the pitch and coming out to play: Lesbians and physical education in sport. *Sport, Education, and Society 3*(2), 145–160.

Coach Abuse.com. Available at www.coachabuse.com. Accessed 15th November 2008.

Coad, D. (2008). *The metrosexual: Gender, sexuality and sport.* Albany: State University of New York Press.

Coakley, J. (1998). *Sport in society: Issues and controversies* (6th ed.). Boston: McGraw-Hill.

Cole, C.L. (1993). Resisting the canon: Feminist cultural studies, sport, and technologies of the body. *Journal of Sport and Social Issues, 17*(2), 77–97.

Connell, R.W. (1987). *Gender and power.* Stanford, CA: Stanford University Press

Connell, R.W. (1992). A very straight gay: Masculinity, homosexual experience and the dynamics of gender. *American Sociological Review, 57,* 735–751.

Connell, R.W. (1995). *Masculinities.* Cambridge: Polity.

Connell, R.W. (2002). *Gender.* London: Polity

Connell, R.W. (2005). Change among the gatekeepers: Men, masculinities, and gender equality in the global arena. *Signs: Journal of Women in Culture and Society, 30,* 1801–1827.

Connell, R.W., & Messerschmidt, J.W. (2005). Hegemonic masculinity: Rethinking the concept. *Gender & Society, 19*(6), 829–859.

Corbin, J. & Strauss, A. (1990). Grounded theory research: Procedures, canon, and evaluative criteria. *Qualitative Sociology 13*(1), 3–21.

Crosset, T. (1986). Male coach/female athlete relationships. First Interdisciplinary Conference for Sport Sciences, Sole, Norway, 15–16 November.

Crosset, T. (2000). Athletic affiliation and violence against women: Toward a structural prevention project. In J. McKay, M. Messner and D. Sabo (Eds.), *Masculinities, gender relations, and sport* (147–161). Thousand Oaks, CA: Sage.

Crosset, T., Benedict, J. & MacDonald, M. (1995). Male student athletes reported for sexual assault: A survey of campus police departments and judicial affairs offices. *Journal of Sport and Social Issues, 19*, 126–140.

Curry, T. (1991). Fraternal bonding in the locker room: A profeminist analysis of talk about competition and women. *Sociology of Sport Journal, 8*, 119–135.

Cushion, C. & Jones, R. (2006). Power, discourse and symbolic violence in professional youth soccer: The case of Albion football club. *Sociology of Sport Journal, 23*(2), 142–161.

Davies, C.A. (1999). *Reflexive ethnography: A guide to researching selves and others*, London: Routledge.

Davies, J. (1962). Toward a theory of revolution. *American Sociological Review 27*, 5–19.

Davis, L. (1990). Male cheerleaders and the naturalization of gender. In M. Messner and D. Sabo (Eds.), *Sport, Men and the gender order* (153–161). IL: Human Kinetics.

Davis-Martin, S. (1984). Research on males in nursing. *Journal of Nursing Education. 23*(4), 162–164.

Deutsch, M. & Gerard, H.B. (1955). A study of normative and informational social influences upon individual judgment. *Journal of Abnormal and Social Psychology. 51*, 629–636.

Dilorio, J. 1989). Feminism, gender, and the ethnographic study of sport. *Arena Review. 13*(1), 49–59.

Donaldson, M. (1993). What is hegemonic masculinity? *Theory and Society, 22*(5), 643–657.

Donnelly, P. & Young, K. (1988). The construction and confirmation of identity in sport subcultures. *Sociology of Sport Journal, 5*, 223–240.

Douglas, M. 2002. *Purity and danger.* London: Routledge.

Dunnig, E., & Sheard, K. (1979). *Barbarians, gentlemen and players: A sociological study of the development of rugby football.* Oxford: Martin Robertson.

Durkheim, E. (1976). *The elementary forms of the religious life.* Translation by J. W. Swain. London: Allen and Unwin.

Dworkin, S. L., & Wachs, F. L. (2009). *Size matters: Body panic, health, and consumer culture.* New York: New York University Press.

Eccles, J.S. & Barber, B.L. (1999). Student council, volunteering, basketball, or marching band: What kind of extracurricular involvement matters? *Journal of Adolescent Research, 14*, 10–43.

Edwards, T. (2006). *Cultures of masculinity.* London; New York: Routledge.

Eisenstein, Z. (1979). *Capitalist patriarchy and the case for socialist feminism.* New York: Monthly Review Press.

Ellis, K., O'Dair, B., & Tallmer, A. (1990). Feminism and pornography. *Feminist Review 36*, 15–18.

Emerson, J. (1969). Negotiating the serious import of humor. *Sociometry, 32*, 169–181.

Emerson, R., Fretz, R., & Shaw, L. (1995). *Writing ethnographic field notes.* Chicago: University of Chicago Press.

Eveslage, S. & Delaney, K. (1998). 'Trash talking' at Hardwick High: A case study of insult talk on a boy's basketball team. *International Review for the Sociology of Sport, 33*, 239–253.

Ewald, K. & Jiobu, R.M. (1985). Explaining positive deviance: Becker's model and the case of runners and bodybuilders. *Sociology of Sport Journal, 2*, 144–156.

Farrell, W. (1974). *The liberated man: Beyond masculinity; freeing men and their relationships with women.* New York: Random House.

Farrell, W. (1993). *The myth of male power: Why men are the disposable sex*. New York: Simon & Schuster.

Field, Tiffany. (1999). American adolescents touch each other less and are more aggressive toward their peers as compared with French adolescents. *Adolescence, 34*(136), 753–758.

Filene, P.G. (1975). *Him/Her/Self: Sex roles in modern America*. New York: Johns Hopkins University Press.

Filiault, S. M. (2007). Measuring up in the bedroom: Muscle, thinness, and men's sex lives. *International Journal of Men's Health, 6*, 127–142.

Fine, M. (1988). Sexuality, schooling, and adolescent females: The Missing discourse of desire. *Harvard Educational Review, 58*(1), 29–52.

Foucault, M. (1977). *Discipline and punish: The birth of the prison*. Translation by Robert Hurley. New York: Vintage.

Foucault, M. (1984). *The history of sexuality, volume 1: An introduction*. Translation by Robert Hurley. New York: Vintage.

Foucault, M. (1988). *The care of the self*. Translation by Robert Hurley. New York: Vintage Books.

French, J.R.P. & Raven, B. (1959). The bases of social power. In D. Cartwright (Ed.), *Studies of Social Power*. Ann Arbor: University of Michigan Press.

Freud, S. (1905).Three essays on the theory of sexuality. *Complete psychological works* (vol. 7). London: Hogarth.

Frye, M. (1999). Some reflections on separatism and power. In J. Kourany, J. Sterba, & R. Tong (Eds.), *Feminist Philosophies*, (359–366). Upper Saddle River, NJ: Prentice Hall.

Gerdy, J. (2002). *Sports: The all American addiction*. Jackson, MS: University Press of Mississippi.

Gervis, M. & Dunn, N. (2004). The emotional abuse of elite child athletes by their coaches. *Child Abuse Review, 13*(3), 215–223.

Girginov, V., Papadimitrious, D. &.Lopez De D'Amico, R. (2006). Cultural orientations of sport managers. *European Sport Management Quarterly. 6*(1), 35–66.

Glaser, B. & Strauss, A. (1967). *The Discovery of Grounded Theory: Strategies for Qualitative Research*. New York: Aldine de Gruyter.

Goetz, J.P & LeCompte, M.P. (1981). Ethnographic research and the problem of data reduction. *Anthropology and Education Quarterly* 12: 51–70.

Goffman, E. (1959). *The presentation of self in everyday life*. New York: Double Day.

Goffman, E. (1961). *Asylums: Essays on the social situation of mental patients and other inmates*. New York: Double Day.

Goffman, E. (1963). *Stigma: Notes on the management of spoiled identity*. New York: Simon & Schuster.

Gramsci, A. (1971). *Selections from prison notebooks*. London: New Left Books.

Granovetter, M. (1983). The strength of weak ties: A network theory revisited. *Sociological Theory*, 1, 201–233.

Grazian, D. (2007). The girl hunt: Urban nightlife and the performance of masculinity as a collective activity. *Symbolic Interaction. 30*(2), 221–243.

Greendorfer, S. (1992). A critical analysis of knowledge construction in sport psychology. In T. Horn (Ed.), *Advances in Sport Psychology* (201–215). IL: Human Kinetics.

Griffin, P. (1998). *Strong women, deep closets: Lesbians and homophobia in sport*. Champaign, IL: Human Kinetics.

Grundlingh, A. (1994). Playing for power? Rugby: Afrikaner nationalism and masculinity in South Africa, c. 1900–70. *The International Journal of the History of Sport, 11*, 408–430.

Halkitis, P.N., Green, K.A., & Wilton, L. (2004). Masculinity, body image, and sexual behavior in HIV-seropositive gay men: A two-phase behavioral investigation using the Internet. *International Journal of Men's Health, 3*(1), 27–42.

Hamilton, V.L. & Sanders, J. (1999). The second face of evil: Wrongdoing in and by the corporation. *Personality and Social Psychology Review 3*(2), 222–233.

Hanson, M.E. (1995). *Go! Fight! Win! Cheerleading in American culture.* Bowling Green, OH: Bowling Green State University Popular Press.

Hargreaves, J. (1986). *Sport, power and culture: A social and historical analysis of popular sports in Britain.* Cambridge: Polity.

Hargreaves, J. (1995). Gender, morality and the National Curriculum. In L. Lawrence, E. Murdoch and S. Parker (Eds.) *Professional development issues in leisure, sport and education.* Eastbourne: Leisure Studies Association.

Harris, M. (1964). *Patterns of race in the Americas.* New York: Walker.

Harris, J. & Clayton, B. (2007). The first meterosexual rugby star: Rugby union, masculinity, and celebrity in contemporary Wales. *Sociology of Sport Journal, 24,* 145–164.

Hartmann, H. (1976). Capitalism, patriarchy and job segregation. *Signs Journal of Women in Culture and Society, 1*(3), 137–169.

Harvey, J., Levesque, M. & Donnelly, P. (2007). Sport volunteerism and social capital. *Sociology of Sport Journal. 24*(2), 206–227.

Heasley, R. (2005). Queer Masculinities of Straight Men, *Men and Masculinities, 7*(3) 310–320.

Hekma, G. (1998). "As long as they don't make an issue of it . . .": Gay men and lesbians in organized sports in the Netherlands. *Journal of Homosexuality, 35*(1), 1–23.

Heywood, L. & Dworkin, S. L. (2003). *Built to win: The female athlete as cultural icon.* Minneapolis: University of Minnesota Press.

Hicks, G.R. & Lee, T. (2006). Public attitudes toward gays and lesbians: Trends and predictors. *Journal of Homosexuality, 51*(2), 57–77.

Hochschild, A. (1989). *The second shift: Working parents and the revolution at home.* New York: Viking.

Holub, R. (1992). *Antonion Gramsci: Beyond Marxism and postmodernism.* London: Routledge.

Howe, D. (2001). An ethnography of pain and injury in professional rugby union: The case of Pontypridd RFC. *International Review for the Sociology of Sport, 36,* 289–303.

Hughes, W. (1994). In the empire of the beat: Discipline and disco. In A. Rose (Ed.), *Microphone fiends, youth music and youth culture* (pp. 147–157). New York: Routledge.

Hughes, R. & Coakley, J. (1991). Positive deviance among athletes: The implications of overconformity to the sport ethic. *Sociology of Sport Journal, 8,* 307–325.

Hughson, J. (2000). The boys are back in town: Soccer support and the social reproduction of masculinity. *Journal of Sport and Social Issues, 24,* 8–23.

Ibson, J. (2002). *Picturing men: A century of male relationships in everyday life.* Washington, DC: Smithson Books.

Ingraham, C. (2001). Heterosexuality: It's just not natural. *Handbook of Lesbian and Gay Studies.* London: Sage.

Jackson, S. & Scott, S. (2004). Sexual antinomies in late modernity. *Sexualities, 7*(2), 233–248.

Jackson, C., & Warren, J. (2000). The importance of gender as an aspect of identity at key transition points in compulsory education. *British Educational Research Journal 26*(3), 375–388.

Jacobs, J.A. (1993). Economic and sociological explanations of gender inequality. *Rationality and Society, 5*(3), 286–397.

Jeziorski, R. (1994). *The importance of school sports in American education and socialization.* New York: University Press of America.

Johnson, R. (1998). *Destined for equality: The inevitable rise of women's status.* Cambridge, MA: Harvard University Press.

Johnson, A., Mercer, C., Erens, B., Copas, A., McManus, S., Wellings, K., et al. (2001). Sexual behavior in Britain: Partnerships, practices, and HIV risk behaviors. *The Lancet, 358*(9296), 1835–1842.

Jones, R.L., Armour, K.M. & Potrac, P. (2004). *Sports coaching cultures: From practice to theory.* London: Routledge.

Kaplan, D. (2006). Public intimacy: Dynamics of seduction in male homosocial interactions. *Symbolic Interaction, 28*(4), 571–595.

Kelly, S. & Waddington, I. (2006). Abuse, intimidation and violence as aspects of managerial control in professional soccer in Britain and Ireland. *International Review for the Sociology of Sport 41*(2), 147–164.

Kelman, H.C. & Hamilton, V.L. (1989). *Crimes of obedience: Toward a social psychology of authority and responsibility.* Yale University Press.

Kimmel, M. (1994). Masculinity as homophobia: Fear, shame, and silence in the construction of gender identity. In H. Brod & M. Kaufman (Eds.), *Theorizing masculinities.* London: Sage.

Kimmel, M. S. (1996). *Manhood in America: A cultural history.* New York: Free Press.

Klein, A. M. (1993). *Little big men: Bodybuilding subculture and gender construction.* Albany, New York: State University of New York Press.

Kong, T. S. K., Mahoney, D., & Plummer, K. (2002). Queering the interview. In J. F. Gubrium & J. A. Holstein (Eds.), *Handbook of interview research.* London: Sage.

Kreager, D. (2007). Unnecessary roughness? School sports, peer networks, and male adolescent violence. *American Sociological Review, 72,* 705–724.

Latane, B. (1981). The psychology of social impact. *American Psychologist. 36*(4), 343–356.

Latane, B. & Bourgeois, M.J. (2001). Successfully simulating dynamic social impact. In J. Forgas and K. Williams (Eds.), *Social influence: Direct and indirect processes* (61–78). London: Taylor and Francis.

Laumann, E., Gagnon, J., Michael, R., & Michaels, S. (1994). *The social organization of sexuality: sexual practices in the United States.* Chicago: University of Chicago Press.

LeVay, S. (1996). *Queer science: the use and abuse of research on homosexuality.* Cambridge, MA: MIT Press.

Levine, M.P. (1998). *Gay macho: The life and death of the homosexual clone.* New York: New York University Press.

Light, R. & Kirk, D. (2000). High school rugby, the body and the reproduction of hegemonic masculinity. *Sport, Education and Society, 5,* 163–176.

Loftus, J. (2001). America's liberalization in attitudes towards homosexuality, 1973 to 1998. *American Sociological Review, 66,* 762–782.

Lyle, J. (2002). *Sports coaching concepts: A framework for coaches' behavior.* London: Routledge.

MacInnes, J. (1998). *The end of masculinity: The confusion of sexual genesis and sexual difference in modern society.* Buckingham, UK: Open University Press.

Majors, R. (1990). Cool pose: Black masculinity in sports. In M. Messner & D. Sabo (Eds.), *Sport, men and the gender order: Critical feminist perspectives* (109–115). Champaign, IL: Human Kinetics.

Marsh, H. (1992). Extracurricular activities: Beneficial extension of the traditional curriculum of subversion of academic goals. *Journal of Educational Psychology, 84,* 553–562.

Marsh, H. (1993). The effects of participation in sport during the last two years of high-school. *Sociology of Sport Journal, 10,* 18–43.

Martin, P.Y. & Hummer, R.A. 1989. Fraternities and rape on campus. *Gender & Society,* 3, 457–473.

Mathisen, J.A. (1990). Reviving "muscular Christianity": Gill Dodds and the institutionalization of sport evangelism. *Sociological Focus, 23*(3), 233–249.

McCaughey, M. (2007). *The caveman mystique: Pop-Darwinism and the debates over sex, violence, and science.* New York: Routledge.

McCormack, M. (Forthcoming). Hierarchy without hegemony: Locating boys in an inclusive masculinity setting. *Men and Masculinities.*

McCormack, M. & Anderson, E. (forthcoming). 'It's just not acceptable anymore': The erosion of homophobia in an average English secondary school. *Sociology.*

McGuffey, C.S. & Rich, B.L. (1999). Playing in the gender transgression zone: Race, class, and hegemonic masculinity in middle childhood. *Gender and Society,* 13(5), 608–627.

McKay, J., Messner, M. & Sabo, D. (2000). Studying sport, men, and masculinities from feminist standpoints. In J. McKay, M. Messner, & D. Sabo (Eds.), *Masculinities, gender relations, and sport* (135–152). Thousand Oaks, CA: Sage.

McNair, B. 2002. *Striptease culture: Sex, media and the democratisation of desire.* London: Routledge.

Meijer, H. 1993. Can seduction make straight men gay? *Journal of Homosexuality,* 24(3–4), 125–136.

Messner, M. (1987). The meaning of success: The athletic experience and the development of identity. In H. Brod (Ed.), *The making of masculinities: The new men's studies* (193–209). Boston: Allen and Unwin.

Messner, M. (1988). Sports and male domination: The female athlete as contested ideological terrain. *Sociology of Sport Journal,* 5, 197–211.

Messner, M. (1990). Boyhood, organized sports, and the construction of masculinities. *Journal of Contemporary Ethnography,* 18(4), 416–45.

Messner, M. (1992). *Power at play: Sports and the problem of masculinity.* Boston: Beacon Press.

Messner, M. (2002). *Taking the field: Women, men and sports.* Minneapolis: University of Minnesota Press.

Messner, M. (2004). Becoming 100 percent straight. In M. Kimmel and M. Messner (Eds.), *Men's lives* (421–426). Boston: Allyn & Bacon.

Messner, M., & Sabo, D. (1990). *Sport, men and the gender order: Critical feminist perspectives.* Champaign, IL: Human Kinetics.

Milgram, S. (1974). *Obedience to authority: An experimental view.* New York: Harper and Row.

Miller, T. (2001). *Globalization and sport: Playing the world.* London: Sage.

Miller, K., Melnick, M., Barnes, G., Farrell, M., & Sabo, D. (2005). Disentangling the links among athletic involvement, gender, race, and adolescent academic outcomes. *Sociology of Sport Journal, 22*(2), 178–193.

Miracle, A.W. & Rees, C.R. (1994). *Lessons of the locker room: The myth of school sports.* Amherst, NY: Prometheus Books.

Muir, K., & Seitz, T. (2004). Machismo, misogyny, and homophobia in a male athletic subculture: A participant observation study of deviant rituals in collegiate rugby. *Deviant Behavior,* 25, 303–327.

Mullen, B. & Copper, C. (1994). The relation between group cohesiveness and performance: An integration. *Psychological Bulletin,* 115, 210–227.

Nardi, P. (1999). *Gay men's friendships.* Chicago: University of Chicago Press.

Neuwer, H. (2004). *The hazing reader.* Bloomington, IN: Indiana University Press.

New, C. (2001). Oppressed and oppressors? The systematic mistreatment of men. *Sociology, 35*, 729–748.

Nielsen, J.T. (2001). The forbidden zone: Intimacy, sexual relations and misconduct in the relationship between coaches and athletes. *International Review for the Sociology of Sport, 36*(2), 165–182.

Nixon, H. (1994). The relationship of friendship networks, sports experiences, and gender to expressed pain thresholds. *Sociology of Sport Journal, 13*, 78–86.

Nylund, D. (2007). *Beer, babes, and balls: Masculinity and sports talk radio.* Albany: State University of New York Press.

Ohlander, J., Batalova, J., & Treas, J. (2005). Explaining educational influences on attitudes toward homosexuality. *Social Science Research, 38*, 781–799.

Papas, N., McHenry, P., & Catlett, B. (2004). Athlete aggression on the rink and off the ice. *Men and Masculinities, 6*(3), 291–312.

Parker, A. (2001). Soccer, servitude and sub-cultural identity: Football traineeship and masculine construction. *Soccer and Society, 2*, 59–80.

Parsons, T. & Bales, R. (1955). *Family: Socialization and interaction process.* Glencoe, IL: Free Press.

Pascoe, C. J. (2005). 'Dude, you're a fag': Adolescent masculinity and the fag discourse. *Sexualities, 8*, 329–346.

Peralta, R. (2007). College alcohol and the embodiment of hegemonic masculinity among European American men. *Sex Roles, 56*, 741–756.

Peterson, G. & Anderson, E. (2009). Queering masculine peer culture: Softening gender perfomances on the university dance floor, in (Eds.) N. Rodriguez and J. Landreau *Queer Masculinities: A Critical Reader in Education.* New York: Spring.

Pharr, S. (1997). *Homophobia: A weapon of sexism.* Berkeley, CA: Chardon Press.

Plummer, D. (1999). *One of the boys: Masculinity, homophobia and modern manhood.* New York: Harrington Park Press.

Plummer, K. (Ed.) (2002). *Sexualities: Critical concepts in sociology.* London: Routledge.

Pollack, W. (1998). *Real boys: Rescuing our sons from the myths of boyhood.* New York: Henry Holt and Company

Pope, H., Phillips, K. A., & Olivardia, R. (2000). *The Adonis complex: The secret crisis of male body obsession.* New York: Free Press.

Price, M. (2000). *Rugby as a gay man's game.* PhD dissertation, University of Warwick.

Price, M., & Parker, A. (2003). Sport, sexuality, and the gender order: Amateur rugby union, gay men and social exclusion. *Sociology of Sport Journal, 20*, 108–126.

Pringle, R. (2005). Masculinities, sport and power. *Journal of Sport and Social Issues, 29*, 256–278.

Pringle, R. & Markula, P. (2005). No pain is sane after all: A Foucauldian analysis of masculinities and men's experiences in rugby. *Sociology of Sport Journal, 22*, 472–497.

Pronger, B. (1990). *The arena of masculinity: Sports, homosexuality, and the meaning of sex.* New York: St. Martin's Press.

Putnam, R. (1995). *Bowling alone: The collapse and revival of American community.* New York: Simon & Schuster.

Raphael, R. 1988. *The men from the boys: Rites of passage in male America.* Lincoln, NE: University of Nebraska Press.

Reis, A. (1961). The social integration of peers and queers. *Social Problems, 9*(2), 102–120.

Reskin, B., & Hartmann, H. (1986). *Women's work, men's work: Sex segregation on the job.* Washington, DC: National Academy Press.

Reskin, B. & Roos, P. (1990). *Job queues, gender queues: Explaining women's inroads into male occupations.* Philadelphia: Temple University Press.

Rich, A. (1980). Compulsory heterosexuality and lesbian existence. *Signs: Journal of Women in Culture and Society,* 5(4), 631–660.

Richardson, D. (Ed.) (1996) *Theorizing heterosexuality: Telling it straight.* Maidenhead, UK: Open University Press.

Rigauer, B. (1981). *Sport and work.* New York: Columbia University Press.

Robidoux, M. (2001). *Men at play: A working understanding of professional hockey.* Quebec: McGill-Queen's University Press.

Rofes, E. (2000). Bound and gagged: Sexual silences, gender conformity and the gay male teacher. *Sexualities,* 3(4), 439–462.

Ross, L. (1999). *The divine nine: The history of African American fraternities and sororities.* New York: Kensington Books.

Rotundo, E.A. (1994). *American manhood: Transformations in masculinity from the revolution to the modern era.* New York: Basic books.

Rubin, G. S. (1975). The Traffic in women: Notes on the "political economy" of sex. In R.R. Reiter (Ed.), *Toward an anthropology of women* (37–85). New York: Monthly Review Press.

Rubin, G. (1984). Thinking sex: Notes for a radical theory of the politics of sexuality. In C. Vance (Ed.), *Pleasure and danger: Exploring female sexuality.* Boston: Routledge.

Russell, B. (1938). *Power: A social analysis.* London: Allen & Unwin.

Sabo, D., Melnick, M. & Vanfossen, B. (1989). *The women's sports foundation report: Minorities in sport.* New York: Women's Sports Foundation.

Sabo, D., Miller, M., Melnick, M., & Heywood, L. (2004). Their lives depend on it: Sport, physical activity, and the health and well-being of American girls. East Meadow, NY: Women's Sports Foundation.

Sabo, D. & Panepinto, J. (1990). Football ritual and the social reproduction of masculinity. In M. Messner and D. Sabo (Eds.), *Sport, men and the gender order: Critical feminist perspectives,* (115–126). Champaign IL: Human Kinetics.

Sabo, D. & Runfola, R. (1980). *Jock: Sports and Male identity.* Prentice Hall: Englewood Cliffs, NJ.

Sage, G. (1990). *Power and ideology in American sport: A critical perspective.* Champaign, Illinois: Human Kinetics.

Sanday, P.R. (1981). The socio-cultural context of rape: A cross-cultural study. *Journal of Social Issues,* 37, 5ñ27.

Sanday, P.R. (1990). *Fraternity gang rape: Sex, brotherhood, and privilege on campus.* New York: New York University Press.

Schacht, S. (1996). Misogyny on and off the "pitch": The gendered world of male rugby players. *Gender & Society,* 10, 550–565.

Schroeder, K. (2002). *Military masculinities,* Unpublished PhD Dissertation, University of Chicago.

Schwartz, P. (1995). The science of sexuality still needs social science. *The Scientist,* 9(2), 12.

Sedgwick, E. K. (1990). *Epistemology of the closet.* Berkeley: University of California Press.

Segal, L. (1994). *Straight sex: Rethinking the politics of pleasure.* Berkeley: University of California Press.

Silk, M. & Andrews, D. (2009). Practising physical cultural studies, *Journal of Sport & Social Issues.*

Simpson, M. (1994). *Male impersonators: men performing masculinity.* New York: Routledge.

Simpson, R.L. & Simpson, I.H. (1969). Women and bureaucracy in the semi-professions. In A. Etzioni (Ed.), *The semi-professions and their organization*, (196–265). New York: Free Press.

Smith-Rosenberg, C. (1985). *Disorderly conduct: Visions of gender in Victorian America*. New York: Oxford University Press.

Southall, R., Anderson, E., Coleman, F., & Nagel, M. (2006, November). Attitudes regarding sexual orientation among university athletes. Paper presented at the Annual Conference of the North American Society for the Sociology of Sport, Vancouver, Canada.

Sparkes, A.C. (1992). The paradigms debate: An extended review and celebration of difference. In A. Sparkes (Ed.), *Research in physical education and sport: Exploring alternative visions*. London: Falmer.

Spencer, C. (1995). *Homosexuality in history*. Florida: Harcourt Brace.

Spitzer, R. (2003). Can Some Gay Men and Lesbians Change Their Sexual Orientation? 200 Participants Reporting a Change from Homosexual to Heterosexual Orientation. *Archives of Sexual Behavior, 32*(5), 403–417.

Spradley, J.P. (1970). *You owe yourself a drunk: An ethnography of urban nomads*. Boston: Little & Brown.

Stangle, J. (2001). Comments on Eric Anderson's Trailblazing, *Sociology of Sport Journal 18*(4), 471–475.

Swain, J. (2006a). The role of sport in the construction of masculinities in an English independent junior school. *Sport, Education and Society*, 11, 317–335.

Swain, J. (2006b). Reflections on patterns of masculinity in school settings. *Men and Masculinities 8*, 331–349.

Tanenbaum, L. (1999). *Slut! : Growing up female with a bad reputation*. New York: Seven Stories Press.

Taylor, V. (1999). Gender and social movements. *Gender & Society. 13*(1), 8–33.

Thorne, B. (1993). *Gender play: Girls and boys in school*. New Brunswick, NJ: Rutgers University Press.

Thurlow, C. (2001). Naming the "outsider within": Homophobic pejoratives and the verbal abuse of lesbian, gay and bisexual high school pupils. *Journal of Adolescence, 24*, 25–38.

Thurow, L. (1985). *The zero-sum solution: Building a world-class American economy*. New York: Simon & Schuster.

Tilly, C. (1978). *From mobilization to revolution*. Reading, MA: Addison-Wesley

Tomlinson, A. & Yorganci, I. (1997). Male coach/female athlete relations: Gender and power relations in competitive sport. *Journal of Sport & Social Issues, 21*(2), 134–155.

Turner, V. (1967). *The forest of symbols: Aspects of Ndembu ritual*. Ithaca, NY: Cornell University Press.

Warner, M. (1993). *Fear of a queer planet: Queer politics and social theory*. Minneapolis: University of Minnesota Press.

West, L. (2001). Negotiating masculinities in American drinking subcultures. *Journal of Men's Studies*, 9, 371–392.

West, C. & Zimmerman, D. (1987). Doing gender. *Gender & Society, 1*(2), 125–151.

Widmer, E., Treas, J, & Newcomb, R. (2002). Attitudes towards non-marital sex in 24 countries. *Journal of Sex Research, 35*, 349–365.

Williams, C. (1989). *Gender differences at work: Women and men in nontraditional occupations*. Berkeley: University of California Press.

Williams, C. (1993). (ed.) *Doing "women's work": Men in nontraditional occupations*. Newbury Park, CA: Sage.

Williams, C. (1995). *Still a man's world: Men who do "women's" work*. Berkeley, CA: University of California Press.

Windmeyer, S, & Freeman, P.W. (1998). *Out on fraternity row: Personal accounts of being gay in a college fraternity*. Los Angeles: Alyson Books.

Wolf, N. (1997). *Promiscuities: The secret struggle for womanhood*. New York: Random House.

Wolf Wendel, L., Toma, D., & Morphew, C. (2001). How much difference is too much difference? Perceptions of gay men and lesbians in intercollegiate athletics. *Journal of College Student Development, 42*(5), 465–479.

Woodward, R. (2000). Warrior heroes and little green men: Soldiers, military training, and the construction of rural masculinities. *Rural Sociology, 65*(4), 6–40.

Woog, D. (1998). *Jocks: The true stories of America's gay male athletes*. Los Angeles: Alyson Publications.

Wright, E. (1996). *Torn togas: The dark side of Greek life*. Minneapolis, MN: Fairview.

Yang, A.S. (1997). Attitudes toward homosexuality. *Public Opinion Quarterly, 61*, 477–507.

Index

About the Author

Dr. Eric Anderson is an American sociologist at the University of Bath, England. He is well known for his research on sport, masculinities, sexualities and homophobia. Dr. Anderson is the foremost researcher on the relationship between gay male athletes and sport. He has authored several books and peer-reviewed articles, including the award-winning *In the Game: Gay Athletes and the Cult of Masculinity*. His autobiography, *Trailblazing: America's First Openly Gay High School Coach*, has also been widely acclaimed. Dr. Anderson also writes about distance running, authoring *The Runner's Doctrine* and three editions of *Training Games: Coaching Runner's Creatively*. Dr. Anderson lives with his husband of twelve years, Grant Tyler Peterson, and his four-legged running partner, Lewie.

Made in the USA
Middletown, DE
25 July 2021